The Price

by

Janice Madden

Published by UNESCO - APNIEVE Australia

All Rights Reserved

Copyright © 2016 held by Janice Madden

This book is entirely the work of Janice Madden, who asserts the moral right to be identified as the author of this work. This book is copyright and may not be reproduced by any process without the written consent of the author, in accordance with the Australian Copyright Act 1968.

Copies may be purchased online at www.janicemadden.com
janice.madden@yahoo.com.au

Second edition published in 2016 in Adelaide by UNESCO-APNIEVE Australia Publishing

National Library of Australia Cataloguing-in-Publication entry

Author:	Madden, Janice, author.
Title:	The Price / Janice Madden.
Edition:	2nd edition
ISBN:	9780994612106 (paperback)
Subjects:	Madden, Eva, 1896-1935
	Murder victims-New Zealand-Biography.
	Women-Biography.
Dewey Number:	364.1523092

The Price is a reconstruction based on historically accurate events.

Cover design and typeset by Ailsa Williams, Yooyah Interactive Pty Ltd

Printed by The Printing Hub, South Australia

A copy of this book is held by the State Library of South Australia and The National Library of Australia

The designations employed and the presentation of material throughout this publication do not imply the expression of any opinion whatsoever on the part of UNESCO or of UNESCO-APNIEVE concerning the legal status of any country, territory, city or area or of its authorities, or the delimitation of its frontiers or boundaries.

The author is solely responsible for the choice and presentation of the contents of this book and for the opinions expressed therein, which are not necessarily those of UNESCO or of UNESCO-APNIEVE and do not commit the organisations.

Ample make this bed.
Make this bed with awe;
In it wait till judgement break
Excellent and fair.

Emily Dickinson (1830-86) Complete Poems.
Part Four: Time and Eternity

Acknowledgements

Janice Madden began the research into the death of Eva Madden in 1991, which led to the publication of the first edition of *The Price* in 2008, after which she decided to publish this second edition. Janice wishes to acknowledge the following places and people who have all contributed to bringing Eva's story to the world in both editions.

Places

Brereton Hall, Cheshire, England, UK
Crewe Chronicle archives, Crewe, Cheshire, England, UK
Jesus College Archives, Cambridge, England, UK

Hastings District Council, NZ
The Maori community of Rotorua, NZ
Wellington National Archives, Te Rua Mahara o te Kāwanatanga, NZ

Ontario Library archives, Ontario, Canada

The Mortlock Library, Adelaide, SA

People

Sandy Balfour, sea captain, artist, writer, Anglesey, North Wales, UK
Consultant Psychiatrist, Cheshire, England, UK
Roger Dunn, sea captain, engineer, marine pilot, Fowey, Cornwall, England, UK
Julia Hamilton, Writer, Oxford, UK
The late Ted Hughes, Poet Laureate of England, UK
Ryan O'Connell, Poet, UK
Doris Oxley, Oxley's Funeral Services, Crewe, Cheshire, England, UK
Emily Sutton, Crewe, England, UK
Frances Willmoth, Archivist, Jesus College, Cambridge, England, UK

Former Prime Minister of New Zealand, Mr Jim Bolger, NZ
Consultant Pathologist, Auckland University, NZ
Christopher Drinkwater, Wellington, NZ
Mr and Mrs T. R. Lowry, Lowry Estate, near Hastings, North Island, NZ
Angus McKinley Sexton of Hastings cemetery NZ and his wife Sharron
Herbert Monk, Rotorua, North Island, NZ
Police Constabulary, Hastings, NZ
Victoria Trembath, Auckland University, NZ

Carole Cracknell, Adelaide, SA
John Gladwell, Adelaide, SA
Samela Harris, Adelaide, SA
Kim Hebenstreit, Adelaide, SA
Monica Leahy, Adelaide, SA
Francis Shephard, Adelaide, SA
Lynda and Ashley Turner, Cowell, SA
Annette Verwey, Cowell, SA
Ailsa Williams, Adelaide, SA

A special thank you to Dr Joy de Leo for her invaluable input to this second edition.
Her collaboration and editing combined with sound professional advice and her personal support have enabled me to produce a book worthy of its subject, Eva Madden.

Contents

Part 1 - Life in Cheshire, England (1896-1924)

Leaving Home	1
Welcome to Brereton Hall	7
The World Changes	38
The Worst Nightmare	45
The End of the War	52
Mrs Wilmot	59
The Turning Point	65
A New Life	77

Part 2 – Emigration to New Zealand (1925-1930)

A Free Spirit	85
New Zealand at Last	106
Life with the Hills	113
Moving On	128
Time's Up	150

Part 3 – Canada (1930-1933)

Canada Bound	155
Fiji Heat	175
Two Hearts as One	183
Aloha	190
Vancouver	198
A New Life Unfolds	208
A Bigger Storm to Weather	233
Picking up the Pieces	249

Part 4 – Home to Crewe (1933-1934)

Crewe Again	258
Summer Months	267
A Visit	273
No Consent	277

Part 5 – Return to New Zealand (1934-1935)

Return to New Zealand	283
Oreka Station	294
Things Change at Oreka	307
Leaving the Lowrys	319
A Body is Discovered	337
The News Reaches Home	348
The Head	357
The Trial	364
The Death of William Price	371
For those left behind	380

Postscript

Finding Eva	384
Reflections	392

Part 1 - Life in Cheshire, England (1896-1924)

Leaving Home

It was time to enter the grown up world, one of struggle and hard work. Eva Madden had always been aware of the need to bring money into the home for her family and continually struggled to make ends meet. It applied to everyone she knew in the working class district of Crewe[1]. Children went hungry and she considered herself fortunate that her father worked and her mother was extremely thrifty. Homelessness was common in England and evidence of such poverty lay all around her even within local families who relied so much on the railway work.

Crewe was a huge railway junction where the spitting, smoking steam trains came to rest before journeying across an England fired by coal and steam trains built and driven by local men. The sound of the engines firing up, their shrill whistles piercing the smoke filled streets was a reassuring sound for it meant food on the table and homes for the railway workforce. Eva's father was a plate-layer, working on the railway tracks and her mother kept a small corner shop. The sound of fire engines was welcome more than the song of a black bird or the chatter of a woodland stream. It was security for hundreds of families and their children were proud that their dads were railway workers at Crewe, which boasted the largest train junction in the world.

Many men had travelled from other parts of Britain including Ireland, seeking work. Eva Madden's grandfather was one of them, setting off from County Wexford, Southern Ireland as a young man in search of employment in England at a small town called Shrifnal where he worked on the land. The money he had earned could barely sustain him, drawing him across the Irish Sea along with thousands of other young

---
[1] Crewe, Cheshire England, one of the most historic railway junctions in the world.

Irish men. He never returned and settled in England. His children moved from the country areas lured by prospects of higher wages on the railways and Eva's father and mother eventually settled in Cheshire.

Now it was Eva's turn to contribute, as she was the eldest child. Many of her classmates had gone before her but she had already had the privilege of remaining at school until age thirteen, proving to be a clever and lively girl, much loved by her teachers. However, there was now no choice for her, merely a sadness, which she hid from her family. Secretly she longed to remain at school.

Her father Joseph Madden told her that she would be leaving immediately as he had found work for her as a scullery maid at Brereton Hall[2], one of the wealthy homes of Cheshire. Martha had given her husband the task of telling Eva with the excuse that she didn't know anything about the hall and Joseph would be required to answer Eva's many questions. His voice trailed away when he saw the tears trickling down Eva's face. He drew her into a hug.

"Think about coming home and telling us all about it Evelyn. Your sisters will be so jealous when they hear your stories of grand occasions and beautiful dresses, especially our Gussie. You will be just like a posh lady living in a great hall."

The crying stopped. Eva was imagining her new life. Maybe she would be able to bear it despite her initial fears. Perhaps it might even be exciting. However, she made up her mind to run back home if she hated it.

Joseph assured her that he would take her to the hall on her first day. He also confirmed that most of her salary would be sent home, as this was Eva's way of helping the entire family. So Eva's life changed forever. Her father tried to console her as her tears began again at the thought of leaving her brothers and sisters whilst her mother withdrew from the uncomfortable situation, unable to comfort her daughter. Her brother George thought it was a wonderful idea.

---

[2] Brereton Hall, Cheshire, England, built 1586.

"Eva, just think. You can save money, your own money in the post office under your own name. I'll look after things here, don't worry. And no more Chapel and Bible readings!"

Joe, despite being older than George, didn't share his sense of adventure. He was speechless. He hated change. He was sure it couldn't have been worse if someone had told him Eva was dying. He ran upstairs crying. Tom didn't understand as he was just a baby, but Eva whispered in his tiny ear, promising him treats on her first visit home. Her quiet words and soothing voice seemed to settle him down again after being upset by all the emotion. As Joseph might have predicted, Augusta sulked. She wanted to go with Eva. There would be fine clothes and Eva would see and hear things that she could only dream of. Eva didn't even care about nice dresses! But Ellen, who'd always been Eva's partner in mischief, clung to her big sister.

"Mam has done this to you. She's making you go away. She's punishing me for saying I don't believe in God! Now I don't have a real sister, just a distant one. Please Eva, please, take me with you. I'll do anything you ask me to and I won't get in the way, ever!"

Martha came into the kitchen as Ellen was pulling at Eva's arm. "Stop this at once Ellen! Behave yourself and show your sister some respect. Be happy for her! We will bless her journey tonight in our prayers."

Ellen pushed past her and ran up the stairs to join Joe. After a while the crying stopped. Eva sneaked up to find them both fast asleep. They lay in each other's arms on Eva's bed. This worried her almost more than the outbursts. Both of them needed her so much. They would be lost without her. Eva stood looking at them, tears running down her face. She wished she was grown up and could take them away with her. Martha had always been so busy with the babies and then the shop, that Eva thought of them as her children and she understood each of them, Joe's silent ways and Elly's defiance.

The Price

Entering into service was a means of reliable employment for a working class girl. It meant leaving behind a family life forever. Once within the confines of one of the great homes of the wealthy, personal life was very limited. Training was often severe and hierarchical. 'Below stairs' had a pecking order all of its own. A scullery maid who worked her way up to be a housemaid was subjected to a life of discipline and obedience to her employers. But none of this meant anything to little Eva as she kissed her brothers and sisters goodbye.

It was a beautiful summer's day in 1910 when she climbed into the horse drawn cart, which would take her the huge distance of ten miles. Most people in Crewe lived out their lives within a few streets of the house they were born in and here she was about to travel across the county of Cheshire. She had never been so far away from home before, except for in her daydreams after reading wonderful tales of travel at school, or imagining the adventures of her friend Ida Hollis's uncle in New Zealand. Of course they were all make-believe and this adventure was real. But she had her Dad by her side so she wasn't scared or anxious.

A great adventure lay ahead. She had longed to enter one of the great homes of the wealthy, if only to serve them. She'd spent all her childhood imagining what it would be like and listening to her father's tales of life at Betley Hall[3] and now she was going to live in one herself. George was right, it was an adventure and she should be excited. It was everything she'd dreamed of. Her father had fed her with images of great gardens, and driveways along which swept coaches pulled by gleaming horses. She wanted to be part of this other world, to hurry home on the few occasions when she was given leave to tell her family stories of life in a great hall. She knew that most of her wage would be sent directly to her mother. Convinced that this would help her brothers and sisters, she finally understood that she needed to do her part and so she accepted a life in service. After all, she was

[3] Betley Hall, Staffordshire, England, now demolished country house.

4

Leaving Home

an honourable little girl with great determination to do well and make her family feel proud of her. It was what all good girls of the day wanted.

So that is how Eva left them, carrying in her wooden box all her belongings including the little presents each of them had made for her. George had handed over a thrush's nest containing four blown eggs. Ellen had given her the king conker[4] that was her greatest treasure. Joseph gave her two battered tin soldiers and Augusta had handed over her peg doll. In contrast, her mother's gift contained the only thing she thought necessary in life; an old bible that she had kept, from when she was a girl. Eva was surprised when she opened a second present from her mother and found a beautiful pearl necklace, which rarely came out of Martha's jewellery box, as well as an ornate hatpin decorated by a single pearl. This was the only sentimental thing Eva had known her mother to do, since she could remember really. The new baby Thomas lay sleeping indoors, but Ellen had wrapped up a little knitted shoe for Eva so that she would not forget him.

Her father gave her a new pencil and a small book in which to record important events and stories of her life in service. Slipped inside the front cover was a photo of him at work. A photograph was a rare luxury to the Maddens and Eva understood this was the only family photograph at that time, so it was a special gift.

"Ah, it's just a silly thing. So my beautiful girl doesn't forget her old Dad who loves her," Joseph protested gruffly when Eva looked up from it to meet his eyes.

The Hollis family from a few doors up the street gave her a small atlas and a wooden globe on a stand. They knew how she was fascinated by faraway places. As she handed the gift over, Ida burst into tears at the thought of not having her best friend with whom to share her secrets.

"Don't do that Ida!" Eva exclaimed. "You'll have me

---
[4] Conker is a traditional children's game in Britain and Ireland, played using the seeds of the Horse Chestnut tree

bawling[5] next! Besides, this will be the greatest adventure of them all. And I'll be back soon enough to tell you all about it!"

Friends gathered around the cart, handing her bunches of wild flowers, a pocket-handkerchief, a needlework case, coins and stamps. Eva felt like a princess going off to a foreign land. She blinked back the tears, waved goodbye and set off for the great hall. As the cart pulled away for the long journey through the countryside to Brereton, she looked back down the street at her beloved brothers and sisters. Little George stood on the step by her worn looking mother who seemed remote, lost in her own thoughts. Eleven year old Ellen stood close to Joe, her round face stained with tears, which was in contrast to Joe, who looked sullen and cross at the thought of losing his big sister. He finally ran to Evelyn, holding tightly to her hand. Augusta stood back from the rest of the family, trying not to cry by biting her bottom lip.

---

[5] Bawling means to cry loudly.

Welcome to Brereton Hall

Once alone with her father, all the questions Martha had expected when Eva was first given the news came rushing out. Had he seen Brereton Hall? Did he know any of the servants there? How big was the hall? Joseph told her all that he knew, keeping hidden his own doubtful feelings concerning his special daughter leaving home. He knew that it was necessary for her to work but he would miss her cheerful ways and laughter, which had brightened up the home.

"No, I've never been inside the hall. But I have been in the grounds a couple of times. I believe it's Elizabethan and probably well over three hundred years old. It stands on its own land and next to it is a little church. Oh, Eva it's a grand place! I think it used to belong to the Brereton family. Well, of course, I suppose. That's where it got its name from and all. I know the gamekeeper Mr Charlesworth who told me a few things about it."

Father and daughter settled into an easy conversation as they journeyed through the summer lanes of Cheshire. The hedgerows were thick with wild flowers. White daisies, 'mother-die' parsley, red campions and tall deep pink foxgloves thickened along the hedgerows as they journeyed deeper into the countryside and away from the smoky town of Crewe. She didn't remember when she'd had this much time alone with her father, and she was savouring every moment, every word, every sight, sound and smell of this adventure.

They passed through the market town of Sandbach, where Eva gazed in amazement at a horse drawn cart, which boasted, 'Model Bakery Machine Made Bread, Self Raising Flour and Confectionery.' A noisy Daimler bus rolled past them on its solid tyres. The sign on the front of the bus read 'Crewe via Shavington' and the boards on the side read 'Nantwich, Crewe, Sandbach, Middlewich'. Eva suddenly felt much happier for here was a means of reaching home once she had earned enough money to pay the fare.

Soon they were beyond Sandbach and heading for Holmes Chapel. As the sun grew hot on their necks, Joseph pulled off the road for half an hour to give the horse a rest and a drink from a canvas bag, which he fixed around the horse's mouth. Eva spread out the small lunch that her mother had packed for them and by the roadside they enjoyed bread, cheese and apples before continuing on their journey. Eva was amazed at how many birds there were once outside the limits of a dirty town like Crewe. As she looked up at the clear sky she couldn't help thinking that every bird in Cheshire was singing for her. She encouraged her father to talk again about Brereton Hall.

"It is a grand house Eva, and you're lucky to get into service thanks to the housekeeper of Betley Hall putting in a good word for me or you wouldn't have stood a chance. So you be a good girl when you arrive and do your job well. Your Mam and me, we're proud of you."

"I'll be good Dad. I'll give you no reason to get a bad name because of anything I do. So tell me more Dad! What'll it be like inside?"

"Well now, I'm not sure. I've never been inside you remember. But if it's like Betley Hall, only bigger, the place'll have lots of posh bedrooms and bathrooms and there'll be a big banqueting hall where rich people come to eat. And Charlesworth told me that there's a library that takes up a whole room. He said that Queen Elizabeth[6] herself even came all the way from London just to lay the foundation stone. So my little Eva is in good company even though some of them will be ghosts!" Seeing the look of concern on his daughter's face he laughed, rubbed the top of her head and reassured her that no one had ever seen a

---

[6] Queen Elizabeth 1st (1533-1603)

ghost! The sun was beginning to dip as they turned off the main road and headed down little more than a track. This took them to the entrance of the great hall. Eva looked ahead but was disappointed. All she could see were great oak and elm trees bordering a long drive. They passed a copse on their left and through it Eva could just see the tower of a church. Suddenly they were out in the open and approaching a great hall that glinted deep red in the late afternoon sun. Eva's heart pounded. She had never imagined that anyone could live in such a huge and beautiful house. It was bigger than Mam's church or her old school and maybe even bigger than anything she could remember seeing in Crewe. She gazed upwards at the two magnificent octagonal twin towers that flanked the arched entrance. In a central panel was the Royal Arms with lion and dragon supporters and immediately below were the Brereton Arms and the date 1585. The rest of the building seemed to be covered in carved stonework. There were stones between the glass windows dividing them, cornerstones and all manner of ornamentation. Eva had always thought that the church she attended was very grand but nothing had prepared her for this.

"Well, our Eva, this is to be your home now. You're a grand lady sure enough."

Turning away, Joseph blinked back the tears that he had fought on and off since they had left Crewe. He knew only too well that a little scullery maid would learn the hard way how to do her jobs within the organised timetable of a servant's life. At least he had the consolation of knowing that he could check on her wellbeing through the housekeeper at Betley. He intended to contact the gamekeeper who often joined the staff at Brereton Hall for an evening meal, vowing that if his little Evie was unhappy, he would bring her home, job or no job. Lifting her down from the cart, he gathered her belongings together. As she started to walk towards the front door, he quietly called to her, "No Eva, this way. Not through the main entrance. Not for the likes of us. It's round to the kitchen we must go."

He set off past the great hall, turning down the drive, which extended past the front of the house, sweeping round to the courtyard at the rear. Beyond the courtyard Eva stared in fascination at the ornate garden and grounds. Great rhododendron bushes with deep red flowers as large as dinner plates, shrubberies and roses that bordered a smooth lawn, huge beech and yew trees flanked a further grassed area. And even farther on grew the mature yews adjoining the church grounds.

Dim gaslights lit up the entrance to a small corridor. This led into a large kitchen, bustling with life as the evening meal was being prepared. Heaped on the wooden table in the centre of the room lay fresh vegetables being prepared by one of the cooks. A girl of about twenty was lifting huge trays of meat from a steaming oven while an older woman prepared pastry. She beamed at Joseph, and wiping her hands on her apron she stepped forward.

"Ah, Joseph! Nice to see you!" And then turning her attention to Eva, "So this is little Eva, is it? Welcome to Brereton Hall my dear. You'll be our new scullery maid I hear. But all that can start tomorrow. Just for now, why don't you sit over there by the fire and watch us all rushing about? This is one of our very busy times." Then, turning back to Joseph, "If you'll excuse me for a few moments Joseph, I'll bring you two cups of tea and cake shortly to fill you up after your journey." She rushed off leaving them sitting by the hearth.

"That's Mrs Wilmot, Eva. And she'll tell you what to do," smiled Joseph, noting Eva's interest.

At hearing the name Wilmot, she felt a pang, remembering Wilmot and Ida Hollis, her friends from Crewe, who she would miss dreadfully. They were one of the few families Martha hadn't minded her children playing with, coming as they did from what Martha judged a 'respectable family'. They had an uncle in New Zealand and when Eva first found it on a globe at school she'd wondered how the people down there stood up and didn't fall off! The Hollis children had never tired of telling tales of their missing uncle, inventing all sorts of stories about pirates, volcanoes and ship wrecks in which the uncle always featured prominently. Ida, Ellen and Eva had become firm friends. Who was she going to invent wild stories with now, she wondered.

Joseph broke Eva's reverie with a little nudge. "She's the head cook and housekeeper here and from all accounts she's first rate. Mind everything she has to tell you. There's nothing she doesn't know about running a big house like this. She's strict, I'll tell you that now. But you must obey her just like you do your Mam. That way you'll learn and you'll be safe. And if you mind her very carefully and learn all you can, maybe one day you'll be running a grand house like this one."

Eva tried to listen carefully to her father, but she was busy trying to take everything in. There was so much happening; the clang of pans, shouting, rushing and tasting of soup from saucepans bigger than she'd ever seen before. A boy no older than her sidled in with a couple of pheasants, which he hung on the hook at the back of the door. A large fat ginger cat retreated under the kitchen table at his approach. Bells were ringing and everyone had red faces. She was reminded of a drawing from one of the Charles Dickens'[7] books from school. Never having been someone who liked to sit still for long, Eva felt instantly that she would enjoy the bustle of this life, even if it meant serving others.

After an hour the meal was spirited away via a little lift that carried it up to places unknown. The noise died down. Tea and cake arrived along with Mrs Wilmot. The large cat, which now felt safe enough, curled up at Eva's feet. Her father and the cook exchanged gossip about Betley Hall. Joseph relaxed, smoking his pipe while Eva drowsed by the fire. It had been a long day, which had taken her to the beginning of another life, one that she was no longer scared of.

---

[7] Charles Dickens, English author (1812-1870)

Her father finally left, but not before kissing the top of her head. He reminded her one last time to work hard and told her that she could visit her family in three months time and again just after Christmas. Eva bit her bottom lip, trying to be brave as she turned to Mrs Wilmot. She was led through the kitchen, past a storeroom and up narrow back stairs, finally emerging into a long corridor. Eva gazed in astonishment at the blue carpet, which ran along its entire length. Carved chairs, oak chests and oil paintings furnished the gallery hall but the ceilings were so high that Eva wasn't sure she could see them in the dim light cast by the chandeliers. In awed silence Eva followed the housekeeper, who appeared not to notice the young girl's reaction.

"Now up we go. This is the second staircase leading to the northern attic. It has three bedrooms and you'll share one of them with the other scullery maid. You also have a small bathroom, which you will share with the other girls. Cold water only up here I'm afraid."

Eva found herself in a narrow bedroom with a sloping skylight for a window. Nighttime showed only a handful of stars and a new moon. For Eva it was symbolic of her new life, her new world. Now her father was gone, so was some of her confidence. She shuddered slightly with apprehension and a little fear. She wondered to herself where this new journey would take her. She wished she had Ellen to talk to.

Mrs Wilmot was aware of her silence and noticed, not for the first time, how tiny this girl was. Part of her wanted to shake Joseph and ask him what he was thinking. But in her heart she knew the slip of a thing was better off with her than in any number of other jobs she might have had to do. "Here's your box," she said briskly. "Now you unpack, have a wash and into bed at once. You'll need to be up at 5am for an early start tomorrow. You'll share duties with Mary, our other scullery maid. You're part of our household now so don't you go getting homesick!" And with a knowing smile she was gone.

Eva was lost in her own thoughts. Carefully she unpacked her few possessions, tears in her eyes as she unwrapped each of the keepsakes from her family before carefully putting them in a cupboard by her bed. She discovered the bathroom. By the time she had finished washing, tiredness had swamped her and she climbed into her bed, noting with approval the flock mattress before her eyes closed and she was asleep.

The following morning she was awakened by a loud noise. It turned out to be the other scullery maid named Mary, singing loudly as she pulled on her uniform. "Hello, Eva Madden! That's your name isn't it?" She threw a uniform onto Eva's bed. "That's yours. Get it on Eva, and hurry up or we'll be late. And I'll be in trouble with Mrs Wilmot for not waking you in time!" And with that she rushed out of the room. But just as quickly she returned. "Eva, since you're to share jobs with me, you can wash the towels," she announced gleefully.

"What do you mean?"

"Go to the bottom of the back staircase. On a trestle table you'll find three earthenware jars with salt water in them. Each jar has the name of the young lady on it. When the young ladies of the house have menstruated, they put their pads as they are called, into their own jar ready for washing. Now it'll be your job because I hate doing it."

This was a surprise, because the bleeding had always been such a secret thing at home. It had always been spoken of in whispers at school and when hers started she had dreaded having a discussion of such a personal nature with as brusque and practical a woman as Martha. In fact, Martha's response had been quite predictable. 'Well Evelyn, you're a woman now. And you must start to act like one. I'll give you some cloths I've hemmed and you'll need to wear them when you bleed. Make sure you wash them every day. And don't let your brothers and sisters know anything about it. Wash yourself in cold water, down in the washhouse when no one else is about.' She'd had so many questions she wanted ask, but the aloofness of her mother stopped her. The subject was never mentioned again. But she did know that if the bleeding stopped that meant that there was a baby in your stomach. And so as much as she hated the monthly ritual, the cold washes, the mess and the secrecy, she felt a massive sense of relief when the bleeding started each month. And now she'd have to clean up after someone else's bleeding.

Eva pulled a face but Mary only laughed. "Don't worry Eva, you'll get to know when to look. And you don't have to wash mine! And I can tell you for sure there aren't any there this morning!" She went on in a more serious tone, "Your other job is to scrub the big kitchen table first thing in the morning and last thing at night. You use the bucket under the kitchen sink. Scrub the top of the table with cold water and salt. Better get going now or we'll be in trouble with Wilmot," and she rushed off singing to herself in a foreign language.

So this is what being in service is all about, Eva thought grimly as she struggled to understand Mary's Welsh accent. As the months went by, the two girls became firm friends. But that first day was a whirl of jobs, done and redone under the watchful eye of the cook, meals in the kitchen, more work, a peep out at the gardens and then the preparation for dinner. Suddenly Eva remembered the night before, which seemed years ago. As the girls tumbled into bed Eva wondered if her brothers and sisters were missing her yet. She'd barely thought of them all day and now it was ten o'clock. Was every day going to be like this?

"Is your family from around these parts?" asked Mary. "From Crewe?"

Eva thought for a minute. "The rest of my brothers and sisters, but I was born in Winsford. What about you?"

"Wrexham. Just across in Wales. What sort of name is Madden? Doesn't sound much like a Cheshire name to me. It's what had me wondering where you were from 'n all."

"Well, my Dad is from Shrifnal in Shropshire. On the railways where he works they call him 'The Irishman' because Madden is an Irish name. But he's never been to Ireland himself. I think maybe his dad was born in Ireland, but I'm not sure. I read in school that lots of Irish came here years ago to work on the railways, so maybe he came then."

"You don't know your Grandad?"

"No. Never met him actually. I heard my dad tell Mr Latham that he lives near Crewe, but I don't think my dad's seen him since the old man left Dad's mother with all the kids."

"What about your Mam then?"

"She's from Shropshire too. Whitchurch. But I don't know anything about her family really."

"So how did your Dad from Shrifnal end up with a lady from a grand town like Whitchurch? And why would they move all the way to Crewe if he won't even venture across Crewe to visit his father?"

"Work brought him here. To Crewe I mean. That's all I can tell you."

It wasn't all she knew but it was all she could tell. The Maddens did not gossip and they certainly did not talk about family business.

"There's a mystery there Eva Madden! And stories to be told, I'll bet. We're going to be friends, you and I. I know it. Now better get some sleep, or we'll never be up in time tomorrow."

"But what about your family? You've asked me all these questions and not given a thing away yourself!"

"Tomorrow Eva. It'll be my turn to tell you everything tomorrow night. Now get to sleep."

And Eva suddenly realised just how tired she was and before she could think any more about her day, her eyes closed and she was sound asleep. Now she was part of this busy scene, part of 'the household' and she felt a sense of belonging and pride despite some of the degrading jobs that she had to carry out. Duty was a word that she quickly began to understand. It meant keeping your mouth shut, waking at dawn, working hard and cheerfully all day long, and making the very best of the shared times around the kitchen fire.

It was by the fire at the end of their long day's work that Mary would tell her stories of the strange goings on in Wales. For Eva's part, she would warn Mary not to flirt and make eyes at the boys who worked in the gardens. Church lessons from her mother about loose girls were hard to forget after all. But Mary would just laugh, twirling her ankles in the air and raising her skirts to bake her legs by the coal fire. To look at them during these moments, you'd think they didn't have a care in the world, but both girls saved their wages, sending most home to their families and Eva set to and made both of them dresses and petticoats for the few occasions when they were out of their uniforms.

Mary was rummaging through Eva's box. "Look at these beads, Eva!" she exclaimed in delight.

"They're in my box, Mary. I have seen them before," Eva laughed.

"Yes, but where did you get them from?"

"From my Mam. I've always had them."

"There's a story here, I can tell. They're obviously from very grand dresses and jackets. Come on, Eva, confess!" Suddenly Mary's infectious laugh filled the room and couldn't be denied.

"I'm not sure there's anything to tell. But I used to tell the other children that me Mam was secretly a grand lady from a great house. Although I never imagined one as big as this one! Course none of the other kids believed me. Arnold Badger used to call me a liar and I would get so angry I wanted to belt him one! But I never did. In any case, I think he was just jealous because he had no Mother at all, lived with his grandmother. But one time he got me so cross that I did something that to this day if me Mam found out she'd near enough strangle me for it. I'm apt to do some rash things sometimes if I lose my temper if I've got to defend myself. To this day I hope my Mam never finds out about me showing off."

"Why?"

"My Mam likes to keep family things private. She hates gossip. This just made the other women in the neighbourhood gossip all the more about her of course. And what I did after Arnold Badger called me a liar probably just made them gossip more than ever."

"Well, what did you do?"

"I yelled at him that I was telling the truth. And then I said, 'It's a big secret you know, but one day a coach will come to our house and we'll all go off in it.' But he still didn't believe me and he was starting to make the other kids doubt too. I couldn't have that. Of course, now I know that thanks to their mothers' gossip that my mother was this big mystery, and they wanted to be the ones that solved it. Anyway, in a huff I told them to wait and I would prove it."

"How can you possibly prove a story like that?"

"I snuck inside and I went to the box Mam and Dad used to hide in the bottom drawer of their wardrobe and took the bag that was inside and hid it under my pinafore. I went outside and made the other children all come up the street away from the house, and when I looked around and was sure I had all their attention, I tipped the bag out into my lap and they instantly believed me."

"Well, come on, tell all! What was in it?"

Eva laughed. "Oh, they didn't say a word! I loved it! It was my Mam's jewellery. Some hatpins, two silver brooches, a ring, that sort of thing. And a small gold locket with a curl of brown hair inside. None of their mothers had anything like all this."

"I'm sure."

"They begged me to put it away. Arnold suddenly said he believed me. My Mam was a lady and now they all knew it. But he begged me to take them back because if my Mam found out that she'd never let me out of the house to play again. So I snuck them back in. But I never had to prove myself to them again. They always believed everything I said was true from then on and they all believed me, even when I told a few white lies!"

"Oh, Eva, that was one way to show them!" Mary laughed. "And what, they never even mentioned it again?"

"Not to me. But a few days later I overheard three of the neighbours talking at the fish cart. The other children had obviously told their mothers what I did and about 'Mrs Madden the lady.' I didn't understand it then, but I do now."

"What were they saying?"

"I'd wager her family fell on hard times,' was one. Another said she'd wager that me Mam fell in love and married beneath her station. But Mrs Gibbs was always after a scandal and had to add her two penn'orth worth. She was a huge old woman, always smelled, and the grime under her fingernails! She never had anything good to say about anything. Anyway, she said my mother was probably a fallen woman, forced at the end of a gun to marry Joseph Madden."

"Oh, Eva that's awful. Bleedin' gossips! They're the same everywhere. If yer can't say anything good, then don't bother at all is what my Mam taught me. But since it's just you and me gossiping here, was your Mam a lady? What was her story?"

"The truth is that I don't really know. It's not something my mother would ever talk about. And my father would never go against her wishes. But she's quite different from all the other women in the neighbourhood. Which means they love talking about her. Her solution is not to give them anything to talk about. So she doesn't really talk to any of them unless they come into her shop." Eva paused. "But there are hints. When she walked me down High Street for my first day at school she told me that she had gone to a grand school. And, of course all the beads and jewellery. And speaking of beads, would you like a couple to decorate your new dress?"

"Really? You'd give me some?"

The mood was lifted again. "Of course. They've

been in that tin for long enough. What use are beautiful things if you don't get to show them off? Go on, choose a couple and we'll see what we can do with them."

Mary squealed with delight and immediately started rummaging. "I just knew we were going to be best friends, Eva!"

Eva looked at her and loved her. Mary was like a sister to her. They were indeed best friends, but best friends didn't make up for the brothers and sisters she'd left behind.

"That Eva Madden, the new scullery maid, she's turned out to be an excellent worker. Cheerful too. And gets on a treat with Mary, the Welsh girl we took on last year," Mrs Wilmot reported to the cook from Betley Hall. "I swear, if I didn't keep those two busy they'd be up to all sorts of mischief together!"

The two women would meet in Sandbach on their rare days off and swap information about the different staff and goings on at their two great houses. "I'd appreciate it if you see that Joseph Madden about the place if you could tell him that I'm well pleased with his girl."

Joseph was indeed doing some seasonal work at Betley Hall. It wasn't easy working six days a week on the railway then working another at Betley Hall, but he still had five young mouths to feed and despite Martha's shop, there never seemed to be any money. Of course, he didn't know just how much money Martha was keeping from him and had no idea that life could have been considerably easier if Martha hadn't been saving all the shop takings. There was usually only work in spring, but any chance to get away from the filth of the railways and into the countryside was welcome.

So the information about Eva settling in well at Brereton soon made its way to the Madden family. Her parents were delighted and proud. Ellen had missed her sister desperately and any news of her was good news. But to hear that Eva was happy there without her almost broke her heart. On two occasions she actually set off to visit

The Price

her big sister, only to be caught by her mother as she was heading off in the wrong direction down Nantwich Road![8] Her fury at being stopped by Martha was beyond belief and she slapped at her mother before dissolving in tears. The only thing that stopped Ellen setting off again this time with a plan for a night escape was a letter telling them that Eva's first visit home would be at the end of October. Ellen was sure she would be able to talk Eva into staying. Surely she would once she knew how much Ellen needed her.

The time finally came when the Brereton Hall gamekeeper safely delivered her to her parents' door. He had made the journey into Crewe to visit his parents and would pick her up and take her back when he returned. Everyone was waiting for her, wondering how she would be. Eva cried when she first saw her family. The time away had seemed like years. She had two days in which to enjoy being with her parents, brothers and sisters. It would go so fast! And baby Tommy was so big! He was soon going to walk and she'd never see it! She enjoyed her new life, but looking at the faces of all the people she loved in the world, she didn't know how she could bring herself to drive off again in only two days.

Joseph could see she was becoming overwhelmed and he gently wrapped his arm around her shoulder and walked her inside to where Martha had prepared an unusually lavish meal for them all. Settling down with her brothers and sisters afterwards, she began to tell them about her life. She explained that her work was long and sometimes monotonous. She peeled potatoes, scrubbed vegetables, helped to clean the large kitchen and sometimes went to market with the cook. No, she didn't get to see the lords and ladies of the house, being as she only worked in the kitchen. Maybe she would in a few years when she might become a maid. She told them that she remembered the lessons her mother had taught her about gossip and didn't join in. She

---
[8] The main road through Crewe from Nantwich.

also told them that she remembered what her father had told her about listening and showing she was trustworthy because that was how people in service would advance. She didn't want to be stuck in the kitchen forever.

Joseph smiled at his daughter and looked on quietly as Eva described her life at Brereton Hall and her hopes for advancement. He knew it would take years for Eva to work her way out of the kitchen, if ever, but he encouraged her to work towards a higher position in the household. He looked at his daughter's hands, red and cracked from constant immersion in hot then cold water and scrubbing with lye[9] and the like. It broke his heart a little and he regretted that he couldn't give her something better. She's just a child, not yet grown, and so smart, he thought to himself. She should have so much more. But coming back to the real world, where his daughter was a scullery maid at thirteen, he just thought, the sooner she can become a maid the better.

Eva was absorbed with having an audience and had no inkling of her father's regrets. She spent so much time working and hardly ever talking, she was glad of the opportunity to introduce new stories to the family. As her brothers and sisters were gathered around listening, she told them about how she had discovered the library, quite by accident, when she was taking a message to one of the maids. It was as her father had said, a great room with two ladders, which you must climb to reach the books. She didn't stay too long. She described the hundreds of books covering the entire walls, the tall glass windows curtained in heavy velvet and the views of the park outside. When she had been there a bit longer and had established herself more, she hoped that maybe she would be able to borrow a book or two to read. After all, it seemed such a shame that all those beautiful books just sat there on the shelves, and it wasn't as though anyone would miss one!

The great house was so different from the one they

---

[9] A liquid obtained by leaching ashes or strong alkali, which is highly soluble in water and made into soap.

sat in now, ignoring the cold, for the fire was only lit in that room on special occasions. Their mother called it thriftiness. As the children grew up, they would call it stinginess and while they would respect Martha's ability to always pay her way, they would never do without life's necessities. But tonight they were impressed just to be in the sitting room. Although the front room was usually set aside only for very special occasions, Martha had relented, allowing the children to sit in there, out of the way. Even the servants at Brereton Hall got a roaring fire at night to keep them warm and had comfortable furniture. For the first time Eva realised that even in the service of someone else, they lived better than almost anyone she knew who was working class. It was something she came to understand well over the years, but for now it was a new lesson, and one she could quickly put aside in her excitement to share her stories with her brothers and sisters.

As Eva began the first of her stories, Joseph got up and quietly left his children to their fun. It was time for his evening pint. "Shall I tell you about the Brereton Bear? Or perhaps the mystery of the floating logs? Maybe not the one about the maid sneaking off each afternoon for a sleep on one of the masters' beds. That would be gossip and you know what Mam would say!"

There were many legends and traditions linked to the Brereton Family and the hall. Eva knew which story they would choose first. The bear was a favourite animal for Ellen and George and she knew their father had already told them a bit of the story. With little encouragement over the years the children would never tire of hearing about the muzzled bear that became part of the Brereton Coat of Arms. All the kitchen staff knew the story. They had related it to Eva several times in gory detail feeling a little disappointed when she wasn't scared. She just stored the tale away to be told at a later date to her family.

"Go on our Eva, tell us the story about the big bear with the chain round his mouth," begged George, who was nursing baby Tom. They all drew closer to Eva. Elly rested her head in her big sister's lap.

"Well all right then. But don't interrupt. Now where shall I start?"

"Start with Sir what's his name losing his temper, just like you Eva really, when you argued with Mam that time," laughed Gussie.

"Be quiet," begged Joe, "Or we'll never hear the end of the story and Eva will be going back soon."

"Right, here we go," and Eva looked around fondly at her little audience. "Sir William Brereton, who was born in 1530, was interrupted at his dinner by his valet and in a terrible ..."

"What's a valet?" asked George, as the others glared at him.

"A man servant who looked after Sir William and even put the correct clothes on the bed and helped him to dress," explained Eva patiently.

"Why couldn't he do it himself?" asked Joe in astonishment and everyone burst out laughing.

"He didn't have to Joe. That's the point. Rich people get everything done for them. Now where were we? Oh yes, he was in a very bad temper and he chased his valet up the stairs at Brereton Hall and murdered him!"

George sat back and sighed. "I know why that happened. He must have been drinking. He was in a bad temper because he was so drunk. A man down by the railway station was drunk the other night and he followed another man into the pub where Dad was and he hit him on the head with a beer mug. Anyway there was blood everywhere and ..."

"Shut up George!" everyone shouted.

"Now shall we carry on?" Eva spoke sweetly, but she was growing impatient. "Sir William must have felt guilty. And before you ask George, that means feeling very bad about killing the servant. Like when Mam goes to chapel she asks God to forgive us for bad things and ..."

"Yes, and she asks God to forgive Dad for drinking," added Gussie with confidence, "even though he says he only has a couple of pints. I've heard them arguing and Dad never comes home drunk."

Everyone looked at each other in horror. This was unspoken family business. Only Gussie would dare voice what the others were thinking. Eva decided to ignore this revelation and plough on. "Sir William went to London to plead for a pardon from the King. The King told Sir William that he had three days in which to invent a muzzle for a bear. Now before you ask, George, a muzzle isn't a chain, it's a metal or wooden cage, which fits over a dog's, or in this case, a bear's mouth." By now George was blushing. His sister was clearly making up for his earlier interruptions.

"If you use a muzzle, no biting can happen. It's quite like the muzzle that Dad's friend puts on his ferrets when they go rabbiting in Betley Woods. It would be much harder to make one for a big bear and it would have to be very strong."

"I think our Gussie ought to wear a muzzle then she would have to keep her mouth shut about our family business," laughed George, getting his nerve back.

Gussie glared at him but refused to flounce off out of the room as she usually would because she wanted to hear the fate of Sir William.

"If it was effective," continued Eva, "he would be allowed to live. If not, the bear would be his punishment! He was shut in the Tower of London for three days and then released with the bear! He threw the muzzle over the bear's head and escaped. From then on the Muzzled Bear became the emblem of the Breretons."

"But where is Sir William now?" asked Ellen, wide eyed after hearing this story. "I think he was very stupid to have even gone to the King and owned up," she added gleefully. "He could have got away with it."

"That was a very long time ago. Now the last of the Breretons has died but he never married so there was no son to carry on his name. He died in 1722 and he was the fifth Lord of Brereton. In 1819 a Mr John Howard bought the hall and it still belongs to his family, but friends of that family, namely Mr and Mrs Moir now reside in the hall."

Young Joseph listened with approval. He thought his sister sounded like a history book, especially with her big words like 'reside' and 'effective'. "Tell us about the land around the hall Eva. Are there horses and can you catch rabbits in the woods? Dad says there is a gamekeeper but does he carry a gun? And do you see the hounds meet for foxhunting?"

"Slow down Joe. One thing at a time!" Eva replied laughing. "First, I have very little time off from my work to go exploring. But yes, there are fields and big woods all around the hall and even a little church that the family visits. There are stables for the horses but I've never visited them. I've seen the coaches pull up and often visitors from beyond Cheshire come to stay. Then the hall is even busier. No one can go catching rabbits on the estate unless they want to risk getting caught by Mr Charlesworth." She paused noting that George's glance prompted a reply. "No George, he doesn't shoot anyone. And he is Dad's friend. He knows you and Dad go poaching. He understands all of that."

"Does he have a firearm?" persisted George.

"Yes, he does carry a gun and I have seen it when he comes into the kitchen with game for the table or when he comes in for a meal with us. He's kind, but a bit gruff. And strict! He has to be or he'd lose his job and he has a family to keep. He lives in a cottage on the estate. But it was him that brought me here today, because his parents live in Crewe."

"Is there fox hunting going on at Brereton?" George leant forward, proud that he knew about such things.

"I was just coming to that part. There has always been hunting on the estate. When they go hunting they all meet outside The Bear's Paw, a pub in the village of Brereton. But I've never been there. On a Sunday you can hear the hounds baying across the estate. Once the fox actually escaped into the woods on the estate! But I only hear all these things by listening to the others talking while I am working. I'm the youngest, so I don't get time to go exploring much."

"Tell us what the great hall looks like," begged Elly. "I was coming to see you once but Mam caught me. I had to stay in my room for two days!" Elly looked triumphant as she revealed this piece of information, proud that she had defied her mother in order to seek her favourite sister out.

Slightly alarmed, Eva worried that she might be making Brereton Hall into a magical place. "None of you must try to visit me unless Dad brings you by horse and cart. You'd get me into terrible trouble." She laughed at the thought of them turning up. "Also there are big dogs that guard the estate at night and you would get bitten."

Everyone went very quiet. Eva laughed, as she knew that would do the trick. "Really. I miss you all, but you can't come to visit me there unless Dad brings you." Smiling, she continued. "One Sunday morning, very early, I came down from my room and through the kitchen to the back of the house. No one was awake so I quietly walked around to the front of the house. It was so beautiful Joe, all wreathed in mist so that the bottom part was almost invisible. I walked over the hoar frost to a big oak tree and just stared and stared. Everything was covered in a light frost, the moon was still in the sky and the only sound came from a few ducks on the pond nearby."

Eva sighed at the memory. Just for that moment no one owned the hall. In her head it was hers alone with not a thing moving. Nothing could take that feeling away from her. Brereton's lords and ladies had disappeared into the mists of time. A scullery maid could appreciate the hall's changing moods as well as anyone she thought as she recalled the early mist lifting to reveal the majestic hall.

For a moment her family stayed silent, sensing not to interrupt their big sister. They loved her, treating her with respect but sensing her silence meant that her thoughts were now private, they moved on to tell her their own news.

The next day they pestered Eva once again to tell them more stories of Brereton but they were unprepared for the very frightening Brereton omen. In 1693 an old book stated that at any time when a Brereton was near to death, trunks of trees floated to the surface of Bagmere, a lake near the hall. Eva told this story to her wide-eyed brothers and sisters. She described the lake, which was by now only trees and a marsh. Long ago it resembled Betley Mere[10], which they had often visited. From its depths they could imagine the dead logs bubbling to the surface as the dawn sun came up. They imagined the horror felt by the Breretons for the death omen fell only upon the heir of the family. The Madden children fell silent.

"What has happened to the mere? Are there fish in there?" asked Joe, which made Eva laugh, breaking the spell.

"No, no. The mere has gone now. Nearly dried up. But the River Croco still flows past the hall."

Her brothers and sisters were in awe of their big sister. She already knew so much of this other world that they could only imagine. Eva was growing up and they sensed big changes in her. Wanting to dismiss the images of her faraway life, they all interrupted at once in an effort to compete in telling her all their news.

As Eva journeyed back to Brereton, she thought about her visit home. Her mother looked strained and anxious. Her father was drinking more than he used to. His habits was reducing the family's already meagre income and Eva wasn't sure whether Joseph spent so much time away from the family home because of Martha or Martha had become even more overbearing because of Joseph's perceived poor behaviour. Ellen had been quick to tell her big sister all about it, but that didn't explain it. Eva already knew that there was an added strain on her mother. She didn't need to be told all the details by her sister.

---

[10] Mere refers to a lake that is broad in relation to its depth.

She resolved that day to help her family all she could. Her mother had been strict, even unreasonable sometimes, but Eva respected her. She'd been a good provider and worked hard all her life. She deserved better. And so did her brothers and sisters. She returned to Brereton determined to work even harder and maybe even forgo her next visit home. Whenever she worked in the kitchen she would always glance up at the words engraved into a plaque above the great fireplace in the servants' hall.

*'Doe nothing this day wherof thou mayest repent tomorrowe.
Knowe Him well whom thou makest of thy councel
lest he betray thy secret.'*[11]

Eva often smiled to herself whenever she read the words. She'd had sayings like that instilled in her all her life through her mother's Methodist teachings and chastisements. She knew the fear that words like that gave to people. She also remembered the argument she'd had with her mother about church when she visited home. She made the mistake of telling her family that every Sunday she had to attend the Moir family service along with the other staff. Her mother disapproved because it was a Church of England service and removed in her mind from Methodism. It was one of the few times that Eva had argued with her. Surely there were other religions, other ways of thinking. After all, there was only one God, surely? Martha hadn't spoken to her for the remainder of the visit.

Their mother had read to them from the Bible every night and as soon as the children were old enough they took their turns reading from the book. At this point each night, their father would mysteriously vanish from the house, but his absence seemed barely noticed by all but Eva and she knew better than to say anything. Much later as she lay in bed, Eva could often hear raised voices, but she never dared come out of her room. If the shouting became too loud she

---

[11] The Author noted the Creed when visiting Brereton Hall in 2001.

would put her fingers in her ears and hide her head under the pillows. Ellen was always fast asleep. She never knew a thing about these arguments and Eva told no one about the grown up world down the stairs.

It wasn't until years later that Eva realised that her father disapproved of the growing religious restraints in the household. He knew it was useless to argue against the rituals that ruled the upbringing of his children. He loved Martha, but he'd known about her strong religious beliefs before he married her, so he had no place to be complaining now. He did not hold with her beliefs but knew that it offered a strong discipline to the entire family and it gave Martha a great sense of purpose. He feared this might be lost when he brought her all alone to Crewe when he could get work on the railway. So he would quietly close the door, leaving his children seated dutifully in front of their mother as she read from the Old Testament. He did not feel any resentment towards his wife. He often made his way across Crewe Hall[12] woods to check a couple of snares, which he would lay after work on Saturdays. Generally returning with a rabbit beneath his jacket, he would enter a quiet house with the children in bed. Martha would usually be sewing by the light of a candle.

When the children were small, Martha tried to convert her husband into a good Methodist. But even though he'd gone to Chapel with her for a while, for the most part she was wasting her time. He strongly resisted her urging him to join the faith, rebelling against the yearly oath and recommitment to God that she took. He was angry when he found out that the children, one by one, were made to renew their membership to the Chapel through words of dedication.

"Martha, it's meaningless. All this stuff cannot possibly make sense to such small children." The exasperation was clear in his voice. Picking up the prayer book Martha had brought home for learning, he quoted

---
[12] Crewe Hall, a Jacobean mansion built 1615-1636.

some of the lines: 'Put me to doing, put me to suffering ... Let me be full, let me be empty ... you are mine, and I am yours. So be it.'[13] Martha, what sort of rubbish is this? I do not want Eva saying those words! Then it will be poor little Joe's turn. He's nervous enough of things he doesn't understand, and mark my words, Ellen will refuse to say it as she grows older."

His voice trailed away as he saw what was happening to Martha. White faced and trembling she stared at him, hardly believing he would mock her God. Instantly Joseph was sorry. He loved her but he didn't understand the religious mania ruling her life. So he never spoke of it again and the children did as their mother wished. Instead, he just removed himself from the situation he didn't approve of.

If Martha disapproved of the Services being Church of England, Eva knew she'd never dare tell her mother about the fun she and Mary had in the back pew away from Mrs Wilmot's keen eye. Mary would nudge and pinch her, making Eva laugh. Then she would flirt with the choirboys, making rude comments. She would cross her eyes behind the cover of her hymn-book until Eva had to stuff a handkerchief in her own mouth to prevent the giggling being heard.

Once, Mary did something quite dreadful. She dragged Eva out in the middle of the service, telling Mrs Wilmot that she was going to be sick. Eva knew it was pretence but was forced to go with her. Under the yew trees and by a grave, Mary lifted her petticoats and peed all over a gravestone. Eva was shocked and disgusted but she loved Mary. She was the one bright star within a solemn and hardworking household.

At night they would lie in their beds under the skylight and tell stories to each other. Eva disguised her family into imaginary characters and unwittingly she was able to share some of her deepest secrets with her. The Welsh girl never suspected that the cold dark house described like part of a Dickens' story was in fact Eva's home. She waited

---

[13] Various lines from the traditional Wesley Covenant Prayer.

for the next telling of the harsh mother, the hungry children and the drunkard father. Eva liked to enhance the family problems. Somehow it made her feel better, lighter, and not so troubled by nightmares.

During the first six months of 1914 every inch of the great hall was scrutinised, resulting in extensive repairs to the exterior. Dry rot[14] had been discovered, seriously threatening its survival. Kitchen life was even busier now. Lunches were prepared for the builders, many of whom travelled from Crewe to re-point the whole of the exterior and to put damp courses under the foundations. The work cost the enormous amount of £3,000, a sum of money that Eva could barely comprehend. But like everyone else in the kitchen she welcomed the fresh faces about the hall for this was how they learnt all the gossip from the surrounding villages.

Despite the extra activity in the kitchen, Eva took the opportunity of the Moirs being away and no guests being expected to make a trip home. She found what she thought were extraordinary changes. In her mind, her brothers and sisters stayed the same age while she was away and life in Crewe went on just as it had before she left. It was always a shock when she went home to see how things had changed.

Joe now had a job at Crewe Railway station as a luggage porter. His wages helped the family considerably. To her, Joe was still the quiet little boy that she'd known. She couldn't imagine him working in the loud, bustling environment of the train station. The way Eva remembered him was a small boy clinging to his mother's skirts as Martha shouted at Ellen or hiding behind his father on their Sunday afternoon walks. He seemed too anxious and shy to go out into the world, but she imagined that just like she had and Ellen after her, Joe had been sent out to work as soon as he was old enough to contribute to the family.

---
[14] Wood decay

George would go down to the railway platforms after school to visit him, forsaking his walks across the countryside for his new love, trains. He was fascinated by the massive steam engines as they thundered through on an express run to London. He would watch the mail train being loaded for Glasgow and on several occasions the gleaming royal train would pass through. It was all he ever talked about. As he stood on the platforms he decided that one day he would drive trains like that.

And leaving school to work on the railway was going to happen as soon as possible. School had never been of interest to George. He was clever enough. Martha had seen that he knew his letters and numbers before he started school, just as she had with Eva, Ellen and Joe, but his classmates were rarely safe from him when he was in the classroom. A born joker, there was many a telling off when one or another burst out laughing at something he'd done when the teacher's back was turned. And then he'd escape whenever he could, shirking responsibilities at home and at school to pick a bunch of wild flowers for his mother or to explore Crewe Hall woods. He'd also loved his father's pigeons and before long had a flock of his own. He tolerated learning, but found school boring, much to his older sister's disgust. He was always looking toward the 'next thing' and with trains it seemed he'd found it. Joe tolerated George's visits to the Station, mostly ignoring the small boy as he rushed about seeing to his work, but enjoying the company for the walk home at the end of a shift.

Compared with the independence of the others, life was very different for Thomas. From the time he was born, Martha had coddled him like she had done with none of her other children. Realising he was to be her last child, she wanted something different for him. Something better. She'd been insisting from an early age that Thomas would at least learn the violin. Her store was doing well, but that hadn't resulted in any loosening of the purse strings in the Madden household in any other way. Martha remained determined that her large family would not eat up the profits of her hard work. Each Sunday as she read to them from the Bible and directed them in prayers, she reminded them again and again that life was incredibly hard in Crewe. 'Cash in hand and savings will mean the difference between the workhouse[15] and getting by. Don't ever think you can rely on anybody else to help you through the hard times. No, you need to make sure you've worked hard and saved while times are good. If you don't, you'll end up in the workhouse.'

Her children didn't starve, but they all knew what it was like to go to bed feeling hungry. Waste was not a friend of Martha Madden and the children got what was adequate for their needs and no more. In the meantime, she continued to save her profits from the store. Eva had watched for years as Martha had carefully counted out the savings each week and hid them in a tin box until she had enough to exchange it for the gold sovereigns that she always hid away in the pouch under her apron.

Eva knew her father had only agreed to taking over the shop because he thought twelve hours a day on her feet might distract Martha from her obsession with religion. The day they moved to the house above the shop was the day that Eva had discovered the contents of the pouch as Martha opened it and handed over one of the sovereigns to the previous shopkeeper in order to purchase the rest of the stock.

"Mam, what do you keep in that little bag under your apron?" she'd often asked.

Martha's answer was always the same. Stern, no nonsense: 'Our security against poverty and starvation, Evelyn. Your father and I do not spend. We do not look to spend. The Lord allows us to feed all of you children. The Lord has given me a chance to keep the wolf from the door. Always remember Evelyn, never rely on any man to provide for you. They can fall by the wayside, take to drink, bring

---

[15] A place for those who were unable to support themselves. Often used by the elderly, infirm and sick.

The Price

us to ruination if they so choose. Make sure you save for yourself. Be frugal like me and always put money on one side.'

Eva had wondered why her mother didn't buy a nice hat and coat like the other women. "I want you to walk to Chapel looking beautiful. You always look so ..." Her voice trailed away as she didn't dare say what she was thinking.

Martha had turned on her angrily. "Evelyn, don't be vain. These things you talk about are only earthly trappings. We are put here to serve God, not to please ourselves. We are his servants. If you have one ribbon for your hair, why would you want two?"

Eva had bowed her head in shame. She felt guilty, but at the same time angry. Why did God always have to get in the way of everything? Her mother must have a small fortune tucked away under her apron by now. She could make the family's life so much more comfortable, but she would never spend on anything other than what was absolutely necessary.

The one exception was Thomas. Martha was determined to invest some money in Thomas whether he liked it or not, setting aside sums each week that would have astonished the others if they had only known how large they were. Martha knew of a music teacher who lived a short distance from their home. At a cracking pace she would march little Thomas off for his violin lesson each Thursday. This resulted in a painful squeaking and scraping of the instrument's strings at every opportunity. And it drove the household, not to mention the neighbours, mad.

The other children felt relieved that they had not been subjected to this ambitious step, always trying to make sure that they were well away from the house before the hideous sounds of practising began.

"It sounds like he's strangling a cat!" Eva said to George one afternoon when they had escaped to Joseph's allotment.

Welcome to Brereton Hall

"More like dragging a saw through slate[16]." replied George. "Oh, slate! I'd forgotten school! Mr Aston will use the cane on me if I don't get home and get my spelling list learned! Ah, but how can I be doing bookwork with that racket going on? Violin? What on earth possessed her?"

"Ah, come on George. You love our Tom," Eva answered. "And it's not his fault we've all apparently failed to live up to her expectations and he has to make up for it!" By now the laugh was creeping into her voice. "Besides, he must be finished with that cat by now!"

Despite the jokes, Eva was not happy about the lessons for reasons other than the awful noise of the violin that now filled their home, turning her visits to endurance marathons. She was convinced that one of the gold sovereigns had helped pay for the lessons. And she was jealous because she remembered how she'd always looked at her mother's purse and longed for some new clothes bought from a shop. She had always had to put up with hand-me-downs from neighbours or home made ones. Why should the gold sovereigns be paying for the lessons Thomas hated as much as the rest of them, when she couldn't have had even one new dress? She also knew that the other children often went to bed hungry and that George would soon have to be earning his keep and contributing to the family's kitty. Not that she thought that would bother him. He seemed to spend every spare moment at the railway station now, at least if he got a job there he'd be getting paid for it!

Like the rest of the family though, she couldn't be mad at Thomas. He was the baby of the family, loved and cuddled by his mother as her last child and protected by George. He grew up a happy child and completely oblivious to the traumas that lay ahead for the family. He was also oblivious to the jealousy that the other children, who had suffered so much at Martha's hand, sometimes felt because of his special status.

Thomas was also unlike the other children in another

---

[16] Used in schools for writing on.

way. He was obedient to his mother's wishes and sat through her Bible reading with unquestioning faith. Despite his love of George and his games, he would ignore it when his big brother started his silly poking and prodding designed to get a laugh out of one or another of the children. And unlike George, he attended the Methodist Church without question, whereas George would miraculously vanish at the start of the meetings. George shared his love of the countryside and trains with Tom, the two of them spending days together either fishing and exploring the woods or sitting by the railway watching the huge engines roar past.

This was a blessing for Martha, knowing that he was in safe hands, as she grew increasingly frail and tired by the enormous effort of running the store and tending to her six children. Joseph away from home more than ever working on the railway, gardening on the estates and on the allotment he'd recently rented to grow vegetables for the family. He provided materially for the children, but was largely absent by this stage of the marriage. In fact the few times that he was at home when the children were awake were marked by frosty silences between the couple and arguments after the children went to bed.

Eva returned to Brereton Hall unsettled by this latest visit home. She felt as if her family was farther away than ever and she was surprised that by now she felt more a part of the household staff of the hall than she felt a part of them.

When she got back to Brereton Hall, young men were beginning to talk about the first rumblings of political unrest in Europe, most declaring that they would volunteer if a war had to be fought. In Britain there was no conscription and recruiting campaigns would be needed if the country were ever involved. Eva's earliest memories of soldiers had been when she had sat astride her father's shoulders outside the George and Dragon[17] pub in Crewe, watching

---
[17] Crewe pub located on the corner of Mill and Brook Street demolished after World War 1.

the reservists marching before volunteering to fight in South Africa[18]. Eva had asked him why they didn't go to fight the dragon instead, the one whose fierce picture decorated the swinging pub sign.

Eva listened to these scraps of conversation in horror. She quickly worked out that none of her family would go to war. Joe and George were too young and her father too old. Mary vowed that she would never help in any war and was mortified when her seventeen year-old brother enlisted, leaving his Welsh village forever. On hearing this news Eva wrote to her parents, begging them to make sure that if a war did start, they'd make sure Joe and George didn't do anything so stupid as put their ages up so they could join in. She thought Joe would probably not be at risk for he was too shy and timid, but if it dragged on for years like the Boer War had, then George, with his mad love of adventure, might just be silly enough to join up.

Her father's return letter contained only three sentences: 'Never. You know I love my boys like I love you and I'll not let them go. Now stop worrying.' So she did.

---

[18] The Anglo-Boer war (1899-1902) fought against Britain in the Transvaal and the Orange Free State, which ended in British victory.

The World Changes

Eva lay back on her bed, exhausted from a long day in the kitchen. She pulled out her notebook from under the pillow and made a few entries. Frowning she reminded herself that she must remember to date each entry. So much had happened since she'd left Crewe.

'Mam and Dad moved from Railway Street to Chambers Street.'

George had told her about the move, carried out under cover of darkness after her dad and Joe had finished work for the day. Eva felt guilty but relieved that she'd not been around to hear Ellen and Gussie complaining about the smell from the cheese factory in Chambers Street and about the rats that were enticed to the factory.

'George says in his letter that Tom has finally protested and given up violin playing.'

Eva smiled at that entry. What a relief! She'd always known it was only a matter of time before her youngest brother came under the influence of George. She frowned as she made the next entry:

'George writes to say that Ellen has started to act really strangely, shouting in the street and not always making sense. Running away twice.'

Eva was worried. Was Ellen trying to reach Brereton? How close they'd been growing up together. She was anxious about Joe and Ellen but what could she do? She abandoned her diary for a while. Too many gloomy thoughts kept creeping into her mind and she was powerless to help. Mary had insisted on meeting her that evening for she had a secret to share. Eva suspected that she was up to something because she kept disappearing from the house when work was over. She headed for the gardens, which were well away from Mrs Wilmot's watchful eye.

"Pssst! Over here."

Mary was standing in the shadows of the large rhododendron bushes, out of sight of the kitchen windows. With a conspiratorial smile she beckoned Eva over to her. "Now Eva, how about doing your bit for the war effort," she laughed, "or should I say the 'anti-war' bit."

"Mary, hurry up. It's getting cold out here, and what are those two sacks bulging with?" Eva had spotted them shoved under the bushes.

"Eva, I had to help them. They're no older than my brother was. They're scared. They're hungry and they just couldn't do it. I don't blame them, I agree with them."

"Mary, who are you talking about? Where are they? I know you mean deserters."

"Eva, help me carry this lot to the woods."

"Well just this once." Eva was very curious to see the soldiers despite knowing that it wasn't the thing to do. "But not now. It's too early. Let's wait for another hour. Then no-one will miss us."

The shadows lengthened and at dusk the two girls set off for the woods carrying even more supplies. Mary had raided the pantry yet again and found more bread. Eva was worried, vowing that she would make this her one and only visit. To her dismay she discovered two young boys hidden in the wet bracken. As they wolfed down the food she turned to Mary.

"They can't possibly be old enough to be conscripted, why they're barely older than Joe and George."

The newspapers, already days old, often made their way below stairs to the household staff at Brereton Hall and were read until they literally fell apart. Eva was horrified by what was written. Reflections on what she read late at night were often thought about as she did her work during the day and filled the conversations around the fire when work had finished for the night. She worried about her gentle and sensitive Joe. She knew that his letters to her only hinted at the effect his daily work was having on him and made up her mind to discuss only the cheerful parts to the staff.

A brief letter from Wales informed Mary of the death of her brother. For days she was inconsolable but then the sorrow turned to anger. She spouted her anti-war views to anyone who would listen until Mrs Wilmot reprimanded her. Mary the scullery maid knew the toll the war was taking on everyone especially Eva, who had woken her more than once with nightmares. Her own grief at the loss of her brother made the nightly ritual torture. So she devised a game to try to lighten the mood around the fire each evening when work was finished. She came up with ridiculous topics to change the subject from the horrors of the war and hoped that they would at least be able to go to bed with a smile on their face. It began when she read out a small item from the paper about the birth of a Lord's new child.

"Says here the poor little thing has five names. Five! What'll he be wanting with five names? Are they going to call him in from play with all of them at once? 'It's time for dinner little Phillip William Arthur Henry Edward'."

Interrupted from their serious and emotional conversations the kitchen staff instantly looked across at her open mouthed. "And I wonder how royalty gives birth. I used to think it would be all such an easy process for them. Couldn't imagine the Queen sweating and grunting and shouting. I actually thought that she'd have to wear her crown through the whole process!" They were laughing now, all picturing a regal birth.

"Imagine the crown falling sideways!" laughed one of the kitchen maids.

Mrs Wilmot tried not to laugh, but you could hear

the smile in her voice as she endeavoured to chastise the outspoken Mary. "Mary Jones, you will not be talking about our Royal Family like that in this house!"

"Why not? It might have taken me a long time to realise it, but I finally worked out that they all have bodies that work just like the rest of us!"

"Yes, that may be so. But it's a terrible thing to say that the Royal Family are anything like the rest of us!"

"Well, how else do you think those lords and ladies have their babies? The way I used to think when I was small, that they are delivered with the meat and fish on a Thursday?"

Now they were all laughing. Eva couldn't help but join in. "I used to think they came out through tummy buttons! And I thought that all the boiling water was to cook them when they came out! You'd think with all the babies my Mam had, I would have known better!

The next night it would be some other topic that Mary would pick out of the paper. And it gave them all some much needed relief from the worrying news that they read day after day. It also served to cover up just how deeply Mary was feeling about the war. Far from being able to ignore the news, she was perhaps the most deeply affected of them all.

Eva lay back in her bed. She imagined Joe and George suffering similar fates as the two young boys out there in the cold and wet. She had helped Mary all she could and made up her mind to continue doing so. She waited for her best friend to sneak in under cover of darkness to tell her about the young soldiers. During the following few days Mary became very bold. The death of her brother had been replaced by a desperate need to help the two lads. She barely covered her tracks, crossing the drive in daylight with the food. Finally she was discovered by Mr Charlesworth, who returned her to the kitchen. Mary owned up immediately and defiantly. In a rage at the injustice of it, she called all who could hear and some who couldn't, every bad word she knew in English and Welsh. The deserters were taken away and Mary was instantly dismissed. So Eva lost her closest friend.

Thousands of young men returned home injured in body and mind. Crewe was no exception, welcoming back the young soldiers, each one bringing home with him horrific accounts of the war. Patriotism turned to disbelief and finally anger towards those who had not been conscripted. Two young men who had run away rather than joining the army were discovered hiding in the Cheshire woods. Their bid for freedom was brief and they were soon captured and imprisoned.

The countryside was changing and it affected the food supply. Although land workers were exempt from being called up for the war effort, many young men made the choice to go. Older men and women farmed the land. Plentiful food wasn't so readily available for most of the population, although the gentry still ate well. Below stairs the menu was far more basic. Mrs Wilmot considered it was her duty to cut back on all luxuries as part of the war effort. And so she turned her hand to rabbit pie, jugged hare, baked pike and eel dishes but found it difficult to make them appetising.

Eva knew well the food that now formed the basis of the household staff's daily meals. It was the food she'd been brought up on and so she shyly suggested what she knew about how her mother cooked them. Suddenly tripe and onions, rabbit stews, jellied eels and pigeon pies were on the menu and being enjoyed by the kitchen staff. Her advice to the cook was quite a success for a girl most thought of as just a scullery maid and all the staff admired Eva's common sense and practical nature.

She was by now carrying out the work meant for two scullery maids and her visits home grew more and more infrequent. It seemed her work was never done and she grew thin and tired. Her beautiful hands that her Dad had always loved to hold when she was a baby were now hardened, always red and cracked and the nails were split and painful looking. She never had them out of water long enough for them to heal and Eva would look at them each morning and then at the empty bed where Mary had once slept. She remembered how Mary entertained her with tall stories told in her musical Welsh accent, and look down again at her hands. Like a weight upon her she realised she was slowly turning into her mother, lonely and becoming broken by hard work.

In 1918 she made only one visit home. Despite her sadness, by now she had grown into an attractive young woman of twenty-two. She wasn't tall like her mother, only five feet and four inches. But with thick, curly brown hair framing a finely boned face, she caught the attention of many male workers at Brereton Hall even when dressed in her plain uniform. However, she had learned how to behave with people from her mother, so she never reacted and rarely even noticed the attention, remaining quite remote, firmly placing a distance between herself and others.

She was a proudly independent young woman whose priorities were now confined to her work and family. Her childhood had long since vanished and the loss of Mary had taken away all the fun and laughter in her life. Eva began to feel very isolated at the hall because she lacked a friend with whom she could share her feelings.

At night, alone now in her bedroom where the empty bed became a constant reminder of Mary, Eva spent more time now writing in her notebook:

'George sent me a letter today. He and Joe have been watching the soldiers at Crewe Station. Joe has become very withdrawn. Ellen is the opposite, shouting profanities, cursing God. Mam and Dad hardly know what to do about her. Am very worried about Joe and Ellen.'
'Written to Mary but there is no reply yet. I hate this war. Everything is changing.'

The Price

Finally Eva pushed her notebook under the pillow and tried to sleep. Everything was changing but just where did she fit into all of it? Well, of one thing she was quite sure. She had to be up at 5:30am for her work. At least there was some sort of order at Brereton Hall even if the rest of the world seemed to be going mad.

The great hall was often occupied. Soldiers and guests from other ancestral homes from across Cheshire and beyond came to stay. Many had stories to tell about the war. Eva waited on young men who were terribly maimed. Two of them raged in a kind of madness that Eva had never encountered. The servants found them as they wandered about in an incoherent state. Eva was very disturbed and not able to comprehend their mutterings and irrational behaviour. Mrs Wilmot had given her precise instructions on how to go about her work as if everything was normal but Eva was angry and upset.

"It would be better to lose an arm or a leg, or even be blinded, than to lose who you are and end up like that," she confided in Mrs Wilmot.

"You're absolutely right my dear," the housekeeper confided in her. "No one can escape this war. One way or another, we all suffer. You're lucky Eva. Your family hasn't been touched by this madness."

The Worst Nightmare

How fateful Mrs Wilmot's words turned out to be. During her only visit to Crewe that year, which lasted for four days, she was very distressed and saddened to find that Ellen had been deeply medicated. Her unpredictable and strange behaviour had grown steadily worse. Eva's fears for her sister proved justified when she realised that she barely recognised her. Martha took Eva into the kitchen and shut the door.

"Evelyn, your father and I need to explain what we've decided to do about your sister. We waited until you came home because we didn't think it was right to disturb your work and we didn't want you to come home to find it had already all happened. We know how much you love Ellen and now you're an adult, we knew you'd want to know everything."

Eva hesitated, wanting to speak out but she dare not. Her mother's voice was steely. She knew this look from her childhood days, knowing that nothing would change Martha's decision. Despite her mother saying that she and Joseph had decided together, Eva knew it would have had nothing to do with her father's thinking. Silently she waited.

"You know full well Evelyn that your sister has been a handful for some years now."

Eva was determined to interrupt as she had already guessed at the terrible decision her mother had made. "She's just full of life, Mam. I know she makes you angry about ..." She paused, choosing her next words carefully, "... about your God."

"Let me tell you Evelyn, you've been away. You don't know what it's come to. It is God's will that this has happened. I have prayed for weeks before we, your father and I, decided what should be done. There are things you know nothing about."

Eva felt a flame of anger. "What don't I know about? And that wouldn't be difficult. This house is so full of secrets that people in it sharing a bed don't even know the first thing about each other!"

But Martha ignored the outburst and spoke very quietly. "Ellen has never started to menstruate. The doctor has been consulted and he said that her behaviour needs medical treatment. She needs to go into hospital." She folded her hands calmly in front of her. Eva stared at her in disbelief.

"So she speaks out. So she has defied you. Mother, she's so unhappy. Why can't you see that? And now you're going to put her in an asylum! That's it isn't it? You are going to sign papers and put her away for ever because she's different."

"Stop this at once Evelyn! Just because you work with the gentry don't think you can come here, lording it about and telling me that I don't know what I'm doing. The decision has been made. I am telling you, not asking your advice."

Eva was white with rage. She left the room, gathered up her bag and coat and slammed the front door. Eva walked round the town for hours, angry with disbelief. She was powerless to interfere even though she knew in every fibre of her being how wrong the decision was. She waited at the top of the railway station for George to finish his shift work. Surely he could make some sense of all this and help her convince her mother to try something else. He came walking from the goods yard, looking very tired. Eva realised that he was growing up into a handsome young man. She also realised how much she loved him. Running towards him, she threw herself into his arms.

"Hold on, hold on. Who is this young woman? We'll have people talking."

His kind words broke down a barrier within Eva.

She sobbed as George continued to hold her, calming her down. "Yes I know all about it Evie. I was the one who went to fetch her when she was wandering about in Winsford. She's ill and Mam and Dad can't help her. We will visit her but she has to go away. She is no longer safe either in the house or in the street. I'm scared for her Eva and she scares everyone else."

"Are you telling me that I have to just accept it?" Eva was incredulous. How could this happen?

"Eva, we've got to trust the doctors. They know what they are talking about love. The doctors understand these things much better than us." Noticing that he was still wasn't convincing her, he sighed and said, "Look at it this way." He took her arm and they walked along together, brother and sister so alike, trying to rationalise such a decision. "What happens if a rabbit or a dog changes and becomes different from all the others? What happened to that snow-white crow we saw over in Betley when we were kids? The other crows pecked it to death eventually because it wasn't like them."

"What has this got to do with my sister?"

"If she continues to wander about the streets of Crewe, doing unpredictable things, keeps going into Chapel when Mam is there, shouting rude things about God, in the end Eva, even her friends will stay away from her and laugh at her. Do you want that for Ellen?"

"But ..."

"Eva, I don't like the thought of our sister being locked away either. But you've been away. You haven't seen how hard this has all been. For Mam and Dad, for all of us, especially for Ellen. She's not happy Eva. Half the time she doesn't know what's going on. My letters to you only said half of it."

On and on he talked, gradually making Eva see the reasons for their mother's decision. Slowly Eva came to realise that George was right. They could visit. Ellen would come out of the asylum one day. People did get better. There was good treatment in there; he was convinced of it. Eva was not so sure, but George persuaded her at least to return to the house with him. Here, they listened to their mother's strong words.

"It must never be discussed either in or outside the house because the neighbours will just think our Ellen's strange behaviour is madness. All of us must remember that Ellen is ill and one day she'll get better but you know what people are like. People already think Ellen is strange, but it's better we don't talk about it at all."

It was decided on the day of Eva's visit that the secret must be kept forever. The first story the family told was that Ellen had gone away to Shropshire to stay with her Aunty Mary. Later the family would tell people who asked that like Eva, Ellen was in service. On no account was it ever to be known that she was in a mental institution. Little Thomas must never be told, but George already knew because he had helped his father bring her back from Winsford.

Eva cried for hours after two doctors took Ellen away, discreetly after nightfall of course, for she was fearful of the treatment that lay ahead for her sister. She tried to reassure her, telling her that she would visit when she could get time off from work at Brereton. Both sisters clung to the hope that this would only be a temporary thing. Little did Ellen know that she would remain in a mental institution for most of her life.

As she lay in bed that night, Eva thought about the stories her father had told her of when Ellen was born and how she had longed to have a little sister. It had been a long wait between babies for those times and Eva knew now that the neighbours had speculated on the reason, everything from Martha banning Joseph from her bed to tragic miscarriages due to Martha's obvious frailty. Of course, it had been the nasty Mrs Gibbs who had taken the gossiping to a whole new level. She disliked Martha and her ways and took great delight in suggesting that she may have visited an abortionist, one of the disgraced midwives who practised in dark, unknown corners of the town. Strange that Mrs Gibbs knew that these women existed, but couldn't name a single one, or where they might be found.

Eva vaguely remembered wonderful times with her father when they left the house so that Martha could rest before the birth. She supposed that's why she always felt close to him. She told anyone who listened that she wanted a baby sister because at least she would have someone to play with. The boys who played outside in the street were far too noisy and troublesome. Her father told her how she had bravely gone all by herself to get the midwife and waited at the bottom of the stairs for him to come home. And how she was so frightened by the cries and pacing from upstairs that she flew into his arms when he walked through the door and rubbed her cheeks against his stubbly face until she got a rash. He also told her how she thought all the boiling water was to clean the baby especially when she heard the first ear splitting yell from Ellen.

She remembered the sight of her mother in the bed and her father holding the baby and thought it all looked like Christmas and the baby Jesus. As her father had lowered the bundle for her to look at, Eva had touched her face and held her hand, her new sister's fingers curling around hers. She loved her instantly. But life in the Madden household had been irrevocably changed by Ellen's arrival. Where the neighbours were barely aware there was a baby in the household when Eva was born, Ellen shook the walls of the terraced houses with her crying, prompting neighbours to call advice over the back wall. Eva remembered the suggestion of a drop of whisky being given on a spoon to help the newborn to sleep particularly enraging Martha. This was the first time that Eva realised how much her mother hated alcohol.

Little Ellen could never be left alone and as her mother was soon pregnant again, Eva was left largely to look after her little sister on her own. Walking by ten months, she couldn't be trusted with anything. If you didn't watch her she'd open the front door and toddle out into the street. In bed she'd pick at the wax dripping of the candle and chew it, often burning her little fingers. Life with Ellen had never been peaceful, but it had always been an adventure.

The worst, but at the same time funniest thing Ellen had done was to humiliate the Crewe Salvation Army Band with her company and to persuade young Joe to join in. It was not long before Eva left for Brereton Hall and Ellen had organised Joe to walk behind the musicians beating a little drum, while she sang as loudly and as out of tune as she could manage. Eva had quickly snatched them from the street and took them home, but not before one of the old ladies of the street had spotted them, resulting in a telltale knock at the door the same afternoon. Their mother was horrified and they were no longer allowed out of the house unless accompanied by Eva, who gave young Ellen a good telling off. A tear rolled down Eva's cheek as she remembered shouting at Ellen. "You see Elly, it's like mocking God. That Sally Army band is playing for their church, so it's like playing to God."

Ellen was not one to be spoken to, unchallenged. "But Eva, I don't believe in God! And neither does Joe! The only bits I believe in are the scary bits in Mam's readings about bushes bursting into flames and speaking, and Lot's wife being turned into a pillar of salt. I don't care about those stupid Sallys and I don't care about church. And I'm not going to church with *her* anymore!"

"You *are*!" Eva shouted, astounded by her sister's stubbornness.

But Ellen had insisted. "I am not! George doesn't go. Dad's at work. And anyway, church is boring. Gussie only goes so she can dress up and wear a fine hat and I always have the job of looking after Tom who falls asleep and sometimes he even slobbers on me! It's all right for you, Eva, you're always so good that you'll fly to heaven no matter what you do. But I'm far too naughty. And you know what Mam says, naughty is the evil devil coming out."

"Not true Elly! You're *not* evil. Don't even think nonsense like that! Besides, I have bad thoughts too. I hate that Mam won't spend any money on nice things for all of us. I feel ashamed when she tells the neighbours that they're cut off at the shop and can't put anymore on tick. I get angry with Dad when he comes home after a pint of beer and argues with Mam. And I don't always think what's said in the Chapel is true or real, but it's Mam's way and we have to go along with it."

Of course, they'd made up only minutes later. But Eva couldn't help but remember her sister saying she thought she was evil and it broke her heart. She was just high-spirited and now she was in an asylum. She lay awake for hours quietly crying. She couldn't bear to think of Ellen in that place despite everyone's reassurances that it was for the best and every time she did think of Ellen her eyes filled with tears. She'd always looked after Ellen and now she was helpless to make things better. And worse, she was forbidden to talk about it to anyone. It was a secret she was worried would consume her.

Eva returned to Brereton Hall looking like she hadn't slept a wink and Mrs Wilmot wondered what could possibly have affected her so badly. Usually Eva came back bursting with stories about the adventures of her brothers and sisters, but this time she was quiet, almost sullen and she was sure the girl was crying when she thought nobody was looking.

The End of the War

The end of World War 1 in 1918 was celebrated across Britain in hundreds of street parties. Nothing had been seen like it since the end of the Boer War. The relief people felt was obvious as they decked out their dull red brick houses with flags and paper bunting, organised parties and stacked trestle tables with as much food as they could collectively offer. The grim scenes on Crewe railway station dragged to a close and Eva hoped that Joe would get over the terrible sadness that almost overwhelmed him. Not just in Crewe, but all over the country, khaki uniforms were hidden away by widows and mothers. They were offered the chance to make the long depressing journey to Flanders to search out the graves of their loved ones, but few among the working classes took up the offer. During the next two years, people of all classes strove for normality in an effort to forget the horrors and wastage of World War 1.

In the houses and halls of the wealthy, great banquets were prepared for guests who travelled from across Western Europe and the colonies to celebrate with their relatives and friends. At Christmas 1918, Brereton Hall staff prepared for a large number of visitors. They would stay for at least a week to enjoy the hunting across the Cheshire Plain, to celebrate lavishly with the finest wines, malt whiskies and food. The festivities would culminate in a banquet served in the magnificent banqueting hall. The staff was frantically opening up the many bedrooms to accommodate their guests. They polished the silver, washed the bedding and dusted the cobwebs from some of the rooms that had not been occupied for years.

The Armistice had been signed on the 11th November, so at Brereton Hall the celebrations were combined with the Christmas activities. A giant pine tree, at least twenty feet tall, was decorated with baubles and bows that had been stored away for years. Guests were amazed when they first laid eyes on it, as they were welcomed at the entrance hall. Some could barely tear their eyes away from the glittering tree to be shown to their sleeping quarters. Coal fires burnt in almost every room, warming the great hall and casting dancing shadows onto the ornate walls.

Eva had worked very hard for two weeks prior to the guests arriving. She watched with pride from the minstrel's gallery as the first of the visitors arrived. She heard the sound of motorcars and then laughter and all the exclamations over how beautiful the hall looked. That night, as Eva lay in her bed beneath the skylight window, she thought about the faraway land that she'd only heard about through the Hollis family. She had only ever known a life that stretched for a handful of miles, but this distant place began to intrigue her, a land that looked like England but had volcanoes and huge sheep farms.

She wondered how her family was, for Christmas times had always been special in the past. She shivered when she thought of the dark little house. It would be joyless and grim with probably no festivities or Christmas food even though she had sent extra money from her wages to her parents. Her father would be escaping into the local pub every evening after work to avoid the almost tangible web of religious discipline that her mother now practised and controlled the household with. Any arguments he might have once had with her were now gone and he just left Martha to her prayers and judgements.

They all needed some way to cope with what had happened to Ellen and immersing herself even more deeply in her religion was Martha's way of coping. Eva thought that her mother saw Ellen's illness as some kind of sin that would be swept away physically by her daughter's absence. These days Martha was always seen in a long black skirt and old white blouse, wrapped around in a thick calico apron and hair dragged back from her strained face. She looked old and worn. Laughter had long ago gone from her life, unlike her eldest daughter who resolutely pursued a life outside the miserable home.

The smile returned again as she thought of George. No matter what happened, he would be out of the house, either in the woods or fields, dragging Thomas with him, on his new milk round or pursuing some vague offer for help on a nearby farm. Like Eva, he was already a saver, determined to have money for himself and the family. Then her thoughts turned to Joe, lovely gentle Joe. No one really understood him. He despised his father, had little to do with anyone and spoke little. But he doggedly went off to work every day. George had said in his last letter that Joe had seemed depressed and preoccupied. And Eva worried about him. Joe seemed so easily injured by the sad and dark things in the world and so unsuited to a life in the misery of the Madden household.

Eva felt a pang of guilt as she thought about the eldest of her brothers. He'd been surrounded by sadness since he entered the world. Martha had been ill throughout the pregnancy and the birth had been difficult. Like most things that happened in the night, Ellen had slept through it. But eventually Joseph came downstairs and beckoned Eva to come into her parents' bedroom to see her new brother. It was a rare treat because even in such a small house where everyone lived so close together, privacy was insisted upon in the Madden household.

"Don't make a sound, our Evie. Just come over and have a peep at your new brother," her father had whispered.

He was so tiny and still and Eva had been scared he was going to die. But the midwife had reassured her, and her father had put the two girls to bed. Eva had lain there for a long time listening to the footsteps coming and going until she felt calm again, knowing that her mother was probably asleep. Finally she had slipped quietly from her bed and tiptoed across the landing to peer in through the half opened door. She had looked first at her father sitting in a chair by the bed and then at her mother propped up on a bolster in the bed, her Bible open on her lap. As she looked in, Eva realised just how much her father loved her mother and over the years when things seemed impossible between the two of them, it was the image that Eva used to comfort herself.

Now she was out of the miserable household, surrounded by wealth and festivities, warmth, good food and stimulating conversation. Yet her parents, brothers and sisters, whom she loved so much, were stuck in a sad and silent house, wrapped up in secrets and unhappiness. Her home had turned into a house of whispers and secrets.

She remembered Ellen as a bright and cheeky little girl, wondering about the madness that had taken her and why it had happened. Shortly before Christmas she had made a two-hour visit to the hospital, but Ellen was heavily sedated, not even recognising her.

But Eva was not in the mood to dwell too long on sad things and once again her thoughts turned to the Hollis family in New Zealand, a bright land where she might one day make a future. If she were to go, maybe some of her family would follow her to enjoy a better life. Maybe one day she might travel away from England, something that she had always secretly dreamed of.

Despite the good mood she was in as she drifted off to sleep, the stress of her family was never far away. Her dreams that night were of dark rooms where the walls were whispering and closing in on her. The floor beneath her looked as though it was made of patterned and broken glass. Looking through the floor, she could see a raging river and logs, great crashing shifting logs, moving and bumping into each other. She couldn't reach the other side where her mother stood waiting. There was blood everywhere, yet her feet were not cut. More whispers and voices called and finally a deep sleep enclosed her, saving her from any more suffering.

Before dawn she awoke to a whispered sound

against the skylight. Fat flakes of snow slid down the glass and the sky was dark with an approaching storm. Eva dressed quickly in the cold of her room, moving quietly so as not to wake anyone. Like her brother George she needed very little sleep, loving the dawn and those first few hours when no one was about.

She made her way to the front of the house to look out across the Cheshire land to the river and beyond to the woods. Smoke spiralled from Mr Charlesworth's cottage but thick untrodden snow blanketed the entire estate, ending any plans for fox hunting. She'd hoped to be able to catch a glimpse of the hunt. She remembered how once when George was old enough their father took him out to stand on the edge of a thick Cheshire wood not far from the dirty town street where they lived. They both loved being out in the fresh air and being around animals and they would just stand and share their thoughts on nature and the subtle changing of the English countryside. Eva had watched them one day as they walked together, waiting for the Cheshire fox to break from cover followed by the hunt riding past. George had been upset for the fox the first time, but Joseph had patiently explained that it was an important tradition that helped keep the countryside alive and after that George loved to go and watch. But there would be no hunting today. Returning disappointed to the hall, she entered through the great oak door, treading silently across the stone flagged floor towards the kitchen. With a sigh she picked up her dusting cloth and started her day's work.

Eva was allowed more visits home but they were not happy events. Now that she had the opportunity to return to Crewe on a more regular basis, she avoided it. Her unhappiness began to show itself in her everyday actions although she struggled to remain cheerful and hopeful. She began to grow impatient with everything and resentful; not resentment for the wealthy lifestyle of those she worked for, but about small things like incompetence among the staff. She felt tired every morning and what little sleep she got was filled with horrific dreams, causing her to wake several times every night. After months of worrying all day and tossing and turning all night, she reached breaking point one day and her temper showed itself in all its fury in the kitchen. She shouted at the new scullery maid who had blocked the sink and caused chaos for everyone else. Mrs Wilmot, who had recently been ill, was struggling to sort out the blockage with the help of Mr Charlesworth.

The following day Eva found the kitchen fire had almost gone out. Once again it was the result of the scullery maid's lack of thought. This time Eva grabbed the child by the shoulder. "You stupid girl! What do you think you are doing? Everything you touch goes wrong!" Then in a quieter and more frightening tone, "You should be dismissed." She proceeded to shake the girl until she screamed and Eva was red with anger.

She allowed herself a few minutes off in the gardens before calming down and re-entering the house. These bad moods frightened her because for the most part she'd always been a cheerful and optimistic person. Resolving never to act like that again and feeling guilty, she looked for the scullery maid to check if she was all right. She heard voices from the vegetable gardens.

"I tell ya' William, she's a real weird one that Eva Madden. She's acting like a grand lady and it's 'Mrs Wilmot this' and 'Mrs Wilmot that,' like she can do nothing wrong! Then she grabs me and shakes me 'cos the fire's snuffed. Keep away from 'er I say!"

Eva turned away before they saw her, knowing that from now on she must keep her growing temper under control. The next thing that people would say was that she was mad, which was something she couldn't bear. Just the word brought visions of Ellen and the way she'd been locked away. She couldn't imagine what people at the hall would say if they knew about Ellen, given her own behaviour recently.

Just thinking about times growing up with Ellen

brought a smile to her face and she resolved to visit her sister as soon as she had a day off. Hopefully she could sit with her in the hospital grounds. Seeing her sister always had a calming effect on Eva, even at the hospital. Perhaps it was the garden and having absolutely nothing to do for an hour or so, but she thought she always felt better after a visit. The longing for her recovery was at times like a physical ache inside Eva. She also made her mind up to write more often to George. They exchanged letters but if she didn't write to him, then she wouldn't get one back. She reminded herself that there were good things in her life and she mustn't lose control of her life or her temper.

Mrs Wilmot

1922 saw a change of management at Brereton Hall. Mr and Mrs Moir left the hall after over thirty years of residency. The coming of Mr and Mrs Norman Howard McLean resulted in many changes in management for the staff, who by now were few in number. Much of the work involved in running the house included domestics doubling up on their duties. For the older members of staff, who were set in their ways, the transition was not easy. It was only the fact that by now Brereton Hall was their home that kept some of them there.

Mrs Wilmot seemed most affected. She found it more and more difficult to cope with the changes. The situation was not helped by the fact that she was now quite sick. What had seemed like a minor annoyance a few months earlier had failed to improve, in fact was growing steadily worse. She rarely complained, but Eva could see that she was constantly in some discomfort and seemed to tire so quickly that she could barely get through her work some days. Finally she had to take a break. She was a widow, whose entire family consisted of one sister in Sandbach, so she went there to recuperate, reassuring Eva that a couple of weeks off would soon put her right. But news soon came from Mr Charlesworth that in fact Mrs Wilmot had cancer and would not be returning. The news devastated her. Everything she had learnt had come from the kind housekeeper who had been like a mother to her. What would Brereton Hall be without her? Eva couldn't imagine her life without the woman who had spent more time with her than her own mother.

The news had a deep impact on Eva, making it even harder to get a good night's sleep and despite her resolve to keep her temper under control, she found herself battling with her impatience on an hourly basis. She really didn't like Mr and Mrs McLean and the new regime with fewer servants only increased the number of errors made by the staff. For the first time in a long time, Eva found herself praying, which brought a smile to the corners of her mouth when she thought of what her mother would say: 'I told you so', or George: 'be practical' or Ellen: 'waste of time', but it made her feel better to pray for Mrs Wilmot, because she worried about her constantly and any help that might be available to her should be provided.

As soon as she was able, Eva gave up a journey home to Crewe in favour of visiting Mrs Wilmot at Sandbach. It was a sad meeting for they knew that they wouldn't be seeing one another again. Eva was shocked by Mrs Wilmot's appearance, but tried to hide it and talk about happy things. But the cook had other ideas. She had grown to love the beautiful little girl who had grown into an intelligent and disciplined young woman under her guidance.

"Now listen to me dear little Eva. And don't you be interrupting me and you can keep your protests too. Let an old lady give you some advice; some personal advice. I've already taught you all I know about running a house and the time for talk of work is over." Eva was shocked. She'd never heard Mrs Wilmot talk like this.

"You follow your dreams. I know that you want to travel and you must." Eva was astonished that Mrs Wilmot had remembered the late night fireside chats from so long ago.

"You're excellent at your job and work can be found for good servants in many of the fine houses in the colonies. All my life I wanted to go to Canada and I always thought that there'd be time to think about it later. Well, here I am and I never did it." Eva listened in silence; her eyes brimming with unshed tears.

"Don't let anything stop you Eva. For years you've

cared about your parents, brothers and sisters. You can still help them, but now have some life of your own. You can only live by your duty for others for so long before your duty is to yourself girl." Eva was crying by now. The tears were silently rolling down her cheeks. How could this woman, who she'd only ever really spoken to about household things, know so much of what was in her heart?

"Your family's burden doesn't have to be yours, young Eva. Yes, I know what's gone on with your family, your father distraught and your mother wasting away. All you bright young children having to go out to work just so there's food in the house and a roof over their heads."

Now the tears were replaced with horror. How did Mrs Wilmot know all this? And did she know about Ellen too? Mrs Wilmot noticed the change on Eva's face, "Oh child, did you not realise what a gaggle of gossips some of us older folk in service are? When you manage a house or estate, as I'm sure you'll discover one day, you can't talk to the people you're boss to, so you talk to each other. At the market or when you can get a few days away to visit a friend or relative on another estate. Not often, but you need to, if you know what I mean." Eva nodded. Since she'd had to supervise some of the staff at Brereton Hall, she'd felt far lonelier than she ever had when she was just a scullery maid and had Mary to share things with.

Mrs Wilmot continued, "Well, what I'm trying to say is that there's been talk about your father, that's all. He used to be such a reliable man. All the estates near Crewe wanted him to work for them on the seasonal jobs, but now he seems lost, much to your mother's distress. It must remind her of her past."

Eva had been staring at the floor, but at mention of her mother, she looked up. Despite her daydreams and stories about her mother when she was child, Eva realised she knew very little about her, other than the town where she had been born. "Wha ...What do you mean?" she managed to stammer.

"You know your mother was a lady, don't you? Surely?"

Suddenly Eva felt very small. "I don't really know anything about my Mam, except for what I've seen myself, Mrs Wilmot," she said very quietly. "What do you know?"

"Oh, Eva! I had no idea. You poor child! Has nobody ever said anything?"

"No, Mrs Wilmot. It's not really Mam's way. And Dad's always gone along with her. We know lots of stories about Dad's family, but none really about Mam."

"Well now. Hmmm. Your Mam was a lady, Eva. Not so rich and grand as those that own Brereton Hall, but from a good family. Life should have been very good for your Mam way I heard it. She went to the best school and had beautiful clothes. Then her father lost it all."

Eva gasped. Suddenly so much of her mother's behaviour made sense. The vigorous nods during the Minister's sermons on the evils of life, including drink and gambling, her lectures to her children during prayers after dinner, the whispered arguments when her father came home late, her advice to each of her children to make themselves financially independent, to save and never have to rely on anyone else. It also explained the bag of beautiful jewellery and the beads that Eva always had to play with as a child. It was just like she used to tell the other children in the street. Only it was a borrowed vegetable cart that had taken them from the street, instead of the grand carriage she had always told the other children would one day whisk the Maddens away to the grand lifestyle her mother had grown up in.

Mrs Wilmot waited quietly as she watched all the emotions cross Eva's face. Finally Eva met her eyes again. "What happened to my mother's family Mrs Wilmot? Do you know?"

"Not all of it. The way I heard it, your grandfather lost the house. The children were brought back from school and they all ended up in a cottage at Shrifnel. How she came to meet your Dad I'm not sure. Perhaps he was doing some work on one of the estates. But it was quite the love affair. There was great opposition to the match because she was marrying beneath her. But to her mind her family had nothing but their name left and so they married anyway and moved away." They sat in silence for a moment. "Have you wondered why you've never met your mother's family? Never heard stories about them?"

"It's just Mam's way, Mrs Wilmot. She doesn't talk about much but religion and rules. She's been a tough Mam to have really. Not like all the other children, with their Mams who love to laugh and sing and gossip. But I do love her and she's worked hard to look after us all."

"Well, now you have another Mam, because I do look on you like a daughter, young Eva. Now don't be crying again. How could I not? I've had you everyday since you were a scrap of a thing. Now, when I'm gone …" and Eva started to interrupt. "Listen to me now Eva. I'm tired and I know you have to go soon. Let me get out what I have to say."

"Yes, of course, I'm sorry Mrs Wilmot."

"That's more like it. Now, you will find through my sister that I have left a little bit of money for you. I want you to promise me that you will buy some nice new clothes with it and one of those lovely hats in the newspaper that you like so much."

"But Mrs Wilmot, I couldn't."

"You could and you will. And I want you to have adventures! And get married. And be loved, but stay away from scoundrels!" She laughed at this last bit. Then quietly, "Do it for me Eva."

Eva was so shocked that she cried quite openly, something she had not done since Ellen had been taken away. Kissing Mrs Wilmot goodbye, she caught the bus back to Brereton.

As she walked up the long drive she remembered that first day when her father had brought her from Crewe.

She was so proud to know that someone beyond her family had so much faith in her. And so warmed by the love that she'd never known the older woman had for her. She resolved then and there to keep the promise made to her dear friend. Seeing out her life at Brereton Hall would not be for her. Neither were the dirty streets and terraced houses in Crewe. Mrs Wilmot was right. Her destiny lay elsewhere.

The Turning Point

It was not for several months after her visit to Mrs Wilmot that Eva had a chance to visit Crewe to check on her family and put her mind at rest after all her worrying. Tucked into her purse was fifty pounds that had been left to her. After a portion of her pay was taken out and sent to her mother each month, it was what it usually took Eva a year to earn and she felt like the richest woman in Crewe. She thought about her mother and how she would want her to save the money, but she was determined to honour Mrs Wilmot's wish.

Crewe had several dress shops and Eva visited each of them before choosing carefully. From one she bought a pair of leather shoes with buckles and a woollen suit with a nipped in waist. As he measured her, the assistant declared that she had a waist measurement of twenty-two inches and could be a model for the men who made the advertisements in the paper! Eva blushed as she was used to getting about in a maid's grey uniform, not being noticed by men.

A high-necked blouse with pearl buttons completed the outfit. She saved some of the money for a hat and some small presents for her family. Then she had her hair cut in a fashionable bob with her curls tucked behind her ears. Finally she put on her hat and looked at herself in the mirror. She decided that she would be hardly recognisable and put on the rest of the new outfit in the shop.

Shyly she made her way to the family home, walking elegantly down the drab streets. She felt like a lady. Smiling to herself, she knocked on the front door. Her mother opened it, staring at her transformed daughter. A sad little smile was her only welcome. Eva followed her along

The Price

the dark passageway into the kitchen. Martha looked at her thoughtfully. Her eyes lit up when she saw the hatpin given so long ago to the laughing little girl who was going into service.

"Well Evelyn, it has not all been of no avail has it? You look very nice. You remind me of me when ..." Suddenly she stopped talking and turned away. Eva felt a rush of compassion.

"Mam! Be pleased for me. Please be happy for me. Look, I've brought you a present." From her handbag she pulled a pale blue silk scarf. "This will look so lovely Mam. Wear it when you go to Chapel."

Martha turned. She took the scarf from Eva, but gently her daughter took it back, placing it round Martha's neck, arranging it in feminine folds about her thin shoulders. "Look in the hall mirror Mam. You look so lovely."

For a few seconds Martha's face lit up with pleasure. Her hands touched the silk around her neck. Leaning forward she stroked Eva's cheek. "You promise me Evelyn, that you'll always look after yourself when you leave us."

Eva opened her mouth to interrupt, but her mother put up her finger for silence. "Yes, I know you're going to leave us. George has told me that your letters to him are filled with stories of places you've read about in books from the great hall's library. And you must go and see them. There's nothing for you here. I don't want you to think I'm sending you away. We'll always love you and miss you and wait for your visits. But go Eva, before you are caught up in this miserable life like me."

"Oh, Mam ...!"

"Just remember one thing. Life works like a balance scale and for everything we take for ourselves, God sets a price. Just like the price in long working hours and the lack of husband and babies has been your price for living in that grand hall. Be free and there will be a price. But if you are faithful and dutiful and keep yourself humble, then it should be a price you will be happy to pay. I pray and I hope it will be so small as missing your family." Eva felt the tears. Martha noticed her daughter's growing emotions. "Now go and catch up with your brothers and sisters, and let me organise a meal."

Eva didn't remember anything so personal ever having been said between her and her mother, and nothing as personal was ever said between mother and daughter again. She also knew for the first time since she could remember, how much love Martha carried for her. It was as if she carried her mother's dreams too.

It was a relief to hear the door bang as Tom, then Joe and George and finally Augusta returned at the end of the day. They made her twirl around to show off her new clothes and Augusta insisted on trying on her new hat. Then they enjoyed their presents from Eva who, as always, entertained them with stories from Brereton. There was laughter in the house once again. After what seemed like hours of talking about the goings on at the hall, Eva took her turn to listen to exaggerated tales of all the goings on back in Crewe.

George had bought a Sealyham terrier for ratting and rabbiting. He called it Peter and had to keep it on his father's allotment because Martha would not allow animals in the house. Eva remembered well the fight that had ensued when her father had brought home a puppy for Eva when Ellen was still a baby and the reaction from Martha to the kitten she'd once tried to adopt. There never had been and never would be a pet in the Madden household while Martha was running it. 'You won't be bringing that filthy thing into my house, young George Madden!' George said in his best impersonation of their stern mother. 'Dogs are scavengers and their only mission in life is to eat. I'll not be having it eat us out of house and home! And I'll not have its fleas in our beds!' he continued, the rest of them falling about with laughter.

Then Tom piped in, "And Eva, did you know that Mam's a magician?" he laughed at Eva's quizzical look.

The Price

"She managed to change George's snow white dog black within an hour!" Everyone burst out laughing again because they knew the story. Eva just continued to look at him puzzled. "Go on. Tell her George!" laughed Tom.

"Well, one day I brought the little dog home. But Mam started with her nagging about not having it in the house, so I tied it up near the back door. As soon as I went out she locked the poor thing in the coal shed. When I got back, no dog! But I could hear him whining and followed the sound to the coal shed. When I opened the door a soot black Scotty dog came out!"

"Black as the coal dust Peter had been rolling in," Tom laughed.

And on they went like that for hours. Eva sensed that the situation at home had improved and she left that evening feeling happier. She thought about what her mother had said all the way back to Brereton Hall on the bus but had no idea how Martha had guessed her secret. Even though her mother said George had told her, she couldn't really imagine that because George was the best keeper of secrets in a family of secret keepers. Eva couldn't imagine George sharing her letters. But there would never really be an answer. What was more important was that Eva realised that maybe Martha had wanted to escape the drudgery of married life many years ago. In any case, Eva knew she had her mother's blessing in whatever she decided to do.

That day was a turning point for Eva. Her mother had given her praise, love and respect. She had kept her promise to Mrs Wilmot. Her brothers and sisters loved her. They had all laughed together. She was finally beginning to dress the way she wanted to, in her first fully shop-bought outfit. So much was falling into place. As the bus took her through the Cheshire countryside she was so familiar with, a lot of the anxiety that had weighed so heavily on her over the past few months began to lift and she made a promise to enjoy life a little more.

She hadn't felt she could for a while, but the visit

home had given her the strength to visit Ellen and she made plans to go on the first day she had off work. Sitting out in the hospital grounds, she breathed the fresh air and felt complete again. As the sisters sat together Eva wove the new ribbons she had brought into her sister's long brown hair and declared how pretty she looked. It was like the old times at home. Eva told her about the dog covered in coal dust and all the other stories she and her brothers and sisters had shared. She described the food at Brereton Hall and from her bag she produced a small tin of salmon and some cheeses for Ellen, promising her that she would visit again very soon and bring some new treats. Before she left she confided in Ellen. They'd shared so many secrets growing up together, so it felt like old times telling her of travel plans.

"Ellen it sounds like such a place! I really think I will go there some day. And then there are so many other places I want to see. Mrs Wilmot told me about Canada and how much she'd wanted to go there, so there's another place on my list. I don't think I should like to visit anywhere where they don't speak English, but there are so many places they do! I could even end up in Africa or somewhere like that one day!"

Ellen just held her hand tightly, not really following Eva's conversation, but knowing that she would never see such places. In fact it seemed more and more that she would never see any of the world outside the hospital again. She was so proud of Eva and a part of her knew she had to trust her to live her dreams for both of them.

It was also around this time that Eva was introduced to the secret girlfriend of George! There was an age difference between the two. George was barely seventeen years old and Edith James was twenty-two but this made very little difference to the couple. Eva was delighted to find that George had discovered a woman who appreciated his bright clever nature and the two women became firm friends.

Typical of George, Eva had discovered his secret

in mysterious circumstances. It had happened during one of her visits home. As usual George invited her to take a walk with him. Only this time they didn't head out across the countryside like they had as small children.

"I want you to meet someone very special, Eva." Then it burst out of him, "She's the woman I'm going to marry!" Eva burst out laughing, looking in astonishment at her young brother.

"What on earth have you been up to George? I thought you spent all your spare time at Betley!"

"Apparently not all of it!" he laughed. "I've met a wonderful girl. And I'm taking you to meet her. Oh Eva, she is such fun, you just can't imagine! I just know you two will be such good friends."

Edith James worked in a flower shop in Crewe. George and Eva peered through the window. In amongst the flowers and carefully making up wreaths was a slight girl. All Eva could make out was her long dark hair falling over her shoulders. George tapped on the window causing Edith to look up. The smile between them told Eva all she wanted to know. Linking arms with George she entered the shop.

"What a heavenly perfume," she exclaimed to the young woman behind the counter.

"Wrong word I think," laughed George. "Nothing heavenly about my Edith is there?" He shot behind the counter and gave the laughing girl a big kiss. "Eva, this is Edith James. And Edith, this is my eldest sister Eva."

The two women smiled at each other and put their hands out. "I'm very pleased to meet you," smiled Eva.

"And it's lovely to finally put a face to the name. It's lovely to meet you too, Eva."

"When you've finished making those dreary wreaths, see if Mrs Chalwin will give you a few moments out of the shop Edith. Now you're introduced, I want you to meet the other woman in my life properly."

Brother and sister waited on the pavement for Edith. She was soon out, pushing her thick brown hair back from her face. She looked at Eva's trim figure and bright smile and liked her straight away. Eva's easy manner with George encouraged Edith to share her feelings at once.

"You know I'm older than George?" she asked.

"Yes, older than me but not wiser!" was the quick reply from George.

Eva looked at the two of them together and smiled. She felt relieved that George had found a girl who obviously cared deeply for him.

"Eva, I want you to know I'm serious about George. I met your mother yesterday. We went back to George's house. My own mother doesn't know anything about us yet. And she won't be happy about it when she finds out!" Then the seriousness left her face and she laughed. "I think that she wants her four daughters with her until the day they die. She doesn't like men at all."

George shook with laughter. "I wonder what she'll think when I roar up the street on my first motorbike?" And as Eva frowned he added, "I do mean to have one."

"Yes, and I shall ride on it!" added Edith, looking at George and laughing. "We'll go everywhere on it, won't we George?"

Here was a girl with spirit and determination, thought Eva. She will need it if she's to walk alongside George, build a home with him and understand the Madden family. Edith worked five days a week in the flower shop. Whenever Eva came to Crewe for visits, the two women would meet to discuss the latest fashion and Edith's love for George. Once Mrs James, Edith's mother, discovered the relationship she was very much against it. Rumours about the Madden family had already spread through the surrounding streets, much to Martha's distress. Eva recognised a very determined character in Edith. She was determined to marry George, she was determined to ignore her powerful mother and she was determined to ignore neighbourhood gossips. On one of Eva's visits she laughingly told her new friend that her mother had threatened George, warning him not to see her eldest daughter.

Shortly after this first threat, George bought his first motorbike, roaring up the street with Edith proudly sitting on the back. It took less than a day for her mother to hear the news. Edith was severely reprimanded, and when her mother saw George again she made quite a scene.

"Come near my daughter again George Madden and I'll tip you off that motorbike!" she yelled.

But George just laughed and sped off on the bike to pick Edith up from work. The relationship between them became stronger every day. Within a few years they would marry secretly, Edith wearing the wedding ring around her neck and returning to her mother's home each day after work. But as soon as the day came when they had enough money saved to set up their own home, it was a secret no more.

For seemingly the first time in years, this was a happy period for Eva. For the first time since Mary had been sent away from Brereton Hall she had a close friendship with another woman. And maybe it even made up a little for the sister she couldn't spend time with. One day they even went as far as to visit the dentist together. Being avid followers of fashion, they had seen the advertisements in the newspapers promoting dentures. *'Create a shining smile'* and other slogans were used. The girls knew some women even had their teeth removed as a sort of dowry so prospective husbands would never have to pay dental bills for their wives. But Edith and Eva's motivation was fashion. They decided to get just their front teeth replaced with a shiny new denture and endured the pain together, holding hands. But what they thought was a brilliant idea was not so well received and shortly afterward when they showed George the partial dentures they didn't get quite the reaction they'd hoped. George was totally disapproving and shouted that teeth must be kept at all cost and that they'd come to regret it. The women were not convinced. As they pointed out, George had incredible teeth, white and even, so he had nothing to worry about!

Presenting a united front to George over the dentures incident only served to strengthen the friendship between the two women and Eva began to share things with Edith that she'd never thought possible. Edith wanted to know the truth about the rumours of madness in the Madden family. It wouldn't change the way she felt about George, she wanted to be his wife no matter what. But if she was to become a Madden, she had to know what it meant to be one.

Eva told her all that she knew, but information on Ellen's medical condition was limited. She had been away too long and it simply wasn't discussed among her family members, so she didn't know a lot more about it than Edith. In return, Edith told her friend her own family secrets. She talked about her eldest brother William, who had enlisted in the war. He had very poor eyesight but he went into the infantry anyway. The Army had been so desperate by then that they would have taken anybody who offered to enlist. A few months later he was killed. Her mother had almost gone mad with grief and had kept the returned uniform, which revealed the bayonet hole in the back of the jacket, locked away in a cupboard and hidden from prying eyes. Maybe George would replace the lost son in time. If the girls' wishes could make it happen, then just maybe. Given confidence by Edith's confession about her own family's difficulties, as the days wore on Eva shared her own thoughts about her family.

"I'll only say this because I know you love George as much as I do. And we both know how determined he is to have a better life. Something brighter than the Madden house he grew up in at least."

"Eva, he talks about doing all sorts of things. Farming, maybe even moving away. But I think we'll end up staying in Crewe if the truth be told."

Eva took Edith's hands in hers. "If he has dreams, Edith, he should follow them. I sat and held the hand of a dying woman once, who had spent her life in the service of others and had not realised even one of her dreams. I don't want that for me and I don't want it for George. There is a life outside my parents' house. And it's bright. And even when you're being told what to do and working long hours every day, it's free."

Edith shook her head. "Eva it's not so simple anymore. George is like the man of the house now. Your father is rarely in. Joe might as well be absent the way he seems to live in his own world all the time. He never takes responsibility for anything. And Tom's too young. I don't think you know what it's really like for George."

Eva suddenly felt guilty. She'd been so concerned about herself and what she'd wanted that she hadn't thought about poor George; what all of it was doing to him, Martha's rules, Joseph's isolation, Ellen's illness and raising Tom almost single-handedly. And Augusta and Joe were never any help to him.

"I'm sorry Edith. He's always so full of mischief and laughter that I forget about what his life must really be like."

"Don't be silly Eva. He doesn't mind really. He loves his family. He even loves Joseph, even if he is an old rascal. He just needs to live two lives, one with me and one with his family. And as long as he doesn't have to talk about the dark things, he can be happy with me in the light."

Eva suddenly realised what a true friend Edith had become. She felt as though she could share more with Edith than she could with her own family. So she decided to confide in Edith what she had yet to tell another living soul. "Edith, I'm thinking about going away. Leaving England even."

"Eva! You can't be serious!"

"I don't fit in here anymore Edith. I know this is my family and this is my home, but I've been away too long. I mean imagine what I am to Tom? I've just been an infrequent visitor his entire life."

"Eva, Tom loves you."

"Tom loves me because George loves me. And

because Mam tells him to remember me in his prayers."

"But ..."

"The truth is, Edith, not even Dad is the same person I left behind. Then he was happy and loved playing with his children. Now we're lucky if we even see him. Even when I come all this way for a visit I never know if I'll see him. I need to go away. I'm twenty-eight years old and most of my pay still goes home to my mother. I don't mind, but there has to come a time when I am not just a breadwinner for my family. I can't come back here now that I've lived another life. I've changed forever and the streets of Crewe are not my streets any more."

"Eva, this is your home. You're always loved and welcome here. You know that."

"I know. But Edith, I don't want to be a working class married woman and live amongst all this poverty. I'm sad because if I go, it will take me away from all the people I love. But really, I couldn't bear one of these dingy houses, the struggle to survive. I look around these streets and I see how so many of the women seem to hide some sort of overwhelming unhappiness. They look faded. And they seem to cover up their unhappiness in duty somehow. Bravado even. I've heard them, 'after all, who'd want to be all la-di-da anyway? Too many rules, and all those corsets!' " Edith laughed. She'd seen it too and couldn't help agreeing with Eva.

"Whew, that turned into a bit of a speech, didn't it?"

"No, you needed to say it all. I think I understand." Then quietly, "George and I have decided to never have children, you know."

Eva was surprised that they had discussed this. She didn't want to alarm Edith, but she felt she needed to touch on the subject of mental illness being hereditary. She had no facts but it scared her. Edith sensed what Eva was thinking.

"I know," Edith comforted her. "George and me, we've often talked about it. My mother is furious of course. She says that there's madness in your family and it's kept hidden. And if I take up with a Madden then it will only be misery for me. She says that no one knows where your sister has vanished to, so she believes all the rumours. I don't care even now I know the whole story."

"I'm so sick of these so called necessary secrets in my family," retorted Eva. "But the way madness is thought of is worse than madness itself, it really is. I'm sure it's some sort of terrible disease. I love Ellen. I know it's a sickness. Other people outside our family don't know. Sometimes I think they imagine that they might catch it if they get too close! It's just so sad for my family."

Edith smiled. "Oh, Eva, you do have a way of putting things sometimes. 'Scared they'll catch it'." Then she hugged Eva before she had to go. "Eva, let's always be friends. Let the Maddens have their secrets, but let's just you and me always tell each other everything! I know that you'll write to us whenever you decide to go away. And even if I miss you like mad, I'll always be able to think about my clever friend out there in the world. We'll always be friends, always. And I will always love George. I'll care for him until the day I die. Have no worries for your brother. He'll be well looked after!" Then she giggled. "Isn't George wonderful?!"

Eva brightened up. She hadn't been able to confide in a girlfriend since Mary. How long ago that seemed. She wasn't sure about sharing everything, but she felt better knowing she had a friend like Edith.

"I need to be getting to the bus for Brereton Hall, but we'll meet again next time I visit Crewe. I heard there's a dress shop in Nantwich with all the latest fashions. We can make a real girls' day of it, both dress up and go there on the bus. And I'll bring you some clothes to try next time I come home. I also have two lovely hats that'll look so pretty on you. I'm quite sure George doesn't know how lucky he is to have you."

They hugged each other tightly before parting. Edith looked back to watch Eva walking very elegantly around the corner. "She looks like such a lady," she sighed.

A New Life

*"FREE AND ASSISTED EMIGRATION
TO NEW ZEALAND"*

The words caught Eva's eye as she waited for a bus back to Brereton one cold autumn evening in 1924. Printed in the *Crewe Chronicle*, it advertised various positions for farm labourers, navvies, ploughmen, shepherds and a few country mechanics. Below in large letters were the words:

*'FREE PASSAGES ARE GIVEN TO SINGLE
DOMESTIC SERVANTS.
APPLY PERSONALLY OR BY LETTER,
TO THE AGENT GENERAL FOR NEW ZEALAND,
7 WESTMINSTER CHAMBERS, LONDON S.W.'*

Her heart began thumping. This was just the opportunity she had been waiting for! She would have been excited if it had been anywhere in the Empire, but this was New Zealand, the place of childhood stories and the land that she had heard so much about from the Hollis family. Within a week she'd written, stating her position and expressing an interest. By the end of that month she travelled up to London for an interview. She had discussed her plans with George and shared her fears with Edith.

"Our Eva! It sounds incredible! If I went I could have my own farm. Own it, not just rent it, which is all I'd ever be able to do here. With crops and sheep!" But then more quietly, "But I've got a good job here." He'd recently started work for the railway as a cleaner. "Before you know it I'll be an engine driver. Besides, Tom's not big enough and ugly enough to look after himself yet! He'd get himself into too much trouble!"

"George, he'd manage!"

"Maybe in a few years, Eva. How about you go ahead and you can tell me what it's like? Maybe I could even farm and drive trains in New Zealand."

"If I go, I'll send you everything you'll need to know, I promise. Ah, listen to us, they haven't even accepted me yet!"

"They'll take you. Of course they will. You'll be off to New Zealand before you know it! And in the meantime, I'll look after things here. And my beautiful Edith, of course!"

Suddenly Eva felt a bit sad about it. She would miss George most of all. "Promise me you'll write to me as often as you can."

"Only if you write back, Eva Madden!" Then more seriously, "I'll look after Dad and Mam. I'll even come with you when you tell them you're going." He also advised Eva not to mention any mental illness in the family, as this would certainly disadvantage her application.

Her interview was successful, and was quickly followed by a medical. She received the results of her medical examination by mail at Brereton Hall: *'Fit and able to take up a working position upon arrival at Auckland'* was the only bit that Eva cared to read. With the results of the medical examination was a paper from the New Zealand High Commission, describing Eva as *'a good clever housemaid of good character, sound health and very experienced at her work.'* She could have told them that!

The next letter to arrive was the notification of her travel plans. She felt her heart flutter as she read that she would make the long sea voyage aboard the *Suffolk*. She would arrive in Auckland on 31st March 1925. Also enclosed was her first passport. She was twenty-eight years old. The passport would be valid until February 1930, when she would have completed the five compulsory years under the free passage scheme. Then she could return to England if that was what she wanted, still a relatively young woman.

She handed in her notice at Brereton Hall, explaining her future plans. She was required to work several weeks' notice. Her employers used the time to try every argument to dissuade her. She was offered extra wages, even promotion, but her mind was made up. Finally she was given an excellent reference, which would enable her to gain immediate work in the new country. So began the emotional business of goodbyes, first from the hall and then with her family and friends.

Eva stayed on at Brereton Hall until Christmas. They were short staffed as usual and needed her for longer. As the Christmas finery was stored away, Eva was already packing her box for home, placing in it the remaininh little presents which the staff had given to her. And the same things she'd brought with her almost fifteen years ago, the hatpin from her mother, Gussie's peg doll, Joe's two old tin soldiers, a very shrivelled king conker from Ellen and even Tom's little bootie. And finally the notebooks from her father that she'd long since stopped writing in. She flicked through them idly, amused by the naïve writings of the young girl who'd arrived there full of wonder at what would one day become routine.

Despite her excitement, this was a very difficult time for her. Some of these people she'd lived with longer than she'd lived with her own family. She had doubts, feeling very scared of the long journey. She questioned her own motives. Was she running away? Or moving towards a better life? But whenever she began to have doubts she often remembered Mrs Wilmot's words. 'Let nothing stop you.'

She talked about her decision with Mr Charlesworth over a cup of tea in his cottage. He was proud of her, urging her to move on as Mrs Wilmot had advised. All the staff loved Eva. Even the little scullery maid, who'd hated her when she first started, but now happily wore the new dresses and pinafores that Eva had made for her, cried on hearing the news. They wanted her to have an exciting life beyond

Cheshire, but how much they would miss her expertise and gentle ways.

For the last time she walked across the grounds to stand under the tree from where she'd looked at the hall when she arrived all those years ago. It was a misty late autumn day and her feet sank into the Cheshire soil. Wild geese flew over her in a 'V' formation. The great oaks had shed most of their leaves and through them in the distance stood Brereton Hall, solid and ancient. Eva stood under the great oak tree and looked out at all she had known since she was thirteen years old and a tear rolled down her cheek. "Goodbye Brereton Hall. You'll be standing here when I'm gone to the other side of the world. You've witnessed more than I can ever imagine. I've been so proud to work here. And you'll always be special to me."

Eva never looked back as she was driven away in the family car, a new wire wheeled motor. She was chauffeur driven all the way to Crewe. The journey by car was a mark of respect for a domestic who had served the hall so well. She was even allowed to leave by the front entrance. Every member of staff stood on the steps as she shook hands with each one of them. The owners of the hall were present too. Mr Charlesworth, his voice just a bit gruff with unshed tears, commented later that he had never known or seen the likes of it in all his time there.

The following few days passed quickly, for which she was grateful. Such a huge journey certainly took a lot of courage. At odd moments in all the frenzied activity, she'd find herself pausing, daydreaming, and wondering. And then she'd come to her senses and realise that she was absolutely doing the right thing. Edith and George gave her two lucky sixpences, which she tucked away in her trunk. She made a list of all the things she thought she'd need and she and Edith packed, and folding the garments meticulously. Eva ticked off the contents on her list.

"Righto, let's check that it's all there. Four aprons, two dresses and my blue tweed coat with the astrakhan collar?"

"Yes, all here," Edith replied.

"Now, pyjamas, silk bloomers, silk stockings and petticoats?"

"Mm-hmm. Eva, there are fourteen pairs of stockings here!"

"Well, I don't know how easy they'll be to get there." Edith smiled and Eva reacted, "Oh, don't laugh at me! Did I pack all five of my suits? And I'll need at least nine hats, several pairs of shoes and a pair of galoshes."

"All already packed."

"Gloves! Gloves! I didn't write gloves down!"

"Don't worry, I've put in two pair of cotton ones and a pair of fur ones."

"How many handkerchiefs are there? Should I buy more?"

"There's twenty. I should think that would be enough for anyone. You only have one nose!"

They both laughed at that and Edith added, "I've also put in your white blouse, your white silk cape and some spare celluloid cuffs."

"All right then. That takes care of clothes. What about these other things? A hot water bottle and an umbrella? And my boot cleaning kit?"

"I've put in two boxes of boot cleaning materials, just to be sure, and a set of brushes. As you said, you never know whether you'll be able to get good English ones where you're going!"

"What else then? I know, I've got a list here, but none of it seems to make sense now."

"Stop the nerves, Eva! Let's see. There's a nice big piece of cotton fabric for you here, your needlework bag, two cardigans and your scarves. And that's it."

"No it's not! We forgot my dressmaking and cookery books!" "Here they are."

And as Edith placed the books carefully in the trunk, Eva looked down at it all and remembered her promise to Mrs Wilmot. She had managed carefully and provided herself with an excellent wardrobe as well as savings to spare. She felt proud and a little emotional. "I don't know why, but I'm glad you were here to do this with me Edith."

Two days before she left by train, she made her way to her father's allotment, sitting on the old bench with him. She remembered the happy times when she and Ellen used to escape to the sanctuary of the allotment. It was wintertime now, so it was greyer than the green she preferred to remember. She looked over the frozen earth, knowing how it would yield food in abundance in the spring months. The conversation between her and her father was difficult at first. She had grown away from him in her desperation to understand her mother.

"Dad, I've been to see Ellen. She's much better. She sends her love to you." She paused, waiting for a reply. She knew that her mother or father had never visited their daughter. It was too painful for them.

His reply surprised her. "Eva, I know that Ellen is making a slow recovery. I have spoken to the doctor you know. There's a possibility that she might even be released some day. I mean, that she may be able to come home."

"Father," admonished Eva gently, "she's not in prison."

"I know, I know. But sometimes it seems to me that we're the ones in prison. Her illness has set us apart and keeping the secret, for all our sakes, has taken such a toll."

"Oh Dad, I love you so much. Why should this happen to us? I can see what all this has done to you. How much has changed." Daughter and father clung together and held on to each other for a long time, lost in their own worlds, watching the breeze blow across the allotment.

In his mind he was remembering the young bride he'd brought with him to Winsford. How the neighbours thought she was fragile and hauntingly beautiful. That she was the silent envy of all of them who initially sought her friendship. How they'd soon decided she was aloof and a bit snobbish though, as it became apparent to all that tried to befriend her that Martha had very little in common with them. She chose to show them through her closed door, remaining remote through her silent, almost secretive ways, which made her the subject of neighbourhood gossip.

Everyone thought them ill suited as a couple. He'd been notably jovial and social, enjoying a pint when he finished work as a plate-layer on the railway tracks. But he worked those long hours never discussing his wife or family business, always cleverly guiding the conversation onto other matters. The privacy on which Martha insisted was his concession to her. It was more in his nature to join in with the rowdy men who talked about their wives and children, telling tall tales of cold beds and colder dinners served by wives who decided that their husband had stayed too long at the pub. He laughed as loud as any as he took his pint with the lads after work usually about tales such as the poor fellow who told a tall story of a wife cross enough to wash his drawers and leave them hanging on a line in the dead of a Cheshire winter and him with nothing to wear. But he never joined in and told stories of his own. He honoured his wife at least that much.

Finally he began to speak quietly. "I do love your mother, Eva. It's just that it's so difficult to reach her. There are things in her past when she was a girl that she should never have been witness to. And don't you go asking me, because I won't be telling you." And even quieter, "and I know that I've let her down. That in the end I haven't been strong enough for her."

"Dad, I know that her sadness doesn't come from you. It comes from her own childhood. She made it hard on you from the start." Joseph looked into his daughter's eyes at this. She went on, "Dad, I know some of what happened to Mam when she was a girl."

He looked shocked and started to speak, but Eva quickly continued. "Mrs Wilmot told me before she died. You know how it is in service. Everyone knows someone who knows someone else. Gossip spreads among the great houses and across the countryside like weeds in a garden."

"Eva, I'm sorry. You weren't ever supposed to know."

"Dad, don't be sorry. I'm glad I know, because it explains so much. And I know you feel like you've let her down. And maybe you have, but this madness, this illness haunts her and not just Ellen." Smiling again then, she said, "I'll write to both of you as often as I can. And I'll send money. Imagine letters from the other side of the world!" Joseph returned the smile and stood up. "Come on girl. We'll be in trouble. Your Mam is making a special tea tonight just for you. She is proud of you Eva. So very proud."

Finally the goodbyes were said except for Joe, who could barely stand to look at her without crying. His sister had been away almost since he could remember, but she was the one bright thing in his life. When life in the family home became too bleak, in would breeze Eva with tales of goings on in Brereton Hall and he could forget for a while. Augusta was far more pragmatic and merely told her sister that she expected regular letters and descriptions of any eligible and well-to-do men that Eva met. Both women laughed as they hugged. The trunk and cases were sent ahead to Liverpool and her father and George took Eva to Crewe Station where they said their final farewells.

"It's only five years. I've been away at Brereton Hall three times as long. It will disappear before you know it!" And with that she got on the train and found her seat. As the train pulled out, Eva looked back at the two figures standing on the platform, her father dejected and looking worn around the edges and George, proud and handsome. She watched until she couldn't see them anymore. She was twenty-eight years old and it was time to start a new life.

Part 2 – Emigration to New Zealand (1925-1930)

A Free Spirit

The *SS Suffolk* was at anchor in Liverpool docks awaiting its cargo of goods and passengers. The papers Eva was given said that she was a steel ship, built in 1902 for carrying machinery and passengers to the Antipodes. But such basic facts couldn't really tell what she was. She was a vessel of dreams with a cargo of dreamers and risk takers, people unlike any Eva had met in England. There were 389 passengers who were to travel on her in all. And they were milling about on the dockside, nervously clutching their cases and few belongings. They were all waiting to board. The actual preparation and final goodbyes had tired many of them. Now they were anxious to leave behind the 'old country' for a brighter and more hopeful future.

Eva looked around her at all the families who still had loved ones they were farewelling. She also looked to see if there were any other young women on their own like her, someone she might have something in common with. She knew she would be fine without it, but some companionship on such a long voyage would be much better.

The day was black and stormy and like everyone on board, Eva was not sorry to see the last of 'Old England' as Captain Matthews welcomed her aboard. Eva saw families with at least six children, all of whom stuck close to their parents. The children stared wide-eyed at the activity around them as the patient line of emigrants began to board the ship. It all seemed to go slowly, as though the passengers were both eager and reluctant to start the journey. Looking at the families, Eva was glad she was travelling alone. She did not have the responsibility of a family. She also considered herself lucky because she had been placed in a two-berth cabin. She only had to share with one other woman, whereas others were in cabins accommodating six or more people in family groups where possible. Her berth was on the starboard side, a fact that she came to appreciate when they stopped at ports in warmer waters. She would stop off at places that only belonged in atlases, experiencing a sea voyage to the other side of the world. As she again noticed that all around her were strangers, she wished she had Edith and George with her.

Several of the children called out, asking questions. One little boy immediately attached himself to her, taking hold of her hand. "Hello. My name is Tommy. My Dad is going to buy hundreds and hundreds of sheep!" And before Eva could get a word in he continued. "We're going to New Zealand, you know. It's going to take us a long time. And then when we get there, my Dad has to organise getting a farm ready. So we can have our hundreds of sheep." Eva had no need to contribute to the conversation, as Tommy chattered on without encouragement.

"Ah, Thomas! There you are! Thank you Miss, for helping him across the deck. My hands are a bit full as you can see. And young Thomas here can be more than a handful all on his own!" Eva realised where Thomas got his chattering from.

"Oh! and where are my manners now? We're Edwin and Mary Bruce. And this as you know is Thomas. He's certainly taken to you, Miss. His little brother I'm holding here is Arthur. We've travelled down from Glasgow, hoping to spend a couple of days resting up. But the ship sails at midnight, so there's no rest for us."

The Bruces both had broad Scottish accents and cheerful faces and Eva took an instant liking to them. "My name is Eva Madden. It's very nice to meet you Mr and Mrs Bruce. And you too, young Tommy," she said with a smile in her voice. It was a comfort to make some friends so quickly. She was delighted to hear that they too would be landing in Auckland until the time came to buy farming land further south.

Below decks she was shown to her cabin, which she shared with another single woman by the name of Bronwyn Jones. Eva recognised her Welsh accent from her friend Mary all those years ago when she first went to Brereton Hall. Amid all the strangeness, she found it comforting. Even though Bronwyn assured her that she had lived in Liverpool for most of her adult life, the Welsh was still there in her voice.

"I'm going out to live with my brother. He moved there about ten years ago. I was stuck at home with my parents, who were heartbroken about 'losing their only son'. You'da thought he'd died! Anyway, they died a couple of years ago, within a few weeks of each other, and I was left with nobody but him. So it made sense to sell off what me Mam and Dad had and take meself to New Zealand to join him."

Eva had just continued unpacking her essentials as Bronwyn talked, not willing to share her family stories quite so soon. But having run into Mrs Bruce and Bronwyn within half an hour of each other, she was beginning to wonder if the whole world talked without stopping for breath! The two women continued to unpack their few belongings, endeavouring to make the small cabin their home for the voyage. Two chairs, a little sink, two bunk beds, a chest of drawers and a wardrobe filled the small space. Eva was used to making do for herself, so she volunteered to take the top bunk, but as she looked up at what would be her bed for the long voyage, she was surprised to see a strange metal object. She took it down and Bronwyn recognised it immediately from her brother's description of his earlier sea voyage.

"What on earth could this be?"

"This, Eva, is a wind scoop." It was a bent oval shaped tube of tin with a hole at each end and Eva looked at it curiously, turning it in her hands.

"What on earth do we do with it?" she asked.

"Well, you open the port hole when the weather's hot," explained Bronwyn, taking it from Eva. "And you push it through so far until the flange holds it firm in the frame of the porthole." She proceeded to do just that until the strange object stuck out of the porthole like a small sideways chimney.

"Now, you see, when the weather is very hot, the wind blows past the side of the ship and it's funnelled in through the scoop, keeping us lovely and cool." Both women burst out laughing as a few flakes of snow were effectively blown in through the chimney.

"I can't imagine that we would ever become so warm," shivered Eva. And Bronwyn quickly closed the porthole.

As the winter night closed in, Eva felt the pangs of anxiety coming back. What lay in front of her? She thought about how much she loved her family. But she felt compelled to make this journey because after never having been more than ten miles from home in her twenty-eight years, her curiosity and longing to travel was overpowering.

She barely ate at her first meal in the mess with the other passengers. Her stomach felt funny, and she wasn't sure if it was from fear, sadness or excitement. The meal was simple and was washed down by sweet tea poured from an enormous old teapot, reminding her of the 'heirloom' as the staff at Brereton had called the ancient pot that was used to brew the servants' tea. Mrs Wilmot's words of comfort came back to her and Eva knew she should feel grateful for this wonderful opportunity. Later that evening she fell asleep in the top bunk bed to the quiet thud of the ship's engine, not waking until just after midnight when she felt the slight rocking that she would become so accustomed to, and which meant that the *Suffolk* had sailed.

Slipping down from the bunk bed without waking Bronwyn, she peered through the porthole into blackness. Pinpricks of light in the distance showed the Liverpool docks. The *Suffolk* cleared Liverpool on February 13th. They were on their way at last. As if in answer to her thoughts, the ship sounded its horn. The eerie sound was swept away into the night.

At dawn they left the shelter of the Irish Sea and sailed past the Tuskar Rock lighthouse to enter the open Atlantic. Now Eva really felt the journey had begun. But the gentle movements of the night had become quite different. The two women struggled to stay upright as they dressed for breakfast as the ship rode through huge ocean swells. Eva listened anxiously to the howling wind. The continuous clatter of the chain steering and the slap, slap of the chain inside the steel box where it was housed on the deck were the only other sounds. There was no sign of the family groups. They had taken some of the breakfast from the dining room, going below to their cabins where the children would be safe.

Eva struggled to the side of the ship to look at the long grey waves stretching to the horizon. Accepting finally that there was no turning back, she remained calm and disciplined, not allowing panic to affect her logic. All her life she had exercised this strong willpower and it would hold her in good stead in the days ahead. Forty-six days of sailing would bring them to their new land. She had to remain calm.

She questioned the crew whenever she had a chance, wanting to know the route that they would take. Glad to find such a pretty passenger who was really interested, they told her about the coaling stations that lay between the United Kingdom and New Zealand, where the ship would 'bunker', which meant taking on coal. It relied upon the fuel to provide the steam for power.

During the first few days of the voyage, the *Suffolk* ploughed through heavy seas, forcing the passengers down below as the decks were awash with huge breaking waves. The sea even managed to make its way aboard the ship, crashing into the lounge and smoking room, throwing one passenger across the room and smashing into a table. Waves washed the decks, everything was tied down and the ship was wet inside and out. Down below in their cabins many of the passengers feared for their lives. But Eva didn't panic, and waited eagerly for the first opportunity to go on deck to see the massive rolling seas.

Eva showed Tommy their route in the small atlas that she had brought with her. They were amongst the few passengers who were not suffering from the terrible seasickness that had driven the others below for days. She and Tommy spent their time playing board games such as draughts and snakes and ladders, plotting their progress on the map and telling each other stories. Tommy described the back streets of Glasgow where he had lived and Eva told him stories of the great hall where she had spent so many of her working years. She was pleased that he was entertained by all the games she had loved playing in the street as a child like *whip and top* and *hopscotch*. Eva even managed to coax a can out of one of the crew to play *kick the can* and orchestrated a game of *hide and seek* for one group of children on a rare calm afternoon. She loved her time with the children and was pleased to provide some respite for some of the parents, who were understandably almost at their wits end from living in such close quarters with their children for days on end.

On calmer days she and Bronwyn had decided that they would sew, each making a cotton dress. Bronwyn shared her memories with Eva, explaining in more detail about how heartbroken her parents had been when her brother had emigrated. Bronwyn had also been sad, but angry too, because she couldn't replace her brother in any way, and angry because he'd left her to look after her sad parents. Eva talked about her parents and family but avoided the subject of Ellen. She felt guilty, but it was as if a door had closed in her mind, a locked door. How could she tell anyone about her sister? It was open to so much misinterpretation. Tales came thick and fast as the two girls sat on deck, comparing families as they sewed in the brisk air. As they cut out the cotton dresses, they wondered if the weather would ever change.

"I was talking to one of the deck hands this morning. He told me that it gets so hot up here some days that you can fry an egg on one of the metal hold covers," Bronwyn said in amazement.

Eva frowned. "That's ridiculous. I can hardly believe it." How soon she would eat those words. Three weeks into the voyage there was an outbreak of measles. Ten children and four adults were infected. They were well looked after in the ship's small hospital, emerging one by one when they were considered fit again. The other passengers were relieved. Nearly everyone had had measles as a child so they weren't going to catch it again. In fact it was one of the 'childhood diseases' some parents deliberately exposed their children to, just to get them over it, but they knew that if an epidemic broke out on the ship as it neared New Zealand, those patients infected, and possibly everyone else would have to remain on board under quarantine conditions.

After what had seemed like months of rocky seas, but had actually only been a couple of weeks, Eva woke with a start, aware that something was different. She could no longer hear the rattle of the chains. She realised that they were in calmer waters. The sun was shining. Suddenly everyone was on deck, pale and exhausted, but triumphant that they had weathered the storms and survived. From now on they felt that the sea journey would be bearable without the terrible sickness that most had suffered. Everyone was in the mood for celebrations. They played games on deck, meeting one another as if for the first time, daring to allow their children to run about without fear of going overboard.

The temperature increased daily, until the small cabin portholes needed to be open night and day. They steamed on flat blue waters accompanied by dolphins leaping around the bow. The children were delighted. Eva finally began to really relax. She realised that for the first time in her life she wasn't required to wait upon others or to be accountable either at work or at home although she did still find it hard not to comment when she noticed less than perfect service from the crew. But she understood the meaning of the word *freedom*. Thousands of miles away from the accountability of her previous life she was a free spirit at last and she loved the control it gave her over her own destiny.

Her friendship with the Bruce family grew every day. They vowed that they would always keep in touch once they reached their new home. Edwin produced an old camera, persuading a crew member to take a photo of the group, promising to send a copy to each of them. Gathered together on a warm sunny day out on the deck, beneath a brilliant blue sky, they shyly grouped together, ten adults and five children, laughing and joking as they arranged themselves for a photograph. Eva stood on the back row between John from Edinburgh and Frank from Liverpool. The Bruce family was seated at the front, Tommy grinning widely and his little brother shyly hiding his face as he leant back in his mother's arms. Later in New Zealand, they would laugh and joke about the photograph that captured their hopes and dreams of a new life.

`The photograph made her think of her own family and so that evening, rather than socialising with the other adults without children, she sat at the small table in her cabin and wrote a letter to her brother George. Writing to her brother made her somehow feel closer to him, and helped keep the realisation that she was alone and heading for the other side of the world from intruding.

On Board the Suffolk, sailing towards the Panama Canal - South America.

My Dear George,
How much you would enjoy this voyage, there is so much to see, hear and smell. To actually sail to such places is unimaginable. At times I can hardly believe that I am doing so.

I am missing all of you dreadfully for it seems an age away when I last saw you and Father standing on Crewe Station waving goodbye to me, but this journey is taking me to new territory and to places that I have only dreamed about.

Once we had left the stormy weather of Liverpool behind, a few days' journey brought us into much better weather. It was such a relief to everyone on board, for everyone has been so sick. The ship had to sail through such terrible Atlantic storms. I felt so sorry for the poor children and in particular for a 9 month old baby who has barely recovered even now!

There are 295 of us aboard who are on assisted passages, but 389 passengers in all. This includes many children who are quickly making friends with each other. At times the decks look like a school playground as they adapt to their surroundings. The Suffolk is well built. She has carried both passengers and cargo to New Zealand for a number of years. She is also loaded with machinery of every kind. Although our accommodation is quite basic, we are all well looked after. You would have smiled if you had seen the huge amounts of butter, flour, meat and other provisions coming aboard for there are many of us to feed. The cooks and stewards must work hard to meet the great demands placed on them. It feels a little strange to not be doing the work myself, but I shall enjoy the freedom while I have it! There will be time enough for kitchens and serving others in days to come.

I am now well acquainted with my fellow travellers for we have to make the best of one another's company. Fortunately everyone is very friendly, as they are mostly family people who are looking for a better life. There is such hope for our new lives. Aboard the ship there are forty-three domestics, many of them much younger than me and looked after by a matron. About ten of us are experienced and travelling on our own, coming from as far afield as the very north of Scotland, Wales and Ireland. There are only two of us from Cheshire it seems.

At first not having much of anything to do seemed very odd, but I occupy myself by helping with two children who belong to Mr and Mrs Bruce, a pleasant couple from Glasgow. Mary is grateful for help with her 6-year-old son named Tommy and he has attached himself to me much like our Tom with you when he was little. I have also spent some time playing games with other children, all the ones we used to play in the street at home and it has brought back wonderful memories. On the warm evenings I sit up on deck and watch as the stars show in the sky. Away from the lights and smoke of a city, they are so bright that it quite takes my breath away. It really is so beautiful now that the rough passage is over.

When we reach the Panama Canal[19], we hope to be allowed to go ashore, if only for a short while. My friend Bronwyn (she is Welsh but lived in Liverpool) plans to buy some silk fabric and so do I. Together we will sew during the rest of the long voyage and each make a dress for the weather will be hot shortly. The ship will also take on more coal ready for the long voyage across the Pacific.

I have learnt to play Cribbage! One of the crew spent time with us, explaining the game, which has since whiled away many an hour. I have also improved in all the card games, which you, Edith and I used to play so many times. Please send her my best wishes for she is a lovely girl George. I do hope you marry her for I think you are very happy together. Tell Mother that I share a cabin with a very nice woman and that I am safe and well. The food is plain and the meat is salted so there is no chance that I will grow fatter. We are well nourished, but looking forward to the tropical fruits the crew keep telling us about. Once we reach South America we will take much fresh food on board. I intend to have this letter posted to you from Colon, which is the next port of call. I promised you that when I reached Auckland, I would open a post office account in which I will place my savings so do not worry.

Before I close my letter to you dear brother, I must tell you

---

[19] Man made forty-eight mile waterway, which connects the Atlantic with the Pacific Ocean via the Caribbean Sea.

of an incident which occurred last evening. It was so terribly hot that Bronwyn and me came up from our cabin, as the heat was unbearable. The sides of the ship are made of steel and so our accommodation had warmed up to unbearable temperatures. It felt as though there was no air left in there to breathe.

A slight breeze on deck relieved our distress. The stars were already showing and a full moon lit up the deck when we were suddenly made aware of something landing near to the bow, and then slapping noises! We hurried forward to discover a number of fish on the deck, six in all, soon to be collected by one of the sailors who told us that we would be having fresh flying fish for breakfast! Have you ever heard of such a thing?!

Please give my dearest wishes and love to my family, I think of you all often, dear brother.

I will write once again when I reach Auckland.

Eva.

Finally they saw land and Eva looked around her in absolute wonder. Her thoughts returned to her life in England, which had been completely drab and colourless by comparison. The contrast was breathtaking. She would never be able to describe this riot of colour and activity, not even in a letter of fifty pages. She was beginning to realise that the experience of travel was a singular almost private affair. That unless you shared it with someone else, you could never really make another person understand the sights, sounds and smells you experience and all the emotion they evoke. And even then, the way you felt about what you saw was yours alone. She felt that morning, as she stared at the huge variety of ships, that she had changed forever. She would never again fit into a small northern English town. But all the realisations she'd had that morning made her feel conflicted, both exhilarated and sad at the same time.

The noises of the jungle penetrated even the solid walls of the ship. The hum of night insects, bird calls and the

The Price

incessant chatter of the people on the dockside entertained the passengers. The sailors loaded up the usual provisions: coal, butter, fresh water and the like. The exception was strange fruit such as mangoes, melons and bananas. All of these would be very popular on the way to Auckland, as none of the assisted passengers had ever tasted anything like it. She knew it was hardly ladylike, but Eva took great joy in eating a fresh mango with Tommy and laughing as the juice ran down their chins and over their hands.

Looking over the side of the ship, Eva and Tommy exclaimed in delight at the activity. A thousand cases were waiting for export on the dockside. Hundreds of coconut trees, each loaded with fruit, lined the sand banks. And the jungle beyond looked like a tropical paradise. Eva longed to go out and explore the new landscape. The crew had even told her about the tiny monkeys that could be found there and Eva would have loved to see one but the passengers were not allowed to leave the ship as the stop was for provisions only.

The crew distributed information and told any passengers who enquired that the Panama Canal should never be taken for granted because it was an engineering feat beyond compare. All the passengers marvelled as they slowly entered the man made channel. It was said that thousands of labourers had died of disease, mostly malaria, or accidents during the construction. So many had died that their bodies could have been laid side by side along the entire length of the canal. At Colon, Eva had heard a strange language amongst the dockers that turned out to be Spanish. The crew had informed the passengers of the history of Panama, and explained that American money was used in the Canal Zone, and that the passage through to the Pacific would take about nine hours. The decks of the *Suffolk* were filled with chattering passengers, all anxious to learn as much as possible about their first port of call.

Just before entering the Canal, some of the crew played a joke on the younger passengers. They explained

A Free Spirit

that the ship would have to move very slowly through the locks and so the engines would not be able to be used. Instead, mules would pull the ship through the locks using great ropes attached to the bow and sides! Surely they must be lying, most of the children said, but the sailors were so convincing that in the end they just had to be believed. The joke went on.

"Now you all know how stubborn mules are. They'll never do anything if they don't want to." The children all nodded, for quite a large group had gathered by now. "So how do you think we get them to pull the ship?" They looked around at each other, puzzled looks on their faces. "Well, we tie a carrot to a big, long stick and we hold it front of them and the mules will pull the ship along as he tries to get the carrot!"

"No!"

"It's true. Look over there. We have all the poles ready. You just need to find carrots and you can help us!" Suddenly the children scampered about, asking high and low for carrots, so they could help tempt the mules. This left the deck clear for the sailors to get on with their work to prepare the ship for her passage through the Canal.

The parents thought this was a great joke because they had seen great machines with the word burro painted on the side. Not knowing what burro meant, several had asked and been told that it was in fact the Spanish word for 'mule'. The little shunting trains that would pull them through the locks were called 'mules' because they were workhorses like the local beasts of burden. The sailors had not lied when they said that the ship would be pulled through into the locks by mules. Only the carrot treats were a joke.

Of course, when the children returned as they felt the ship moving again, the sailors informed them that they were sadly too late for the mules and that they would have to be pulled through by machines instead. And now the donkeys would go hungry because they hadn't earned their keep. But the children weren't sad for long, because the action of the locks and all the machines were just as fascinating to most of them as any mule might have been.

Tommy stood close to Eva as they stared with curiosity at so many strange buildings and people. His father had handed him a map, one of many given out by the crew, and Eva explained some of the interesting facts to the small boy. Suddenly she gasped, examining the map more closely. She traced her finger. A large lake near to Colon led to a dam that was planned to enlarge an artificial lake named Gatun. The lake and a long highway that linked to the railway were both named MADDEN![20]

"Look Tommy!" she exclaimed. "Here's my name!" She spelled it out carefully to the excited child.

"Eva, it's your lake! You are the lady of the lake!" chanted Tommy. "Just like in the story your Dad taught you!"

Tommy had been restless and unable to sleep in the heat the night before and so Eva had told him the story her father used to tell his children when they were small. Joseph had them convinced that Betley Mere was home to the magical Lady of Shalot[21]. Eva had described the yellow lilies that grew along one side of the pool that looked like flags and how they were there to welcome the Lady of Shalot home. How she was so beautiful that sometimes grown men had fallen down in a faint just at the sight of her.

She smiled as she remembered how she'd begged Joseph to show her where the Lady lived. But he'd explained that only very quiet children who never put so much as a toe in her mere had any chance of seeing her. Of course, it had all been a way to make sure the children had not played in the deep pool of water, but it had seemed magical to her then and still held the enchantment of a favourite childhood moment. Tommy had found it just as captivating. Now he was convinced it could be true. After all, here was proof.

---

[20] The main drinking water reservoir for the cities of Panama and Colon providing 40 per cent of the water required for the operation of the Panama Canal.
[21] Poem by Alfred Lord Tennyson, (1832). *The Lady of Shalot*.

His Eva was beautiful and here she had her own lake.

"It's true Eva! It's true!" With that he rushed off to tell his entire family. The strange coincidence made Eva wonder why her name stood out among so many Spanish words. A lake and a highway, both carrying her name! She stared across the mountains, longing to see her namesake but knew it was impossible. How could this be, so far away from home? She felt comforted, identifying with this strange land of pioneers, construction and bravery. People here had taken chances and risks in the hope of building a better life. All this had been occurring whilst she had been quietly living her life at Brereton Hall.

As the *Suffolk* steamed slowly along the canal, the wild jungle that grew to the water's edge amazed Eva. She shivered slightly as she tried to see beyond the thick entanglement of green. Suddenly all desire to get off the ship and explore was gone and she was glad that she was safely on board and happy to wait for the safety provided by a town. Here, she could walk on dry land for the first time since leaving England. That would come at the end of the day's journey through the Canal at Balboa and everyone on board was excited about their arrival because they would be allowed to go ashore for two days. Each evening they returned to the ship for evening meals and accommodation, tired from their explorations. Apparently there was a fierce storm raging in the Pacific Ocean and all shipping was delayed until the weather settled, lengthening their stay in port. Nobody minded. Any break from the monotony of shipboard life was welcome.

The *Suffolk* docked along with many other ships, waiting for the all clear. Eva accompanied the Bruce family as they explored the small market stalls that lined the dockside. Edwin even parted with a penny to a street vendor so he could take a photograph of Tommy with a tiny monkey on his shoulder. It had taken a few minutes to convince Tommy that it was a good idea, but once the monkey was actually on his shoulder, he was squealing with delight. Growing even

The Price

more adventurous, Eva and the family set off into the nearby town, walking in unbearable heat.

The humidity swamped them, leaving their European clothes wet and shapeless and as they trudged the dirt road they were startled by strange birdcalls. The tropical rainforest seemed to loom over them on both sides. It was bright green, impenetrable and exotic but it made all of them feel rather uneasy. This was a world of the unknown, the unexplored. As they all became more unsettled, Edwin called a halt to their short-lived adventure. Despite their eagerness to explore, they were relieved to turn back. This place was too different from England to feel safe.

Tommy had loved the adventure in port and as they sailed out of Balboa, he stood on the deck looking wistfully at the retreating harbour, which was by then bathed in the last of the sun's rays. In Panama he had experienced something that he would tell stories about for the rest of his life. He had seen jungle and monkeys and birds so colourful and strangely shaped that they almost defied description. What an experience for a six-year old boy from a village near Glasgow and a woman who, prior to travelling to London for her interview and medical, had never ventured more than ten miles from the place where she was born.

Eva and the Bruces stayed on deck as the sun went down and soon the ships in the harbour became nothing more than pinpricks of light, finally giving way to an inky blackness only broken above the horizon by bright stars. Within hours life aboard ship began to take on an easy rhythm as the passengers settled back into the routine experienced by all those who take long sea journeys. They now rested when the heat was unbearable, ate when they were cooler, relaxed and appreciated the long silences which came with a mysterious ocean. Eva wondered at the vastness of the waters they were journeying across. She watched the dolphins, bird life and sharks that followed the ship, each hoping to get an easy meal from the waste that was released at the stern.

England's winter colours were replaced in the immigrants' minds by bright blues and greens. The memories of smog, rain and sleet, which brought with it the freezing nights, were dimmed by the warmth of the sun and the sea breezes on their faces. The sun beat down every day, warming the ship like a metal oven, squeezing thoughts of their homeland out of them. They could now only look forward to their dreams of the future. Even Eva began to let go of some of her more painful memories, including those of her sick sister. She was timelessly slipping into another world.

Although it wasn't talked about, many passengers experienced a feeling of relief as they neared New Zealand for they were now thousands of miles from home, but not yet on dry land. They desperately wanted the reality of New Zealand to give a sense of purpose to their long sea journey. The decision to leave, to make such a journey to a new land now needed to materialise into practical details such as homes, clothing and work. One week out of Auckland the sailors spotted whales, which brought everyone out on deck. It gave them a sense of optimism to see the great mammals surging through the ocean, some passengers even seeing them as a good luck sign.

Eva came up from her cabin early the following morning to be confronted by raging seas. The decks of the *Suffolk* were awash with the suddenly icy waters of the Pacific Ocean. The peaceful, dreamlike weather of the tropical and equatorial zones was gone. And so was the languor and good humour they brought with them. She pulled her shawl tightly round her, leaning against the rigging. Now that New Zealand was such a close reality, she felt suddenly and inexplicably completely alone. A dreadful feeling of emptiness washed over her and as she stood there her tears were whipped away by the icy wind.

She was experiencing homesickness for probably the first time since entering service. Her decision to leave behind the 'Old Country' now left her feeling sad and isolated. Behind her lay her entire life, lived out in a northern town of England, surrounded by sisters and brothers, mother and father. Later she had worked in a great Cheshire Hall, establishing a comfortable daily pattern of life for herself. Why had she done this? Too late now to retreat, to claw back the familiarity of her life, she had plunged herself into something so vast, that she felt her entire identity slip away.

She started sobbing. Oh God, what's going to happen to me? Who's going to care for me and love me? What am I looking for? I know the streets of Crewe are dingy and I was just a servant but it's enough for everyone else. Why couldn't I be satisfied with what I had? I'm so afraid! The sadness and fear slowly gave way to anger because she hated to be wrong. She had argued about her decision to leave with her parents, her brother George and finally the owners of Brereton Hall where she worked. She remembered standing in the entrance of the hall, angry that people should try and stop her. She would go to New Zealand no matter what. Her tears had been shed in silence and alone. She hated everything she had left. She could only look forward. But to what?

Watching the grey swelling seas, her mind travelled back to her childhood. Her mother dragging her along to the Methodist Chapel in Mill Street, her temper hidden for fear of a sharp slap, her muttering the Methodist oath but at the same time swearing against it, her fingers tightly crossed behind her back. So this is where her stubbornness had brought her, alone and scared. She had punished herself but she vowed that she would never admit it. She would tell no one.

Vaguely she looked out at the rough seas. No whales were visible today, despite some of the migrants spotting one the day before. The ocean rolled on, anonymous just like her. This was more than just a journey across oceans she had taken. It was the beginning of a journey to becoming a new person. She just hoped she'd recognise this new Eva when the journey ended. She looked down at her gloved hands and realised that she was gripping them so tightly in her anxiety that her fingers were beginning to hurt. Forcing herself to let go, she looked up as something moving on the deck near one of the gunwales caught her attention. Struggling forward against the wind, she saw it was a huge sea bird straddling the planking. It flapped its ten-foot wingspan as it awkwardly tried to right itself.

Eva moved closer to stare at its grotesque movements, feeling as sad for it as for herself. It belonged to the freedom of the air and it too was trapped. She had no fear as she stepped forward to kneel against the great bird, talking softly to it, crying tears into its sodden feathers. Then she gathered its huge body into her arms and rocked back and forth on the deck. She did not realise that all it suffered from was seasickness, as often happens when an albatross[22] lands on a ship. She felt the fast beating of its heart, many times faster than hers, but somehow in unison. It gave her great comfort in this alien place, the two of them stranded in a storm of distance.

"Oh God, please let us be free and our lives be good," she whispered.

Angry shouting from behind her disturbed both woman and bird. Leaning awkwardly she struggled to turn in the wind to face a deck hand. He drew back and she realised he was scared. Eva stood in front of him, frowning, watching his every move, and instinctively knowing that he disliked the albatross and her.

"Miss, you shouldn't have touched him! He's a bad luck sign, that's what he is."

"Don't be so ridiculous, he's a beautiful bird and I'm going to set him free," she retorted in the most imperious voice she could muster.

---

[22] The Wandering Albatross has the longest wingspan of any bird (up to eleven feet) and rides the ocean winds and glides for hours without rest or even a flap of its wings. They have a special place in Maritime Lore and superstition, most memorably evoked in Samuel Taylor Coleridge's *The Rime of the Ancient Mariner*.

The Price

"Don't you know what you have in your arms? Drop the blasted thing over the side, quick, before anyone sees you!"

Eva, sensing the panic and urgency in the lad's voice, drew back, fearing that he might take this symbol of her freedom from her. Determinedly she climbed onto one of the lifeboats, holding tightly to the great creature and barely taking her eyes from the deck hand. Gaining a steady foothold, she buried her face in its feathers and whispered a blessing, and then with all her strength she pushed its great body up and over the side of the ship. For a brief moment, it appeared to dive, and then regaining its balance with several powerful movements of its huge wings, it took control of its flight and soared upwards. Eva and the deckhand watched in silence as it soared higher and higher until its grey shape was hardly visible. Eva trembled with emotion but feeling triumphant, she stepped down and faced the trembling deck hand.

"Just what was that?" she questioned as she brushed her hands against the bodice of her dress.

"That, missus, was an albatross and us seamen believe that every one of them is the soul of a dead sailor. Some stupid fools try to catch them by baiting a piece of tin shaped into a triangle. The bird's beak gets caught then they haul them aboard. Use the webbed feet for tobacco pouches and the wing bones for making pipes. Fools they are not to listen to the old stories."

"What are the old stories?"

"It's very unlucky if one of them damned birds lands on a ship and even worse if you touch one."

"What rot!" retorted Eva. "I don't believe any of those stories. It was just a bird that was trapped."

The deck hand stared at her, incredulous that she was ignoring his warning. "You remember Miss that you touched it. I'd shut up about it if I was you," he frowned. "Don't say nothing to no-one." And with that he quickly moved away from Eva as if she were contaminated.

Yet the incident remained with Eva for days, comforting her in a strange way. She remembered some of the Brereton Hall stories, including the one of the floating log that predicted the death of one of the Breretons. She had heard many such yarns and she certainly wasn't about to be disturbed by this piece of nautical rubbish. She kept the incident to herself and the voyage continued without mishap until land was in sight. New Zealand at last.

New Zealand at Last

The Suffolk sailed into New Zealand waters on the 31st of March 1925. Although it was already autumn, the weather was fine and warm and the summery day made all the immigrants feel happy and hopeful again. They chattered excitedly as they saw the greenery and sunshine. The fresh sparkling harbour cheered them all. Even the crew, who'd seen the sight many times before were infected with the good humour. The contrast to Liverpool on the dark and stormy night that they'd left couldn't have been more startling. Eva stood on the deck, drinking in the smells of this new land. The gloom and sadness that she'd felt only a couple of days before melted away. She was here and she would be all right.

For over six weeks the ship had been home to everyone. Children had played together on the decks. Strong friendships had been made but there was little regret about leaving her behind. Many of the Scots boys wore the kilt to mark the special occasion of their arrival, looking fine and healthy as they collected their belongings. They set off for various parts of Auckland. The Scottish girls wore sailor hats with checkered tops. Men were neatly dressed, predominantly in double-breasted coats.

Passengers crowded the decks for their first look at the land they had travelled so far to see. The 295 assisted immigrants dressed as smartly as they could manage, all anxious to give a good first impression on landing. Many of the boys wore 'Oxford bags'[23] which were very popular in England. These fashionable trousers were extremely comfortable. They had been reassured by members of the

---

[23] Loose-fitting baggy trousers, favoured by members of the University of Oxford during the early twentieth century from the 1920s to around the 1950s.

crew that some of the boys in Auckland wore them too. Many of the women wore Russian boots that were popular in England at the time, brown in colour and up to the knees, giving comfort but certainly not elegance.

Everywhere people were calling out to each other in different dialects. The ship was alive with good cheer. Addresses were exchanged, promises were made and a few tears were shed as the travellers prepared to go their separate ways. During the long voyage there had been much discussion about the types of employment each family would pursue once they arrived at the colony and everyone on board had some sort of plan. As the ship slid into her berth, children rushed to her side, parents following anxiously. The cacophony of voices grew.

"Look at that!"

"How green it is!"

"Look, you can see to the bottom of the ocean!"

"Thank you God for a safe voyage!!"

"Stop crying mother! We're here in our new land. How can you be sad?"

"No, we can't go back. We're here to stay."

"I think I can see my brother waving."

Eva stepped through the crowds. Everyone was talking, waving, weeping with relief, and kissing one another goodbye. Handshakes and exchange of addresses, photographs and keepsakes all identified the travellers as one huge family during the time it had taken to make the journey. They had shared things with one another that normally would never have been spoken of. A young man and woman stood by the rail, arms entwined. Their meeting and falling in love had all occurred on the *Suffolk*. With their parents' blessings they were to be engaged.

Eva was once more alone. She kissed Bronwyn goodbye, shook hands with the Bruce family and twirled Tommy in the air. There was a tearful farewell as Eva hugged Tommy for the last time.

"Now, I've given you that address where I'll be

The Price

working in Wellington?" And on taking a nod for a yes, she turned to his parents. "Write to me as soon as you have an address. Let me know how you're getting on. And I especially want news of this little man!" And with a last hug she sent Tommy on his way.

She waited for her baggage to be unloaded, and then she took a cab to the YWCA[24] in Queen's Street, in the centre of the city. Her accommodation and service position had been arranged by Immigration in London. Eva was relieved that at least she had a room and some kind of identity. Her name was checked off on a list and at last she was free to rest. But despite having a moment to catch her breath and rest in a bed on dry land again, she felt strangely nervous. Now that she had finally arrived, nothing seemed real to her. Soon she would be travelling south to Wellington, another unknown destination. She knew that she had to eat and sleep, otherwise her mind would race and feelings of loneliness and panic would begin to crowd in and she'd eventually be left feeling ill.

A bowl of soup and bread helped her to settle. She stepped outside the hostel into the main street of Auckland. The heat was tangible. She tasted the dryness of it. She remembered the humid air in Panama but here it was dry and very hot. Her pale skin prickled within minutes. She brushed strands of wet hair from her forehead, reminding herself that she must wear a hat for protection as a warm breeze bowled papers along the wide street.

Several gentlemen passed by, lifting their hats. She heard a strange English accent as a mother chastised her child. The sun beat down relentlessly from a blue sky. The matron of the hostel had referred to a drought, cross because fresh vegetables were scarce and expensive. She was brought back from her reverie by the sudden awareness that her feet were burning. The pavement was so hot that she could feel the heat through her shoes. She'd never imagined such a thing! Her stockings were totally inappropriate. Trying to

---

[24] Global network for women to be accommodated safely worldwide.

recover her composure, she noticed that people smiled as they walked past. Then a family of immigrants from the *Suffolk* recognised her, calling out to wish her well. Eva felt safe but so alone, despite the friendly greeting. Impressions were crowding in on her, each one caught for only a fraction of a second, like the heat through her shoes, before moving on to the next one as she tried to take it all in.

That night she lay listening to sounds she was not accustomed to. Even in the city she could hear the song of the crickets, a strange birdcall, smelled the scent of flowers not yet identifiable, and sensed that this young city had only recently grown from the wilderness. It was just so different from anything familiar. And nothing seemed old here. The word 'immigrant' seemed appropriate to everyone. It was a new land, a colony on the edge of the world.

Back at Brereton, she always felt that her roots were deep in the thick Cheshire soil. She was standing at the end of generations of people, tradition, class systems that had evolved and perpetuated regardless of the people. Here, she was standing right on top of the earth, no roots, no background, and no family stories, no graveyards filled with ancestors, just Eva Madden. It was a frightening thought.

The following day Eva made her up mind to apply herself in every practical way possible. Just to be here was enough without turning everything over and over in her head. She volunteered to help with the meals, general domestic work and even the laundry that at home she had normally handed over to kitchen staff. She briefly returned again to a routine she felt comfortable with. It was stabilising, enabling her to look ahead and appreciate that she had crossed the world safely.

The matron paid Eva, so impressed was she by her work. They talked together about her position in Wellington and she was offered work at the hostel if ever she came that way again. Eva had made the first steps that an immigrant must make when settling into a new country. She had made an effort to fit in, to work and make new friends and she felt satisfied with herself.

Within a few days she was ready to make the long journey by train, travelling south from Auckland to Wellington, along with many other immigrants. The day's journey by steam train gave her a lasting impression of the North Island. As they pulled out of the city, day was breaking and she sat back in anticipation of the long journey through strange countryside. Used to the flat Cheshire plain, lush with summer grasses, she was surprised to see mile upon mile of green and yellow hills which rolled endlessly to the skyline. She supposed they would turn bright green when the drought broke because even at the end of summer, there was still plenty of grass. The hills were small and steep and cattle and sheep grazed at bizarre angles on every available slope. Rough roads wound round the contours of the land, occasionally leading to holding paddocks. She spotted small hotels and stables housing both drovers and horses.

The entire landscape, as far as Eva could see, was reminiscent of England. Yet the hedges, ditches and woodlands were absent, replaced by miles upon miles of wooden fences. These were built tightly together and wired from end to end to mark out the vast areas of land. It reminded Eva of a child's drawing, simple and uncomplicated. Soon the train passed large houses built in the style of early colonial architecture. Basic in design, featuring a verandah on the ground floor with dormer windows above, just about all of them were built from wood. Each home was surrounded by spacious landscaped gardens strongly influenced by architecture from 'the old country'. Eva was very impressed by the pleasant scenery and housing. She couldn't take her eyes from the windows as she watched the fast moving clouds cast long shadows across the unchanging landscape.

Towards Taupo, she was astonished to see a huge volcano rising threateningly from the simple pastoral landscape. Could this green and innocent land possibly hold such fire in its belly? The Hollis children had always included stories about volcanoes in their tall stories of New

Zealand when they were children, but she'd never imagined it would be like this. Eva gave an involuntary shudder as the train thundered past. She felt that she had an awful lot to learn about this country whose fires boiled close to its surface.

But then her thoughts returned to Crewe, now so very far away. The noise of the steam train evoked memories of the smoky northern town where she had lived out so much of her life and which held her family, so precious to her. Was she escaping from the inevitable drab existence of a single woman in service, experiencing a little of the wealth enjoyed by the upper classes? Or was there a deeper reason for her seeking faraway places?

Thinking back to her last lonely meeting with Ellen in that bleak visiting room at the hospital, Eva felt an overwhelming sense of loss for her sister, trapped in her world of make believe. She had tried to explain to Ellen that she was making a journey across the seas to a colony far away. But Ellen had simply held her hand, talked about her next visit and when she could come home to be with her family. Her lucid thoughts emerged in fragments, aided by the electric shock treatment she'd received. Eva still had no real idea whether Ellen really understood that she'd gone away and wouldn't be visiting again. Why? thought Eva. What caused her to lose her mind?

She had also felt very worried about young Joe. She had seen little of him during those last few days in Crewe. And when he said goodbye he had seemed so emotional and sad. Her last memory of him was of a gentle but remote young man, donning his jacket and setting off to Crewe Station for work. In vain she had looked along the platform as the train had pulled out for Liverpool. There was no sign of him. She remembered the knowing look on her brother George's face as the train pulled out.

"Don't worry, Eva, he's busy. But he's thinking of you. We all love you. If you ever feel lonely, just remember that." Why was she feeling so guilty now? Was this something that all immigrants felt when they leave their families?

Under cloudless skies the train sped on through Hawke's Bay, passing through greener fields. Eva recognised the long groves of poplars growing across the Heretaunga Plain. They were trees from the Old Country. Even in the twilight she could make out the bright yellow gorse bushes that were thriving on the sides of the steep hills. Maybe the early English settlers had brought it out as a hedge plant?

Eva had read that Wellington, the capital city of New Zealand, had grown from a settlement on the harbour's edge and despite the logic that it was the capital city of the country, she had been worried that she was going to a place that would be primitive and without a town's real comforts. She noted with approval, and a little relief, several large buildings and paved roads everywhere as the train drew nearer to the station. Finally it pulled in at Wellington.

Life with the Hills

Gathering up her belongings, she took one swift look into her purse mirror to straighten her hat, smooth her bobbed hair and adjust her dress and jacket. Then she alighted from the train, a slimly built young woman, looking no more than twenty years old. Dark brown hair escaped in wavy fronds from her fashionable hat, the brim of which was pulled down over her forehead. Her widely spaced, deep brown eyes shrewdly took in the busy activities on the platform.

A luggage porter helped her collect her trunk and cases from the train's luggage compartment. He then took her to a taxi, which drove her to Park Street, unloading her belongings at the door of a well-established house belonging to Mr and Mrs Hill. Eva's nerves about meeting her new employers left her unable to take in the sights and sounds of the town as they drove. Her pulse was racing, but she was unaware as she struggled to deal with the thoughts racing through and crowding her mind. She swallowed hard and could barely thank the taxi driver as he knocked on the door, unwilling to leave his passenger just standing on the pavement. Within minutes the owner of the house greeted Eva for she had sent a telegram from Auckland and was expected.

Introductions over, Mrs Hill tipped the taxi driver to carry all her belongings to a small room off the first landing, which would provide her with accommodation for the next twelve months. Mrs Hill was well dressed, in her late forties and most surprisingly to Eva, was quite informal and pleasant as she showed the house to Eva.

As she had done many times in her life recently, Eva unpacked her belongings, glancing round the room.

Her nerves settled and she smiled as she noted the homely touches such as flowers that had been added for her arrival. A servant would never have been given such consideration in England. Her window looked out over the rooftops of houses, which dwindled in the distance. The forested Tararua mountain range formed the distant skyline. As the last of the day's light faded, the lights of Wellington lit up both streets and houses.

Eva quickly worked out that with the twelve-hour time difference Crewe would now be bathed in wintry light as people awoke to a cold morning. She would write a long letter to her parents and George as soon as she was settled for there was so much to tell. She was here, she was all right and her new life had now truly begun.

The following weeks were hectic as Eva was swept along within a new household. She quickly learned the living patterns of her employer Mrs Hill, who commented to friends that Eva brought that indefinable Englishness to her work that the settlers who had never forgotten 'the old country' so craved. Their view of the British way of life saturated their lifestyles and revealed itself in the furnishings of their homes. They may as well have been in England for they insisted on that indefinable middle class atmosphere controlling everything they did.

Eva smiled as she expertly went about her duties as housemaid. She drew the heavy curtains back each morning in the drawing room to reveal nets that were the envy of several of the more gossipy neighbours in the middle class suburb. She smoothed the velvet cushions that were poised on the edge of the high back chairs, served lunch at midday, and the traditional scones, jam and cake afternoon tea at precisely four o'clock every afternoon. Donning her finest cap and frilled apron, she served dinner in the ornate dining room, checking beforehand that the table had been laid correctly with the finest silver.

As she served cups of tea in the sitting room and

went about her work, Eva was for the most part silent and always remote towards her employers. She listened to their trite conversations about the gossip of Wellington, finding out whose son was being sent away to either school or university in England and who was allowed to be invited into their closely knit group of admirers, followers and friends. She was a witness to the antagonism and envy resulting from their so-called middle class lifestyle as they amused themselves with the planning of afternoon teas and the latest fashionable clothes to be worn at their next party. They discussed the local hunting scene, to which they aspired, but played no part in, as their income was a little too moderate. They congratulated themselves on their participation as patrons and benefactors of local causes.

Sometimes their informality amused her, but at other times she found some of their more snobbish ways irksome. For example, Eva smiled politely but seethed inside when they roared with laughter at one of their after dinner jokes. The story was retold from a cartoon they had seen in the local paper. It showed a new domestic climbing through the serving hatch and dropping the dinner plates in front of the startled guests as she exclaimed, "Do I have to come through this hole every time?"

Why is it, she thought that these people seem to need to believe that domestic work relates to someone who is unintelligent? In fact, she knew that they rarely considered servants as people. Servants were a status symbol, merely a way to ensure an easier lifestyle for them in fitting with the social class they considered they belonged to. They knew nothing about her, that she had been reading at three and had spent fifteen years at Brereton Hall with access to its brilliant library, that she knew more about etiquette than they did, yet they somehow knew that they were her superiors.

She was aware of the straying eyes of Mr Hill, who followed her every move. She was watchful of him without him realising it. He was an attractive man who spent little time in the home. Business took him away on many

The Price

occasions, sometimes for days. Eva didn't actually meet him until she had already been in Wellington a month. Once he came into the dining room as she prepared the table for dinner. He hovered, seeking an opening for a conversation. Eva didn't respond to his stares, keeping the table between them.

"Well, Eva, is that your name? Or is it Evelyn? Such a pretty name."

"Thank you Sir."

"There is no need to be formal with me Evelyn. I am your employer yes, but I would like to also be your friend if you would allow it."

"Thank you Sir."

"No more of that. Call me Gordon. I would be happy if you would do that. It would please me."

Eva did not reply. She looked at him across the table. She pitied him. He was not in love with his wife. He was bored, he was lonely and his wife was ugly and gossipy. She knew all of these things. It would be easy to start a friendship with him. In fact, for the most part she quite liked him. But it was a dangerous path to follow. She'd seen the likes of him before, men who cheated on their wife and expected domestic staff to provide all the services he required and Eva was more cautious than that by nature and training. She was relieved when the cook sounded the gong for dinner. The conversation ended as Mrs Hill and guests entered the room.

"Oh, yes. Eva. Managed to get her from one of the great halls in England, you know." It was a comment made more than once by Mrs Hill in her constant quest for superiority over her guests and neighbours. The Hills approved of her seeming lack of interest in men, her efficiency, intelligence and attention to duty and paid her well, something else Mrs Hill sometimes had occasion to let slip to visitors. They preferred to keep their own colonial bred dream of England untouched. Servants did not think or feel. They were there to serve.

As for Eva, she was on a mission to save as much money as she could. She had heard from her brother George about his similar plan to invest all his savings. Brother and sister, from opposite ends of the earth, began a disciplined mission to take them beyond any chance of falling into the clutches of poverty. But unlike their mother, they decided to do it without sacrificing comfort and all pleasure in life.

As month after month passed by, Eva took most of her weekly salary to the post office in Wellington, depositing it in a savings account. She became a well-known figure to the staff and some of them commented on her discipline as she deposited the exact same amount of money each month into her nest egg. Finally, at the end of November 1925 she achieved her first goal.

The postmaster called her to one side. "Miss Madden, I couldn't help noticing that you now have a full £100 deposited with us. With such a sum in such a short amount of time, it's obvious that you have a goal in mind. So I feel I should advise you on how to best make your money work for you. If you buy an investment certificate with your £100, in five years when it matures, you'll have earned some interest. If you mean to keep it here with us for that long, it will be like extra money for free. In the meantime, it would be lodged at the post office for safekeeping."

Eva wasn't sure about five years. She didn't even know if she'd be in New Zealand in five years time. Once her five-year immigration contract was finished, she may just go straight home to England but putting her money to work for her certainly made sense. And she could always send for it if she was back in England by then, so she agreed. If she needed money, she knew she could have another £100 by July of next year at her current rate of saving, so she felt quite secure.

"I agree. Thank you for letting me know about it. What papers do I need to sign to arrange it?"

A few minutes later Eva walked from the post office smiling. She was richer than she'd ever been and more than that, she was an investor! She was free, independent and able to manage her own affairs. She took a moment to savour what she thought was a huge achievement given the world she had come from.

Starting on her long walk back to the house, Eva was surprised to look up and see a line of well-dressed boys lining up, waiting for a bus. She was intrigued because they were obviously immigrants from 'The Old Country' as she'd come to think of it. Piled around their feet were bags containing their few belongings and they looked uncomfortable and out of place. She couldn't help but ask them where they were going. It turned out that they were the sons of British sailors who had been killed in The Great War. The entire batch of young men was waiting to be picked up and taken to Flock House, which was a property near Wellington. There, they would be taught how to be farmers in their new land. Eva knew a little of their loneliness, but couldn't help but admire their families for letting them go so far away to find a better life.

That night she wrote to George.

27th November 1925, Wellington.

Dear George,
Thank you for your last letter, which I received on 17th September, my birthday. Now I am 29 years old!
I miss you all and how I long to see you. But I must be patient for as I keep reminding myself, my assisted passage[25] out here means that I must work for 5 years before returning home. How are Mother and Father? Please send my warmest wishes to them and tell them from me that I have sent money over for Christmas so that life will be a little easier.
I was delighted to hear that you have finally married dear little Edith. I am so happy for you both for she is the sweetest person and will make you a wonderful wife. I was saddened

---

[25] A scheme whereby a government encourages people to emigrate by agreeing to pay for their ticket on condition of remaining in the country to work for a period.

Life with the Hills

to hear that you had to do this in secret and glad that it is now fully disclosed. Her mother probably objected as a result of silly rumours about our dear sister Ellen. She fears madness runs in our family. Even out here, I see and meet many people that you could call mad. They are walking about free!

You have very little to say about Joe. Is he still working on the railway and is he still so very quiet? He had so little to say to me before I came out here. I fear that family events weigh heavily on him and he appears to have so few friends. Tell him that I am asking about him and give him all my news on New Zealand.

What a very good idea to rent a house in Wistaston, right out in the countryside with the prospect of buying some farming land. I know that has been your dream for so long. I still feel a little unsure about Edith living an isolated life on a farm. She is a town girl and we have often laughed about her fear of the dark! I am sure you will resolve things between you. Mother will be well pleased for in her own quiet way she loves Edith.

You were asking me about coming out to New Zealand to buy land and farm. I can only tell you from my limited observations for much of my time is spent in service. As yet I have not looked further afield than Wellington itself.

New Zealand is indeed a beautiful country and does resemble England in many ways. But you must not look for spinnies, hedges and ditches here. Imagine great tracts of land, which unfold for miles. I think that you would need money to invest, although land is still cheap.

I have enclosed two newspaper cuttings. The first one is the sale of a good small farm for £2000, 39½ acres of very best land, all flat, and about £700 cash wanted, with the balance on a long-term mortgage. The second one is for 40 acres and a house for £1500. At least it will give you a fair idea of prices.

From what I have observed, sheep and cattle predominate on the land. The farms are vast and called stations. Little *villages to be found in Cheshire do not exist here. The far spread communities try to appear to be very British. The social classes are more diluted due to the necessity of having to mix with most members of the community or there would be no society at all. The population is far sparser than that in Britain although certain snobbishness exists amongst the wealthier people.*

The farming community appears to hold the power here and farmers have the control over the economy, politics and social attitudes. Thousands of returned servicemen have been put on the land but as in England, there is still much unemployment here. Many farmers borrow huge amounts of money to invest. I always fear what would happen if they could not meet their debts. Mother's frugal attitude towards money has certainly followed me here! Do tell her so and assure her that I am very careful with my savings. I know it will please her.

Only today I saw a large group of young boys who had just arrived in Wellington, the sons of dead British sailors. They will be trained over here to become farmers. Anyone coming out here must be struck by the areas of land which are yet unused. Much of it is still covered by fern and Manuka and other parts are overgrown by blackberry bushes, ragwort and pennyroyal. Other areas are swampland and need draining. It is a land for settlers who are not afraid of hard work.

Tell Joe that there is also a huge profit to be made in rabbits for some farmers have abandoned sheep farming in order to engage in the more profitable business of rabbit skins!

I have heard much talk of the native people here and have seen quite a number of Maoris in Wellington itself. They are a handsome and proud race. I fear that the colonial pastoralists of sixty years ago acquired large areas of land by ruthlessly exploiting the Maori people who were not aware of legal matters. Of course I do not discuss this. I listen to my employers who discuss such matters. Their wealth comes from the grocery business and they are not so

Life with the Hills

concerned with the buying of land.
I am of the opinion that society in New Zealand firmly believes that a woman's place is in the home and there is very little scope for working class women outside family life. I hear much talk of it from my employers. Their grown up daughters preoccupy their time in household duties.
I am quite the oddity here. I do not really think that my employers see me as an independent woman but rather just as a domestic. I give them no opportunity for discussion on this matter. However, I am glad I don't have to answer to a husband like the women here do and I am proud to be independent of any man and that I can make my own way in the world unencumbered by a home or children.
Maybe this is not good news for Edith. I know that she would like to see me settled in a home with a family. It must be a wonderful thing to have a home of your own George. I admire you for saving towards one but I think that path is not for me!
Here in Wellington I am somewhat protected from the elements, but farming would only be for the toughest person. I have heard stories about flooding in the north. During the torrential rains the smallest streams can become raging rivers. It is a much wilder country than England, even though towns and cities are being built. Society seems only just to be developing and hasn't taken on a character of its own. It tries to copy the English ways.
There are many immigrants still arriving by ship. Some have experienced far rougher voyages than my own, including immigrants from India who have arrived in this city ready to set up fruit and vegetable stalls. I have heard my employers speak very disparagingly of them.
Maybe they see them as some kind of threat to their own well-established businesses. I don't know, but the more I hear them talk about Maoris and the new Indian immigrants, the more determined I am to see these in the opposite light. Maybe I'm just being contrary, but the Maoris, after all, had seemed to do all right before the English came and have

been lied to over and over since. And the Indians just seem to be hard working immigrants like me who just want a better life than they can find in their homeland.

Referring to Wellington, I say city, but after visiting London and Liverpool, Wellington appears to be a very pretty town built on the edge of the harbour.

You have talked for some while about investments. You will be pleased to hear that two days ago when I visited the post office I was informed that my savings, including the little money I had brought out from England, had reached the grand total of £100. I invested it in a certificate to be kept at the post office.

As I now have some real savings, I have named Mother as my next of kin should anything happen to me. I doubt this, behind the lace curtains in Park Street! I know how pleased you will feel for even at your age I know you are as frugal as me.

Please keep me informed of every member of my family, including Ellen. I believe Augusta still visits her. It is hard to believe that Thomas is now working and Mother can have support following those difficult years when we were all small. Please give Mother and Father all my love. Tell them I think of them often and that I am safe.

I am well and blessed with good health. The epidemic of infantile paralysis that broke out in April now seems to be under control, which is a great relief to everyone.

We heard on the wireless that there have been several cases in Britain. Are there any cases in Crewe? I am relieved to know that all of you are well and look forward to more news from Crewe soon.

Your loving sister,
Eva.

The first Christmas spent in her new country was very lonely, although she was delighted to receive a letter and small gift from the Bruces. Tommy was even able to write a few words to her by himself in his shaky hand. It was the one real bright spot and reminded her when she was most tired, that she wasn't completely alone in her new country.

Eva spent most of her time making sure that the household celebrations were successful, working for long hours. It was with great pride that she counted up her wages in the first week in January and made her way to the Wellington Post Office. It started out like every other trip she made to the Post Office, but the 7th of January 1926 was not a date that she would forget very easily. As she stood in the queue inside the building, she felt a small movement beneath her feet.

An old lady in front of Eva turned around and caught hold of Eva's arm. "That," she whispered, "is the beginning of an earthquake!"

Before Eva could question her, the entire building began to shake. Someone screamed. The shock set off the chimes in the General Post Office clock. The trembling lasted for five to six seconds and then the floor began to move! A wave had passed through the entire post office! Several people stumbled. There was an eerie silence among those present, as they waited to see what would occur next. The building rumbled and shuddered. Then nothing!

People started to smile and laugh with relief. They rushed outside to see what had happened in the street. Strangely there was no damage apart from a few chimneys that had crashed to the pavements. A startled horse, which was attached to a four-wheeled vehicle, had started to bolt but it was soon brought under control.

Eva shook more than the Post Office had just done. She made her way back into the post office, making her deposit. So that was an earthquake! She marvelled at the acceptance and calm of everyone around her. Was she the only one whose heart was pounding? As she walked back towards the doors she stared at everyone. Smiles of relief showed on people's faces. So she wasn't the only one who'd been scared. This made her feel a bit more normal. It was a natural phenomenon, which everyone seemed to accept as part of life in New Zealand. Eva must learn to accept it too if she was to feel comfortable with her life here.

Her banking done, she stepped outside, hesitant to cross the road. Someone took her arm, guiding her gently. It was Gordon Hill. He too had experienced the shock. Now they had a talking point beyond her duties. "Are you all right? I was concerned for you," he said gently.

"Yes Sir." But Eva's voice shook. She was alarmed by the quake, but just as alarmed by Mr Hill approaching her.

"You're shaking Eva! Come on, let's go and sit in a tea house until you feel better." He guided her to a table and ordered tea and sandwiches. Eva was confused. It hadn't been a planned meeting. Mr Hill is simply being kind, she assured herself and yet she was uneasy.

Unintentionally, the ice had been broken. They had common ground on which to build a friendship. His fascination with Eva Madden grew but he knew that if he made demands on her, she would leave their employment. He did not want that. He wanted her around where he could watch her. In short, he was fascinated by Eva.

He decided long ago that he would never leave the boring security of his house bought with his ugly wife's money. He knew where he was comfortable and secure. Yet he sensed a passion in this mysterious woman. Why was it that she was more middle class than his chattering wife? He desired Eva Madden. He didn't love her, wasn't even sure he knew what love was, but the more remote she was the more he wanted to make love to her, possess her again and again, wake up next to her, and watch her while she slept. Yet he could not as much as touch her because to do so would be to risk losing everything. She didn't suspect his lust. If she had any idea of it, she kept her feelings about him hidden.

Eva made every effort to please Mr and Mrs Hill. She knew that Mr Hill looked leeringly at her when he thought she wasn't looking, but she was completely unaware of the depth of his obsession. She simply went about her work asking few favours, attending to their every need and taking very little time off for herself. But the summer proved to be everything the cook had warned her about. The hot nights prevented her from sleeping. The house heated up unbearably and warm winds brought the fear of fire to the outlying areas of the city. She developed a cough that she could not cure, despite all the old remedies that she had brought from England. She grew extremely thin and as she smoothed down her starched uniform, she realised that her family would barely recognise her.

Gordon Hill still recognised her though. And as familiar as he was with her body and daily appearance, he soon noticed the weight loss and fatigue. He was concerned for her. He desperately wanted to approach Eva, but his obsessional desire for her held him back. He feared losing the one woman he wanted more than any other. His business trips were quite prolonged as he sought other women. But no matter how many women he had when he was away from home, he could not forget little Eva. She was constantly in his mind. He knew so little about her. Several times he followed her from a distance, knowing that she made trips to the post office. He watched her go in, come out and walk wearily back to the house in the heat. He watched her turn away and cough in the dining room. Once he caught her slumped in the chair in the sitting room. He could do nothing. He dare not approach her.

In the evenings she had taken to walking down to the harbour. The cool breeze eased her exhaustion. She walked along the waterfront where she could look out over Oriental Bay. She made a habit of walking as far as the band rotunda and then turning back, anxious not to become too tired. One evening as she approached the rotunda she recognised Gordon Hill sitting reading a newspaper.

"Miss Madden, How lovely to see you. Sit in here next to me and tell me how things are going with you. You're

The Price

not too tired? We're not working you too hard?" He spoke kindly. Eva was pleased to see him for the truth was that she hadn't made many friends in Wellington. She didn't share her feelings with anyone. Gordon Hill had done her no harm so despite it being most improper for an English servant to sit with her employer, she sat down, smiling at him.

"I've been very tired lately. It's not the work. I think it's the weather. Once the autumn winds are here I'm sure I'll feel better."

He was silent. He stared at her pale thin face. Dare he take the risk and tell her? "Eva, I've done something you must not be cross about. Please promise me that you won't be angry with me."

Eva looked at him in astonishment. He was her employer. How could he be talking like this? She felt sorry for him. "I cannot promise until I know what it is."

"I've been to the post office. I've placed an extra £50 in your account."

Eva was shocked. What he would want in exchange was the first thought that flashed across her mind. "Why? Tell me why!" she demanded.

"Because you work so hard. You're far better at your job than any of the household staff of our friends. You deserve to have some money of your own. Mrs Hill and I are lucky to have you in the house. Really! I wanted to thank you. Because you make us both so happy."

Eva stared at him. There was a long silence. Then she spoke, wearily and almost in a whisper. "A long time ago I was given £50 by a very dear friend and it changed my world. Your £50 is a wonderful gift but I cannot accept it. I'm sorry but it isn't right. It just doesn't feel right."

"Please Eva. I beg of you. Take the money. I want you to have it. No one knows that I have done this. Buy some blasted cough medicine with it. Buy a lovely dress or a new hat. Send it home to your family. But do not refuse it. You have more than earned it. Keep it. Please."

Eva felt confused. She was not well. She was being

too proud. She should not argue over such a generous gift. Finally she sighed and looked up at him. "I will accept it, just this once, but never again. No one must know. No one." And then standing up again, she said, "Thank you, Mr Hill. I must walk back now." Before any more words were exchanged, she stood up feeling unnerved and shaky but very determined to make her own way back to the house.

Moving On

The citizens of Wellington were celebrating. The main road between the capital and Auckland had finally been completed to ensure an all year road route. Eva was aware that many changes were taking place. Even in the short time that she had been in the country she was aware of a huge building program. She knew that the rugged countryside to the north of Wellington was gradually being broken in for sheep farming, which meant the felling of thousands of trees. Progress was visible everywhere. But Eva found little to celebrate.

It was during the late summer that she realised that she had gone slightly deaf in her right ear. It had started with an ear infection. Now she had to incline her head slightly to the left to hear properly. She did not disclose this to a living soul as it could most certainly jeopardise her employment. Eva instinctively felt that she was becoming drained and exhausted. It took longer for her to get up and begin the day and for the first time she found herself longing to finish work so she could rest. Coupled with the fact that she was homesick, that gnawing feeling that welled up inside her at unpredictable moments, she felt great pangs of loneliness. She had no friends here, no social life and nobody to talk to about anything but business and it was starting to tell. She was extremely irritable but fought hard against losing her temper, remembering the dreadful incident at Brereton Hall all that time ago when she'd shaken the scullery maid.

Sometimes she longed to wear fashionable clothes, go out and seek company. But it was simply not the thing to do though for gossipers were the same the world over and Wellington was still a small town. Mr and Mrs Hill's friends would be bound to hear and she would be to blame for bringing them into disrepute. Brushing her wavy brown hair in the mirror she stared back at her reflection, a Madden face, high cheekbones, intelligent brown eyes and pale skin. She longed to see more familiar faces that looked like her.

When her duties were finished she would sometimes dress up in one of her loveliest frocks, wear makeup, try on her finest hat and go for a walk. But more and more often as she put on the clothes, she realised she had lost too much weight. She must not get any thinner. She could hear George's words, 'Hullo, bag of bones. We'd better feed you up.' It was not lack of eating. It was a Madden trait. She had seen this happen in her mother. Joe had also grown too thin with worry on several occasions. She lost interest in food. Only certain meat or fruit appealed to her. This could not go on. She had a dreaded sense of something not right in her world. Not the world of New Zealand, but something deep within her.

The nightmares began again. She seemed to be forever wandering along roads that had no destination. Her sister called out to her. Her brother Joe was waiting for her. George was angry. She was glad of the early dawn each day, the net curtains blowing across her bed, as she lay drenched with perspiration, despite the cold of a Wellington winter.

In the spring of 1926 Eva received a long letter from her brother George. She hid the letter for days, taking it out in the privacy of her bedroom to read it again and again. It gave her the answers she was seeking. From across the world came the voices that haunted her. She could hardly bear to believe the contents of the letter. Finally she replied. She was grief stricken over the content but realistic enough to know that her brother would be waiting for her answer.

September 14th 1926

My dear brother George,
I received the terrible news from you just over two weeks ago. Yesterday I destroyed your letter lest it should fall into

the wrong hands. I am resolved to burn all my family mail in future for as much as I love to receive them, I trust no one with the contents of your letters.

I am deeply saddened to hear about Joseph's incarceration into the Mental Hospital at Chester. You say that for four months he has suffered an attack, which has left him in a peculiar mental state. I can only assume that his removal from the Nantwich Poor Law Institution must mean that he is very seriously ill and cannot be contained in a local hospital.

Dear God, George, what is to become of him in such a dreadful place? Why, I ask myself, is he suffering in this way? Where is the God of whom Mother speaks so convincingly? What has been the cause of such an attack? You say that he has cut himself with a razor. Since then he has deteriorated in his mind, slipping into a stupor from which there appears to be no return.

In one of your earlier letters you mentioned that he had moved from Mother's house to live with Augusta and her husband. He became very disturbed during those miserable mealtimes when mother would insist on the Bible readings. It brings back memories to me, George.

When we were children, Ellen and I used to kick one another under the table. Ellen used to try and make me laugh much to Mother's disapproval. Joe would sit and stare into space, having very little to say. He always seemed to be in a world of his own. Yet when he was comfortable and interested he became a happy, noisy child.

I am so fearful of this dreadful illness, which has taken our brother and sister away from us. What does it mean? When I was at school we would make fun of each other's names but now I fear that the name 'Madden' has a more sinister ring. You say that no one has visited him, yet you made the journey to Chester to consult with the doctor and to read his progress report. What a fearsome thing to do my dear little brother George.

I can forgive you for not seeing him. The very thought of him wandering about in a listless manner, full of strange sounds and incomprehensible actions would be too much for you to bear. I am resolved never to marry for I am fearful of having children. I know you think this too.

I will try very hard to put this out of my mind for I am helpless in the situation. Mother and Father must be bowed under with such terrible events. It is a wonderful thing that you have Edith with whom you can build a home, safe from such darkness.

No matter how bad the news is, George, please keep writing for I feel so very far away and so very useless.

With love,
Eva

In her few spare hours Eva did what many a young woman of better means would have spent more time on. She sewed, making herself several lovely dresses of the latest fashion. She stitched and darned, checking through her wardrobe, which she had slowly added to, making sure that she was short of nothing.

She was terrified to dwell on the news from home, fighting her mind in order not to think about it. Only in her restless sleep did it revive, presenting itself in great shapes and night fears that caused her to wake with a pounding heart. Kneeling on her bed, she looked out at the lights of Wellington, questioning her own existence. More than once she questioned why she had signed to come to New Zealand for five years when her family needed her so much. Her mother had been right; all freedom came at a price.

During the day she worked hard, eating little, saying nothing if she could help it. Gordon Hill found a very different Eva when he returned from a business trip to Australia. He was shocked by her appearance. Angry with his wife, he questioned her. How had this been allowed to happen? She'd barely noticed. So long as Eva performed her duties to her usual impeccable standard then her physical and mental state was none of her concern. She was Eva's employer, not her family. He resumed watching Eva closely, but could find no explanation.

Once when she had left the house, he sneaked into her room. He looked at her neat clothes, examined her belongings, and checked for proof of anything that might explain her deterioration. Nothing. In despair, he sat on her bed, holding her nightdress to his face. For the first time in his life, Gordon Hill wept for someone other than himself. He became convinced that his little Eva was consumptive. He would insist that she see his doctor.

That night he waited until dinner was over. Mrs Hill was leaving to play bridge with her friends. The cook was at her sister's. It was an ideal time. He climbed the stairs to Eva's room, bending to listen at her door. There was silence. He knocked. No answer. Gently he turned the handle and looked in. Eva was lying on her bed in her petticoat. Her small hands were folded beneath her left cheek. Her breathing was uneven.

"Eva. Eva, wake up. It's me, Gordon. I need to talk with you."

She stirred uneasily. Suddenly she was awake, clutching the bedclothes to her throat in fright and anxiety. He backed towards the door. "Forgive me Eva, but I had to speak to you. What's wrong with you? You're changed, sick. Let me help."

Eva slipped her dress on but sat down again on the bed. "You should not be in my room. Do not address me as Eva. It is not appropriate," she said, unable to meet his eyes.

Suddenly months of watching, worrying and fretting welled up and he couldn't help himself. "Eva, don't send me away. I love you." He was almost convinced of it himself. He stepped towards her.

Eva jumped up from the bed, angry at the intrusion. How dare he come into her room? She was unhappy, miserable and homesick. She did not need this complication in her life.

"Eva. Listen to me. Life is too short for obsessions, ups and downs. Turmoil. Let us have what we can. Now."

Eva's heart was pounding. She did not hate him. Despite the way he had looked at her, he had been the one really kind person she'd met in Wellington. But she feared where this might lead.

"That, Mr Hill is not life! That is pretence. That is trying to hold two hearts and in doing so, crushing one. That is not love. No! It is just your selfishness. Your desire to have me, but I will not be a mistress."

"But I don't love my wife! She bores me. She's ugly inside and out. She doesn't understand how I feel." He moved a step closer. "But I have no choice. I have to stay with her Eva, please come to me. I am so lonely. I think of you every minute of the day. I will look after you, I promise. Care for you. You no longer need to work. You can live near to me. You can always be there for me."

His voice trailed away as Eva came towards him. He'd never seen her angry and ever the watcher, he was fascinated by this new side of his obsession.

"And I would be a secret? Is that what I'm worthy of? To live my life hidden away, not recognised. You desire me Gordon, but you know nothing of love. You love yourself."

"This is not true. I love you Eva."

The temper that she had been fighting to control for weeks threatened to engulf Eva. She stamped her foot in anger, speaking bitterly. "You say you have no choice. Of course you have a choice. You're choosing now. You are the one who has the power, makes the decisions."

He tried to stop her but the avalanche of words, long waiting to be said to other men whose eyes she had felt on her over the years, now poured out of her in a torrent.

"You are asking me to be your mistress. Is this what your £50 was a down payment on? In a few years you'll want someone younger. What of me then? I would have no security. No future. I could not walk hand in hand with you, openly. I would be a hidden thing in your life. A secret!" She shouted the last two words so loudly that Gordon backed towards the door in awe of her.

"I will never be your possession to sharpen the edge of your boredom. I would rather die first! If you had me, you would convince yourself that you must stay with your wife. After all you would say, she's done nothing wrong. You would stay in your ridiculous marriage. Because that is what it is, a sham. It would take a very expert whore to keep your marriage together Mr Hill. And I am not about to be that whore."

Now Eva was talking very quietly and precisely. Years of thought on these matters were finally being spoken aloud. She had seen the suffering that followed such a decision. She had witnessed several of the maids at Brereton whose lives had been wasted by believing men like him.

"You would even go into the church. Seek absolution. Come out as a repentant sinner. The church loves that. They would have served their purpose. And I would be the sinner! For 'tempting' you! Get out of my room and lust after someone else. I want none of it."

Gordon thought she was finished, but she went on. "It would be so easy now, because I have so little. But later it would be terrible. I may even have an illegitimate child by then. I am lonely Gordon, but not as lonely as you. You are lonely because you don't answer your true longings. You are not honest. Now get out."

Eva leant against the wall, exhausted. Gordon stared at her in admiration and longing. He could not believe that she was refusing him. He stepped forward to touch her. Instantly he was reeling backwards from the sharp slap across his face.

"I said get out!"

Eva shut the door, pushing her trunk against it. She heard Mr Hill's footsteps going slowly down the stairs. She was exhausted. Her energy had finally left her. She lay across the bed and wept. Finally she sat up, smoothed her hair and washed her face at the hand basin. She must leave immediately. She could not tolerate this situation. The opportunity presented itself the next morning. Mr Hill had left again on the pretence of business. Mrs Hill was in her most pompous and persuasive mood. Little did she know that she lived a life of pretence and lies.

"Eva, my dear. Come into the drawing room. I wish to speak with you." Her tone of voice indicated nothing wrong. "I propose to lend you out to my dear friend Mrs Bidewell. Her daughter is to be married within months and her domestic is useless. There are the engagement parties, the preparations, the wedding. You would be ideal. I feel so sorry for her. She simply cannot manage with those useless maids."

Eva's immediate answer surprised her. She thought there would be at the very least a degree of regret. She was after all an excellent employer. But the answer she got was, "I would be most happy to serve Mrs Bidewell. I'll pack immediately. Thank you Ma'am."

In service at yet another wealthy home, Eva unpacked. She wrote to Crewe with her change of address, commencing her duties the following day. She continued to save, even more fiercely than before. She decided to invest the gift of £50. It would be too difficult to hand it back. She would make sure that she never came into contact with the Hills ever again.

Her savings continued to grow and with it her curiosity to see more of the world. During her brief time off, Eva discovered several walks but if time allowed, she would endeavour to reach Day's Bay, which lay on the eastern side of Wellington Harbour. Here she walked in amazed silence through the tracks bordered by giant tree ferns and many native trees, all so different from the Cheshire lanes of England. She avoided the walk to the rotunda. Finally a long awaited letter arrived for her from Crewe, putting her mind at rest.

The Price

March 1927 Crewe.

Dear Eva,
We are all well here in Crewe.
I hope this letter reaches you soon as sea mail takes so long. There is news of an airmail service to be developed once there is reliable travel by airplanes. We have news here of so many small planes attempting the long voyage across the Atlantic to America, New Zealand and Australia and it will only be a matter of a few years before people will be able to fly to distant places. Then you will not seem so far away.
It has been a terrible winter here in England. Across the country there has been a lack of coal. It has been even worse than when we had a coal strike. Thousands of families have been unable to keep warm. Coal merchants blame the railway companies and in return they blame the merchants. We have resorted to bagging the coal that has accidentally 'fallen' from passing steam trains. I am now promoted to fireman and am assisting in this!
Our winter was very cold. England was covered with snow, which looks beautiful from the inside of the house but restricts movement about the town. There were many broken legs and arms as people tried to walk the icy streets. Mother survived it as she made only the very necessary journeys to the shops on Nantwich Road. In March influenza swept the country resulting in over a thousand deaths in London alone. In many ways we are fortunate in Cheshire. Although the weather is very cold, we seem to escape the massive snow, which hits the Pennines. As yet we have not experienced the heavy flooding which the south is suffering from and you may have read about in the newspaper over there.
I have a clear view of the land as I travel on the engines between Crewe and London. Crewe is not such a bad place to live compared to London, which I walk about for several hours at least once a week before steaming back north. The poverty is terrible. I have encountered beggars on the streets and some of the houses have five families living in them.

There is a small tearoom near to Euston Station and I sit in there many a time, listening to the working or unemployed men. Times are hard, very hard in this country Eva. I think that you are best out of it, in a land of opportunity.
The family are all well and send their love. Brother Joe is of course still in hospital. I have not made a visit this last winter. It is a depressing and unchanging situation. The doctor tells me that visits from family disturb him greatly. Try not to dwell on these matters but look ahead to your own life.
I was sent to Bangor, North Wales for 8 weeks, to work as a cleaner on British Rail. Interesting experience but I felt out of place even though I walked on Anglesey, an island just off Bangor, and enjoyed seeing the wildlife there. However I found North Wales to be a lonely and inhospitable country. Once off the job and back in the boarding house I felt alienated by the Welsh language. In Crewe at least I am in a place where English is spoken everywhere!

Love from George and Edith

During April of 1927 all the domestic staff in New Zealand were talking about unionism. News of the formation of a North Island Domestic Industrial Worker's Union spread on the usual grapevine that seemed to operate among people in service the world over. Word was that this union would protect the many men and women in service across the island. Each migrant ship brought in more workers, some of whom had been treated very poorly.

Eva decided to join this union as soon as possible as it improved her working conditions and pay. Membership meant that she would receive one full day off each week, overtime would be charged over forty eight hours a week at the rate of time and a half and she could choose to save her days off and take fourteen days on full pay, every three months. Christmas Day, Boxing Day, New Year's Day,

Good Friday and Easter Monday would all be double pay. It was all the talk amongst the other domestics in Wellington. Eva attended several meetings on the new union. She earned £2 a week and welcomed these changes, thinking of all the hundreds of hours she had worked for no extra money in the past year alone.

Through the newspapers and at the meetings she had heard alarming stories about nominated migrants who for various reasons had lost both job and support. A picture in the local paper showed two immigrant children out on an isolated farm. Their father had been killed in a farming accident and the entire family was starving. The children were dressed in flour sacks for clothes!

She settled into her new work with the Bidewells, her health improving as the autumn came. Her outburst towards Gordon Hill had relieved her of most of her pent up frustration and she was pleased with her decision to change employers. It gave her a feeling of power. Money could buy most things but not Eva Madden!

As she went about her routines, she watched as people came and went from New Zealand, homesick for the land they dreamed of and returning to a New Zealand they then preferred. The wealthy journeyed to the home country, but within a few months they were back, pleased to settle once again into their homes. More than once she wondered what she would do when her five years were up, but she no longer worried about it. It was very easy to keep family secrets from thousands of miles away. Eva could even imagine in lighter moments that everyone was well and happy at home. It was a dangerous mind game to play but the only one that eased her troubled thoughts. She only let herself think about the truth of her family's situation at night in her bed. Then the tears flowed for her confined brother and sick sister and her poor brother, who had assumed responsibility for them both when he was so young himself.

The hard economic times had even touched faraway New Zealand. Eva was distressed to see many men in

Wellington, all seeking work. Some of them had even called at the houses where she worked seeking odd jobs, but nothing was available. Finally they were sent out to farms or to other rural jobs, glad to be able to feed their families even from a distance. Eva watched them with great sadness. She remembered the struggle to survive when she was a child and always tried to give them at least a cup of tea when they called at the houses where she worked. Her childhood had equipped her for harder times, and she continued to save. She now had ample money with which to return to her homeland but what was there to go back to?

As the cold damp winter set in, the tiredness Eva had experienced during the summer with the Hills returned. But it was different somehow and her chest seemed to ache with it. It had come on gradually so she barely noticed it at first. The pain in her chest grew until it was unbearable. Finally on her day off, she sought out a doctor. The diagnosis was rheumatism of her heart. The doctor ordered her to come for fortnightly visits and to rest whenever she wasn't required to work. He actually recommended time off to rest, but he knew what times were like and what risk sick workers took when the market was oversupplied with workers. So he also prescribed a sedative, which helped her to sleep, and insisted on an end to Eva's long walks around the hills of the city. Deciding her family had enough to worry about back home, Eva decided to keep the news to herself. And she certainly didn't tell her employers. She was a woman on her own and she needed to work.

As Eva went about her business in town, she saw more and more men wandering about, drunk, with a bottle in hand. They didn't even bother to do their drinking in a pub behind closed doors. It amazed her that even when lives were desperate and there was no money to put food in the mouths of children, there was still money found for drink. It made her feel as though she detested men, but she detested drinking even more.

In the midst of Eva's illness and her growing disquiet

about the times in which she was living, the next letter from George arrived. It was August 1928 and she still had almost a year and half to serve of her five year contracted stay in New Zealand. There was a terrible finality in his letter. He obviously saw his brother's madness as something that was permanent and a problem that the family had to just accept and hide away from society. This must be for their sakes and for the future generations. Another secret!

Eva sat for a long time on her bed, reading and rereading the words, tears streaming down her cheeks. She tried to come to terms with it and quieten the anger and frustration she felt but she just couldn't help demanding an explanation even when she knew there would be none forthcoming.

2nd July 1928

Dear Eva,
It seems that you have been away from us for a very long time. Yet we are happy in the knowledge that you are doing well in that bright new country you write about. We are all so proud of you. We look forward to your return so that we can once again listen to your adventures.
You ask me to tell you about Joe and so I must do so honestly. Do not grieve too much Eva. There is nothing we can do to help him. I have travelled to Chester on my own and called in to see the doctor at the hospital, informing myself on our brother's progress. I will simply relate this informed documentation to you as it was given to me. You will see that all is being done in difficult circumstances.
None of the family has visited Joseph. His circumstances have been too upsetting, his behavior too extreme. Once he entered the hospital he was observed to be confused and dull. On occasions he shouts out suddenly and for no reason, making the doctors suspect that he is suffering from hallucinations. His bodily health is good but he is still peculiar regarding food. Sometimes he will eat a lot, at

other times he refuses to eat or drink. Other times he will eat only certain foods.

Last year he escaped whilst working in the grounds of the hospital. He wasn't recovered until a month later when he was found in the countryside none the worse for his travels. Just about the whole of the country was iced over with huge snowdrifts. Across Cheshire there was flooding and I feared that he had been drowned. The hospital had informed the police of his escape. They contacted me about the matter.

Mother and Father are too old and distressed to deal with these matters. I have put my name down at the hospital as the person to be informed of any developments. Evidently he settled down well but not for long. He escaped yet again. He was recovered the next day, wandering on the outskirts of Chester and this time he was placed in the locked ward of the hospital.

Then he became the subject of melancholia. The doctor thought that he was hearing voices. On several occasions he had to be confined to bed for his own physical safety. The doctor assured me that no harm had come to him on these occasions. He has a habit of breaking windows, glass in picture frames, glasses and flowerpots. Now he cannot be left for a moment. I did ask if this was his mental frustration at being so closely confined but was assured that it was part of his illness.

I have kept all details from the rest of my family. Thomas does not even know, thinking that his brother is working away in Manchester. Joseph and Martha witnessed the first attack. The only other person to experience his mental state was Augusta. She is deeply disturbed by what has happened and she still believes that he will one day come out of the hospital and live with her again. I have advised her that the doctors do not hold out hope for a recovery but we have differed to the point of arguing. At this point she has not made a visit but insists that she will do so soon.

I beg of you Eva, put these dreadful events behind you. Get on with your life. There is no explanation for his mental state. Although you and I believe that it could be hereditary, we have no medical proof. Dwelling on such matters, looking for abnormal signs within ourselves will only lead to unnecessary suffering.

Mother and Father are silent on the matter now for they can do nothing. They are reassured by Ellen's growing stability. Your photograph gives them great strength. I often catch mother looking at it. You know I visit them practically every day and Edith is a regular visitor.

I have told Edith in no uncertain terms that we shall have a childless marriage for I cannot take any risks with future generations. The medical world does not know sufficient about such states of mind. The best that can be afforded is being done for our brother. Take comfort in the fact that he is in a safe place and being watched over day and night.

I note from your last letter that you may return to England by way of Canada. It is yet another vast country that affords great opportunity and it would be a good idea to extend your journey in this way. I envy you for my little Edie refuses to step away from Crewe, let alone New Zealand or Canada!

My dreams of a farm are fast vanishing. We are both happy in our new home, which is in Crewe, and we travel a little further by motorbike each time we venture out. Edith's mother is just up the street and although she is very fiery and at times we clash, she loves her daughter very much. I am not so sure about the son in law! Edith is near to her when I am away at nights on shift work and prefers it to being in the country.

Whenever you have time, write to us and I will give all your news to mother and father.

Love,

Your brother George.

So finally George was getting ahead. He was still such a young man, but to have achieved what he had was a testament to his strength of personality and Eva was proud of him. The letter, on the other hand, was read many times before she destroyed it. She committed every word to memory for if it fell into her employer's hands the whole of Wellington would eventually find out and her days of plentiful employment options would be over.

She did her best to take George's advice and put the Joe situation out of her mind, but being cooped up in the house was not helping her in this task, so defying doctor's orders, Eva took up gentle walking again. After all, she felt much recovered from her heart condition, and rarely felt any chest pain at all. But on a windswept Sunday in September 1928, she returned from a walk around Palmerston North to a situation that took her to breaking point.

The cook, a bullying woman who constantly moaned about her work conditions, confronted Eva the minute she walked through the kitchen door. She set upon Eva, spotting her coming into the kitchen. For some time her anger towards the maid had grown. She hated the way Eva dressed up for her Sunday walk, like she was a lady. And she'd been with the family since she was twelve, but nobody ever noticed her work. She was sickened by all the praise heaped onto the swanky English maid. Finally, she was determined to have her say.

She sourly observed Eva's ladylike ways, her little fur hat, neatly buttoned coat and leather gloves, looking her up and down as though a prostitute had just walked through the door. "Now who do you think you are, Miss Fine and Mighty? Strutting about the main street of the town pretending you're a lady. Well, you're not, you're just a skivvy like me and don't forget it miss high and mighty Eva Madden!"

Something inside Eva exploded when she heard her family name. Swirling around she slapped the cook hard on the cheek with a dainty gloved hand. Then without saying a word she strode out of the kitchen knowing full well that she had just lost her position. The cook had been with the family since she'd left school and she would weave such a tale about Eva that she would simply have to go. That night

The Price

Eva cried tears of rage, thumping her body with her fists in her anger. Her homesickness and sense of loss swamped her. She'd done nothing to provoke such an attack. She lived her days in virtual silence. She had no friends here and there was rarely any conversation with her employers. Sometimes she wondered if she would forget the English language. How could she have so offended this woman? And worse, how could she so stupidly have lost her temper like that?

She sobbed quietly for hours, alternately sad and angry. It was only later when she got up to wipe her face that her hand passed involuntarily across her breast as if in protection. Suddenly she was aware of a small lump in her right breast. Touching it gingerly and rolling the pea-sized swelling under her thumb and forefinger, she realised that she had something far more worrying to care about than the silly cook. There would be no more sleep tonight.

The following day she sought advice from the doctor who had treated her for her heart troubles. He sent her immediately to another doctor who ran a small hospital in Grey Street, Palmerston North. Here she met with Dr. Cyril King. The fragile and well-spoken young woman impressed him. He examined her, deciding to operate immediately as he feared she had a small tumour in the breast. Eva assured him that she would pay cash for her stay in the Northcote Private Hospital and she was admitted the following day.

The day passed by in a whirl for Eva. She had just enough time to return home to pack a small bag with nightdresses and toiletries before reporting to the hospital. She didn't see the cook, merely leaving a note for her employer stating the fact that she was being admitted to the hospital for surgery for a medical condition and that she would contact them regarding her resignation and collection of her belongings when she was released. She then rushed to the post office, withdrawing £20 from her savings account. The staff was very curious, never having known Eva to withdraw money before. But she was a Madden and Maddens didn't talk about personal issues and so they were left in the dark.

Finally, after rushing about for what seemed like days, Eva signed into the hospital at four o'clock and was shown to her ward. As she climbed into her bed she took a deep breath and took stock of her situation. A day ago she'd been worried about losing her job and now she was worried about losing her life. She decided that if the diagnosis was cancer that she would pay her debt to the New Zealand Government and spend her money to go home. The thought of dying here, so far from her family was more than she could bear thinking about.

The operation took place the next morning, and much to Eva's surprise and relief, with a successful outcome. A small tumour was removed. Apart from the news that the tumour wasn't cancerous, the only other good news was the discount of fifteen shillings she would receive for paying cash for her surgery and five day stay in the hospital. The hospital stay gave Eva time to rest and reflect. She decided that the cost of the stay was a fair price to pay for just the rest if nothing else. It wasn't like a fine hotel, but once the worry of the surgery was over, it was almost as good as a holiday. The doctor visited daily and talked to her in his gentle voice about her weight loss and heart condition. He recommended medicines, which she dutifully took. She actually looked forward to his daily visit. It was the most she had talked to anyone in ages and the fact that he cared about her welfare was an added bonus.

On the second day of her stay an enormous bunch of flowers had arrived. The single letter G marked the white card. Eva left them in the room when she was allowed to leave. No part of Gordon Hill would go with her. Once again the calm and logical side of Eva's character had seen her through this crisis. This enabled her to return confidently to Palmerston North to collect her belongings.

She had fought and won a far bigger battle, one that many women in Crewe had lost owing to ignorance and lack of money. Eva felt triumphant and in control of her future, convinced that her independence had led her safely through a crisis. From now on, her health improved considerably and her confidence grew. So now for a fresh start with a new employer.

Mrs Abraham of Palmerston North proved to be an excellent employer who treated Eva well, recognising both her intelligence and refinement. Their relationship became more one of friendship than one between employer and employee. Mrs Abraham appreciated Eva's quiet sense of humour as she told her what many of the immigrants thought about how life should be lived in New Zealand. She was also concerned for Eva's health, keeping a close eye on her and giving her time off in which to read and sew. In return, Eva diplomatically changed the household routine around, ensuring that everything was run efficiently and economically. She took on the task of household management of the bills, which were never a penny out, much to Mrs Abraham's pleasure.

With more time off, Eva discovered the joy of 'talking pictures'. Like her brother George, she was a great admirer of Charlie Chaplin[26]. This new development in cinematography delighted her. Eva spent many hours at the cinema enjoying and laughing out loud at the films. It was the greatest tonic she could have had.

She and Edith and George continued to contact each other. Finally, some letters arrived from her family that she dared keep. He told her about new films that had already been shown in England.

Mrs Abraham would talk constantly of the new land of Canada. Her brother had been over there buying up land in Vancouver, which was growing rapidly. She was convinced that this was the land of opportunity. Summers were hot and mountains nearby thick with snow, but the place was prospering. Work was available, property cheap and immigrants made welcome. She had sewn the first seeds

---

[26] An English comic actor, film-maker and composer who rose to fame in silent movies (1889-1977).

of interest in Eva's mind. Where large houses were being built, housemaids would be needed. Her job could carry her to many places if she chose to go. Eva could see all the unemployment in New Zealand. Swaggers[27] were crowding the roads. Unemployed men and women were constantly looking for work. It was time to go home and ease the homesickness that she constantly felt. She could do this by travelling through Canada.

A letter arrived from the Bruce family. They asked if they might visit Eva for a few days whilst they looked at property north of Wellington. She was delighted, meeting them at the station and happy to see their familiar faces. Tommy rushed to greet her. He was 10 years old now and as tall as Eva. Eva had planned a happy day together, taking Tommy to Wirth's Circus, which was on tour from Australia. Then on to the zoo to show him the Indian elephant named Lilikutta. This large leathery animal had been in Wellington for two years, and was trained by its Indian keeper to give rides.

Eva couldn't wait to see Tommy's face up there on the elephant. She knew that his life had been filled by hard work on the small farm. And all too soon he would have to leave school and work with his father on the land. It was good to see him laugh with excitement as Lilikutta stopped in front of him. Miraculously it gently lowered itself to the ground, folding its front knees, to allow Tommy to ride with the keeper. Arthur was of course jealous of his big brother, but at his age, he was far too afraid to ride the elephant with him. Slowly Eva, hand in hand with Arthur and accompanied by the Bruces followed, laughing and talking until once more a triumphant Tommy slid to the ground. Eva clapped with delight as he ran to her, too excited even to speak. In amazement he watched as the keeper spoke again to the elephant. Once more it rose on its great solid legs then proceeded with dignity along the road.

Eva treated the family to ice creams and cool drinks

---

[27] Unemployed homeless people seeking work during the Depression.

from the zoo kiosk. Sitting together Eva told him all about how the elephant came to settle in Africa and India. It was a story she had made up herself as a child to amuse Ellen, Joe and the Hollis children.

One day her father had brought home some wooden toys. They had been given to him by one of the housekeepers at Betley Hall, where he'd been doing some pruning work. First from the sack were two wooden elephants, which Joe had seized upon immediately, but the bigger prize was still to come. Next to emerge was a wooden Noah's Ark! It was painted red and was far too big for a child of Eva's age to carry about for long. So Eva sat the small group down on the front step of their house to show it off and graciously allowed all the other children from the street to look at it. She had felt proud that her father worked in grand places and could bring her such marvels. At that stage she had no understanding that her father was just a lackey to people whose exalted position was only achieved through an accident of birth. And to her, the occasional toys her father salvaged were still marvels, not the cast offs she might resent later in life.

Many afternoons were spent playing with the ark. Eva would tell the story of Noah, lining up their toys along the gutter, including the wooden elephants. She had many friends and she would weave such stories of the floating ark sailing to distant lands that parents had trouble calling their children inside as the sun went down. And now she was passing on the same stories to Tommy and Arthur.

"Of course Noah knew that the elephants wanted somewhere very big and very hot. They wouldn't like to stay in England with the foxes and badgers and hares at all. So on his family sailed until they found a place in Africa that Mr Elephant thought would be just perfect for him and his Missus to make their home and start a family." Arthur thought the story was brilliant and as they got up to begin the walk to the train station, he said he couldn't wait to tell all his friends at school about Mr and Mrs Elephant going to Africa."

Finally the Bruces boarded the train exhausted and as the train pulled out of the station, Tommy looked wistfully at Eva. She waved them goodbye. Tommy called from the train, "One day I'm coming back to Wellington, Eva. And then I'm going to take you out for the day!" And with a last kiss blown to the wind they were gone.

Eva was left alone again, her stomach and heart filled with the pangs of homesickness. There were decisions to be made. She knew now that she wouldn't stay in New Zealand after her five-year requirement. She may come back some day, but there were decisions to be made about her future. She knew with certainty there would be other happy days ahead for her, maybe in New Zealand, but maybe in Canada or even back in Crewe. Her day with the Bruces reminded her that she was without family here and that she did after all have something to go back to.

Time's Up

Eva knew that her five compulsory years in New Zealand were practically up, freeing her from any obligations to the Government of New Zealand. She was now able to become a New Zealand citizen and allowed to leave without first having to reimburse her fare to the government, longing to return home for family reasons.

Her time spent away from England had inevitably changed her. Longings for travel had been fed by stories of the great land across the sea. She felt that she could visit Canada, maybe work for a while and then cross by train to the east coast and sail home. The idea continued to grow, Eva confidently knowing that now she could pay her own fare to Vancouver. If things didn't work out, she could call a halt to this new adventure, returning to England whenever she wanted to.

In December of 1929, Eva found the very thing she was looking for: *Booking details for Canada*. She snipped the information from the *Auckland Weekly News*, to study it later when she was off duty. That night she read all the information carefully and finally decided to make a booking with the company.

The new year of 1930 made up Eva's mind. She was no longer a young girl with few means. She had considerable money in her bank account, a wealth of knowledge concerning her job, excellent references and a great deal of confidence. She knew that she could have quite easily had involvements with several of the husbands in the homes where she worked, but her pride and strict upbringing never allowed her to stray into that domain. Voicing her anger and fears of such a situation to Gordon Hill had given her strength. An employer or anyone else who had power and money would never control her. She had placed herself in an invulnerable position by hard work and thriftiness, and despite how much she had resented Martha's frugality when she was a child, she now thanked her mother for teaching her the rewards that came from saving.

It was in this frame of mind that she sat down on a warm summer's night in January to reply to her brother George's latest letter from Crewe.

January 1930, Palmerston North.

Dear George,
I trust that this letter will find you all well at home and that the winter is not treating you too harshly. I am sorry to hear about Mother's sickness. I believe that when spring comes and the weather is less harsh, her chest will clear. If not, I know you will seek 'informed opinion' as you so often put it! Tell Edith that I have no plans for marriage or even a liaison with anyone out here although I have had admirers. I have been far too busy working and saving to think about socialising. However, I have continued to preserve and build on to my very satisfactory wardrobe. Indeed, the wool and cotton garments that can be bought here are of extremely high quality. Unfortunately, the opportunity to dress fashionably does not arise very often for me.
I am delighted with the two photographs that you enclosed and tell Edith that she looks like a film star! I am very proud that I have such a handsome brother and my best friend looks very beautiful.
I am not lonely out here. In so many ways it is very like England in attitude and habits. I am of the opinion that the New Zealander regards himself as a British subject first and a New Zealander afterwards, so complete has been the connection with Britain. It is a very young country and I know it will need time to develop its own national spirit.
Now I must inform all of you of my plans for the future. Today I applied for a passport with which to leave New

Zealand. My 5 years are now up and I can travel without fear of re-imbursement to the government. I am now a New Zealand citizen with a passport, which will be good for use until the 1st March, 1935.

I intended to come straight home but have since changed my mind. I will travel via Canada, maybe work for a while in Vancouver and then cross Canada by train. Tell Mother I do not propose to stay long in Canada. It is merely another way of reaching home and perhaps paying for the journey. Just think George, by the time I reach home I will have seen so many countries!

I have already looked into bookings. I will most likely travel on the 'Niagara', which is a Canadian Australasian Steamship. I propose to make the journey from Auckland, leaving on the 8th April, arriving in Vancouver on the 25th April, a journey of only 17 days.

In answer to your question about the Hollises, I have searched and asked but can find no trace of Mrs Hollis's brother. Do tell her that I have not cut all my connections with New Zealand. It has a charm unlike any other place I have ever visited and I intend to come back here one day. I have left a bank account here containing my savings.

Regarding my dear sister Ellen. I am pleased that she has been able to return home for a while but do hope this does not place an intolerable burden on Mother who is not strong at the best of times.

The added shock of Joe's illness and the fact that he remains permanently committed in hospital must be so terribly distressing to Mother and Father. You tell me that they are not advised to visit. I am personally glad of the distance, which makes it even more difficult for them.

Sometimes I feel selfish being so far away. Yet I feel that Mother and Father are proud of me as a single woman being able to support herself and travel at the same time. This must be a rare thing indeed in Crewe. Do let me know if they need anything. I trust that the money I sent for Christmas has arrived safely.

Time's Up

Your investment in a house has been a wise move indeed even though it is not the farm you envisaged. Living nearer to her own family can give Edith the security she needs when you are working night shifts on the railway.
Continue to stay well George. I can imagine how hard you work. Give my best wishes to Edith. I am pleased that Father's retirement from the railways is allowing him more time with Mother. She will like that.
I enclose the address of the YWCA in Vancouver so that any letters can be collected from there upon my arrival. I love to have news from home and will write to you directly I enter Canada.

My best wishes, Eva.

PS. I say at the beginning of my letter that I am not lonely. This is true but I do on occasions grow homesick. I long for England, which has become a very special place.
Did you know that the strangest experiment[28] was carried out here only two years ago? I read about it in the newspaper. A number of nightingales were brought to New Zealand, caged but then set free. It was hoped that their beautiful song heard in Surrey from which they came, would be part of the bird song of New Zealand!
I heard no more of the birds for months but I suspect that they too grew homesick and made their way back to the woods of England. Only the other day it was reported in the newspaper that a man who originally lived in the South of England went out into his garden one evening for he recognised a bird song from his childhood in England. It was at a place named Mount Eden near to Auckland where it is thickly wooded.
Sure enough two nightingales, which had been introduced and liberated in Auckland, were heard singing for over half an hour! They commenced singing at dusk.

---

[28] Experiment in the 1920s to introduce nightingales into New Zealand from Surrey, England, because of their beautiful song. (See: www.nzetc.victoria.ac.nz)

I too feel like the nightingale and it is time that I returned home. I think part of me will remain here though for I don't think I can ever forget this beautiful country. It is so similar to England on the surface and yet so different from within!

Part 3 – Canada (1930-1933)

Canada Bound

With growing excitement Eva visited the booking office of the Canadian Australasian line to enquire about paying her fare. *The Niagara* sailed from Sydney to Vancouver, stopping off at Auckland, Suva, Honolulu and Victoria. Once the decision was made, it all happened very quickly. She gave her notice to Mrs Abraham and prepared to leave New Zealand, packing her treasures in her trunk and suitcases yet again.

George had written to her about the growing unemployment in Great Britain, clinging to his job on the railway and fearing redundancy. Although initially interested in settling in New Zealand, he had drawn his horns in, partly because of the economy, partly because of his responsibilities to his own family and partly because of Edith, who needed the security of her own family. Eva was sorry. She knew that George could have loved the life out here and done well for himself, but now his choices were limited.

As for her, she had untold freedom, daring to do what so few women had ever done, living independently and travelling beyond most women's dreams. Yes, there were sacrifices to be made, as her mother would have said, God's price, no babies or a little home in Crewe where a man would support her. But Eva had seen little in that life that attracted her and had known from a young age that she wanted something else. She was confident in her decision to stay away from most of what life in Crewe would have meant for her despite the sacrifices.

The next day the Bruces travelled into Auckland to see her and it was an emotional farewell.

"Och Eva! I'm sad to be seeing you going," said

The Price

Mrs Bruce, the regret clear in her voice. "I know we barely get to see you, but your letters are such a joy to all of us and without you here I feel like we're losing a piece of home here in New Zealand."

"But I'm not even from Scotland!" exclaimed Eva.

"Oh, but you know what I mean. You've been a part of this new life from the beginning. Tommy will be heartbroken, won't you lad?"

Tommy was trying to be brave and grown up. But the excitement at seeing Eva and showing her how grown up he was, was balanced with sulking about her leaving for good. "Now I'll never get to take you on an outing in Wellington."

"Well, you never know Thomas. I don't know that I'll stay in Crewe forever. I have a shiny New Zealand passport and I may just need to use it to come back to you!"

"He's just cross because he thinks he'll never get another Christmas present from you," piped up Arthur.

"Shut up Arthur!" Mary Bruce was not going to have her boys speaking like that. "You'll not be using language like that in polite company. Your father and I didn't raise you to be ruffians! Now settle down and enjoy this visit quietly."

Eva had the last word on the subject. "I promise you letters from everywhere I visit and Christmas presents every year till I return. As long as you promise to never ever, ever forget me."

Two days later the *Niagara* sailed into port from Sydney and Eva collected her sailing ticket from the dockside office, ready to leave. Looking down at the ticket, she realised that this was more than a piece of paper she held. It was a passport to adventure, to a new phase in her life, and her spirit lifted. Talk was rampant among the waiting passengers. The inward bound ship the *Aorangi* was being held in quarantine in Auckland Harbour, suspected of carrying smallpox. Most people waiting to board the *Niagara* were worried about a delay because of health checks. Like everyone else, Eva was relieved when the word was given for boarding, watching as the first class passengers were allowed up the gangplank first.

Unlike the *Suffolk*, the *Niagara* ran on oil instead of coal and every effort had been made to make all accommodation comfortable from first class to third class. Eva felt that the £62 she'd paid for the journey would be well worth it, despite it having taken her months to earn it.

As she gave her details for the Canadian Shipping lists, she thought about her family situation, taking care to reveal nothing that might come back to haunt her at a later date. Eva felt dishonest about lying on two answers. She had given the wrong address so that no contact could be made with her parents. She also declared that there was no mentally defective person in her family. But this was how it had to be from now on in order to survive in any country without a finger being pointed at her. She knew she would never find work and may even be denied entry to a country if she was honest about her brother and sister's mental illness.

Eva was shown to the cabin she shared with another young single woman. She'd hoped to get a cabin to herself, but as a third class passenger, knew that it was unlikely. Her bunkmate introduced herself as Catherine Main. She was travelling back to Scotland through the United States. Tears were shed, farewells made and as Auckland slipped away into the distance, the ship headed for the Pacific. It was the 8th April and despite nobody to farewell Eva, she cried a little too. She knew that for her own sanity she must continue to travel on and on, for this would be her way of coping. At the back of her mind she had already made the decision to find work in the growing city of Vancouver instead of starting the journey home immediately. This would come later and when she felt ready. She would then make the journey across the great colony of Canada to sail for Liverpool and home. If nothing else, she would see it for Mrs Wilmot.

Turning away from the railing she began to look around her, as she stood by herself on the deck. Involuntarily she was looking for people travelling alone like herself, but

The Price

also missing the exuberant welcome she had received from Tommy Bruce when she'd boarded the *Suffolk* five years before. People were milling around, introducing themselves to each other, smiling in anticipation of the journey that lay ahead. Eva noted that she was as well dressed as any of them and couldn't hold in her happiness. No longer in her domestic role and dressed in dowdy uniforms, she felt as free as a bird. Turning again, she leaned over the side of the rail and looked down into the surging sea sliding past the ship and smiled broadly. Finally all the nerves were gone and the excitement took over.

Looking back up at the still chattering passengers, she saw the man a little way off, leaning against the rail and looking thoughtfully about him, a well dressed man wearing a trilby hat, warm inside a thick coat with his collar turned up, partially hiding his face. But it was his notebook that had first caught her attention. He struggled against the wind, endeavouring to write something down. She stared again, noting his forehead creasing in exasperation as he attempted to turn a page for further scribbling. Suddenly, the entire book was lifted from his grasp by a gust of wind and the pages flew into the air, briefly coming to rest far below on the crest of a wave until they finally sank. Involuntarily, Eva burst out laughing at the escape, despite a great deal of arm waving and a panicked look from its owner. He turned to see who was the cause of so much laughter. Eva quickly looked away, silently and resolutely staring into the waves. But the cheeky smile couldn't be hidden.

"Well Miss, I am sure glad that the loss of my thoughts gave at least one human being some joy." And with a broad smile he moved over to her side, towering above her.

She noted his American (or was it Canadian?) accent, and the warmth and sincerity of his voice as he extended his hand in a warm strong handshake to introduce himself. He stooped slightly to look at Eva's face beneath her warm woollen blue hat pulled over her curls.

"The writing which now lies fathoms below

belongs to Morris Miller, born in London, raised in the USA and returning to work in Vancouver. Er ... my family lives near Napier," he added as way of an explanation. Then he extended his hand to shake hers.

Eva was at a loss for words. Her entire lifestyle had moulded her into an observer. She was completely unused to being the centre of anyone's attention. But her reservations were swept away that day along with all her years of telling herself that she would be a fool to become involved with others. For the first time she was not taking any risks. She didn't have to think about her status and the restrictions placed on her through her work. She felt a great weight lift from her. A slow, shy smile replaced words. She placed a tiny-gloved hand into his, and looking up directly into his eyes, she spoke for the first time.

"I wasn't laughing at you, but you were so intense, scribbling away for the ocean bed," she smiled gently. "I hope it wasn't too important, the notes I mean."

"Ah, it was meant to be," he shrugged, moving thoughtfully to her side, protecting her from the increasing wind. "And maybe they're better off down there. Otherwise I would never have met you, Miss?"

"Evelyn Madden. Travelling from Auckland where I have spent the last five years. On my way home to England, but stopping off in Vancouver, probably for work. Then I'll take the rail route across Canada."

"Miss Madden, am I hearing correctly? A young woman on her own, coming such great distances? Finally, crossing the world! That's what you'll have almost done by the time you reach home!" He laughed again. The little crease in his forehead deepened.

"Please call me Eva. That's the name my friends and family call me by. But tell me please, for I am intrigued. What was written on that small notepad that is now food for the fishes of the Pacific Ocean?" Serious now, she stared thoughtfully at him. Her wide brown eyes weighed him up, her hand lifting to secure her hat.

The Price

"A poem, simple and brief. Well, hardly a poem, but the beginning of one, about the two new lands both carving out separate identities." He laughed apologetically. "I must explain. I'm a reporter for a newspaper in Vancouver. Whenever I get the chance, I like to dabble in prose and poetry. Although it brings very little to the dinner table!" he laughed. "These are fascinating times. They call for observation. Unfortunately, articles for newspapers are given over to factual accounts. So I allow myself the luxury of free writing whenever I am given a chance."

Eva listened carefully and silently. All of her life she seemed to have been close to libraries of books but had never been given the opportunity to become acquainted with the writers. For a brief moment her thoughts dwelled on the great library at Brereton Hall and the little girl pulling down *A Tale of Two Cities*.[29] She knew of this other world but it was beyond her grasp. She felt a little nervous. She liked the man who stood in front of her waiting for her response to the information he had given of himself. Involuntarily her gloved hands came together in a small nervous action, noted by her companion. Then her hat went bowling across the deck, relieving the tension. The chase that resulted in its capture left both panting and laughing.

"On that note, I think it may just be time for us to go below, prepare for dinner and get out of this wind. And it looks as though rain's coming too."

Eva was glad to follow his lead and as they made their way to their cabins they were both quietly amazed to find that they had been placed next to each other, Eva in number 12 and Morris Miller in number 13. This started them laughing again, but even more nervously this time.

Eva spoke first. "Next door neighbours? Looks like it. Can you believe it? How's your cabin-mate?"

"I don't have one actually. I splashed out on a second-class ticket this time. All that means is that I pay a little more for the privilege of having a cabin to myself.

---

[29] Book by Charles Dickens (1859)

But that's probably a good thing. I'm a dreadful snorer I'm afraid!"

They both laughed and then slightly embarrassed by this unexpected proximity to each other, Eva quickly entered her cabin. Morris paused, reassuring himself that they would meet over dinner.

Once inside her room, Eva leant against the door, feeling totally exhausted. What on earth was she doing? Where was she going? Had she just engaged in flirting? A woman of her age? What was she going to do now? She could hardly hide for seventeen days. And why was her heart pounding? Why was she so drawn to this stranger? Her newly found confidence was quickly disappearing. Opening her case she began to unpack her clothes. Then she saw them, the two tiny battered tin soldiers that Joseph had given to her all those years ago when she was leaving for service at Brereton Hall. During her many moves, her other small keepsakes had been mislaid but for some strange reason she had managed to hang on to Joe's present. Tears blinded her and she threw herself onto her small bed. She screwed up the corner of her pillow in her fist in anger as she thought about her brother, trapped inside his mad world, forever escaping through broken windows and smashing glass. She felt trapped too, by the secret she kept. Finally she had cried out all the tears and sat up, taking the two small figures in her hand.

Well Joe, I will be happy. I will travel on despite your prison. Despite no explanation for what's happened to you and Ellen. I will make the journey. Somewhere, somehow you'll be happy for me. If not in this world, then the next. She bit her lip anxiously. She didn't really believe in the afterlife. And she knew Joe didn't either. Maybe this was a journey she had to make on behalf of her family. Sitting on the edge of her bed, holding the toy soldiers in her hands, she drifted into her own thoughts. We go alone Joe, wherever we are, even if we are in the so-called reality of the normal world. But what is reality Joe? George tells

The Price

me that you hear voices, that you have no link to reality anymore. But what is it? I see reality in things rather than people. The stars I saw over the Indian Ocean were my reality, the great grey albatross winging his way over the waves, the vast sweeping skies of New Zealand. All of these things are more of a reality than the silly conversation and social expectations between people.

Startled by her own thoughts, Eva slowly prepared for dinner. She would sit by the side of a man who made sense, who could think and talk about other things other than day to day living. She glanced into the mirror before she made her way to the dining room. Looking back at her was a young woman wearing a sequinned dress, overlaid with a very delicate pink wrap. Her hair was brushed back, held in place by a silver hairpin. Her pale complexion, brown eyes and small straight nose reminded her of so many of her family, a small piece from one, a feature from another. Her hands and feet were small and slender. Never would anyone guess that she had worked and at times drudged as a domestic for all those years. She frowned. Could she honestly tell her charming companion that that was what she did for a living? Finally, she sighed and said, Ah, Eva. What are you doing? Time to get going. And she tore herself away from the comfort of the mirror. Carefully shutting the cabin door behind her, she headed nervously up to the dining room.

The room was crowded with passengers, seated in groups of up to ten at well-laid tables. Eva smiled. She could see several mistakes in the overall setting of the places. Even here she could not quite get past the more than twenty years she had spent as a servant. Suddenly she felt overwhelmed and she started to back out, to head back to her cabin. The room reverberated with loud noise and laughter. This was not her world to participate in! What was she thinking? The panic began to rise and she turned to go. But then she saw him. He was standing by a table, waving his arm in her direction and pointing at a seat. Several of the ladies glanced first in his direction, seeing a handsome man dressed in a distinguished dinner suit. Then their eyes followed the direction of the wave, alighting on Eva, a slight but enviable woman standing quietly by the door. Eva swallowed hard, gulping back her nerves and walked towards him and smiled. But the slow shy smile broadened to a laugh as he bowed in front of her. Drawing out a chair he said laughingly, "Please be seated Madam."

Eva placed her small jewelled bag on the table as she had seen ladies do so many times. She had been in grander dining rooms than most of these people would ever know. Playing the part he had created for her, she sat down on the edge of her chair, her back rod straight. Beneath the table her hands twisted nervously together but she appeared completely composed and elegant to everyone around her. That was soon to change as Morris nudged her foot under the table, looking directly at a large man who insisted on trying to fill Eva's glass with wine despite her firm protests.

"My partner does not take alcohol," Morris said quite loudly.

From then on the room seemed to fall away as they began to talk, exchanging observations freely, discussing wide-ranging subjects from politics to the latest fashions, from earthquakes to the deepening recession across the world. Their company at the table was included in the conversation by Morris. He was skilled in encouraging others to voice their opinions. As the meal drew to a close there was a companionable conversation flowing between all six of them.

Eva was glad she'd worked in homes with good libraries she'd been able to use and newspapers that she'd had access to, nevertheless, she wasn't highly educated. But she needn't have worried, because whenever he felt that Eva might not be fully aware of the subject, Morris drew her thoughts and the conversation, in another direction. He studied her small sensitive face, the curving lips that tightened when she felt that she was being drawn into a

The Price

conversational trap, her eyes blazing when the fate of the American Indian was discussed. He loved the little twitch of her nose when she laughed and above all, her hands, which expressed dismay if the stories turned to injustice.

"What it seems to me is that the people who settled countries like America, New Zealand, even Australia, want the same sort of class system they escaped from in England. In England the working classes toil in poverty and filth until their short lives are over, so that the upper class, who barely give any more consideration to the lives of the working class than they would to a rodent, can exist secure in the knowledge that they live the 'right' way. They seem to think it has nothing to do with an accident of birth that they were born to grand houses and a life of luxury, while another was born the son of a coal miner with blacklung. Well, it seems to me the same with the way the Indians and Maoris are treated. If I could only count the number of times I have heard people say, 'They don't want to live like us, so they only have themselves to blame for their position in the world.' When the reality is, there is no equality because people protect their own position of superiority and don't allow others to climb up."

Eva suddenly realised the others at the table were looking at her as if she had started speaking a foreign language. Or as if she had suddenly jumped up from the table and danced a one-legged jig. And she felt a blush creep up her neck and into her cheeks. All those years of listening to the pompous conversations of the wealthy had formed some very definite opinions. She just hadn't thought she'd express them in such a public way. But Morris saved the day, by steering the conversation into lighter waters. The awkward silence that followed Eva's outburst was soon followed by jolly laughter again.

He couldn't help looking at her. Even when he was appearing to pay full attention to the person he was talking with, he remained aware of Eva from the corner of his eye. What a puzzle this woman is, he thought to himself. He did not embarrass her about occupation or family. He had already looked at the shipping lists, discovering that she was single, aged thirty-three and a domestic.

When he swept her up onto the dance floor to show her off, he treated her respectfully and gently. Eva blessed the times at Brereton Hall when she and the Welsh girl Mary had practised their dancing steps to the music in the kitchen during the great balls which had been held. How proud George would have been to see her now. How he would have approved of Morris Miller. His politics, his compassion, his humour and his writing would have gained great respect in her brother's eyes.

During that first evening, Eva learnt many things about Morris Miller. He had travelled to the Yukon, living in the mining towns. He told her about the great white moon which shone over their camps and the howling of the wolves in the forests. And the bears that sometimes came right into town to scavenge for an easy meal. He explained the rapid growth of Vancouver from a small town to a thriving city due to timber, prospecting, mining and many other associated industries. The mansions of Shaughnessy were built in the residential centre of Vancouver's old money and without telling Eva that he already knew she was a domestic worker, he imagined that Eva might look for work there.

His ancestry pulled him back to London on several occasions. He loved the theatre, plays and operas, so he often sought his birthright in a country supposedly the centre of more sophisticated entertainment where he could freely attend the productions he loved. But his real dream was the great, unexplored land of Canada and more recently New Zealand. He and Eva discussed the 'Old World' heredity that drew them back to England. The deep roots of both culture and family were strong in both of them.

Morris slowly began to discover Eva by working around the closed doors that held the secrets from her childhood and young womanhood. He sensed the aloofness in her. Her loyalty to her family, and the hesitation and avoidance in discussing anything personal when she fleetingly described her childhood in Crewe was tangible. She laughed with delight when she discovered that he had actually visited Crewe, or at least the railway station where he had spent two miserable hours in the dead of winter whilst waiting for his train to London. She referred to a brother who worked on the railway as a fireman, in the hope that he would one day become a train driver. But that was about all he discovered.

The pride and passion in her voice revealed much to Morris Miller, whose job after all was to extract facts from individuals. He was a good reporter, but more than that he had great respect and compassion for his fellow man. He was able to extract the finest stories from people through tolerance and forbearance, not the bullying tactics and deception that reporters of his generation were renowned for. He instinctively knew that the young woman had travelled a difficult and painful road. It was not one she was about to share easily with any human being.

Certainly Eva Madden was a well-travelled woman. But she was remote. She never once really allowed him near to her quiet self-taught opinions. Yet her eyes shone, her laughter filled his ears and her arm was tucked into his as they returned from the dance floor. She was simply the most enchanting woman he had ever known. Later that evening they went up onto the deck to look at the black smooth ocean that bore their ship to a new land. Eva felt safe with Morris, who wrapped her in his warm coat. Then laughingly he lifted her high onto the edge of one of the lifeboats so that she could look down on him.

"I will do as you command," he joked, staring up into her eyes, seeing the disbelief and amusement in her as she wavered on the edge of the boat. "Anything, anything for so fine a princess."

"Poetry! If I am Princess of the Sea, then I shall have a poem that speaks of the ocean!" she shouted, laughing.

On command, Morris began to recite verses from

The Tale of the Ancient Mariner[30], loudly and dramatically. Other passengers wandering by paused in amazement to stare at the woman wrapped in a big coat standing high above her companion.

> *"At length did cross an Albatross,*
> *Through the fog it came;*
> *As if it had been a Christian soul,*
> *We hailed it in God's name."*

Eva was spellbound. She stared down at this strange and fascinating man who dared to lift her high above the other passengers only to quote a sea story to her. She was also intrigued about the great bird for the moment she had held five years ago on her voyage to New Zealand was still clear in her memory.

> *"God save thee, ancient Mariner!*
> *From the fiends, that plague thee thus! –*
> *Why look'st thou so?' - With my cross-bow*
> *I shot the ALBATROSS."*

Eva by now had sat down on the edge of the boat, listening carefully to his words. She felt a sense of doom. Others gathered around too to enjoy the recitation spoken in a rich Canadian accent. Eva was unaware of anyone else around her. She could only stare at her companion as he recited verse after verse of Coleridge's poem.

> *"And I had done a hellish thing,*
> *And it would work 'em woe:*
> *For all averred, I had killed the bird*
> *That made the breeze to blow!"*

Eva shivered in the night air as she imagined the terror on

---

[30] Coleridge, S. T. (1798) The Rime of the Ancient Mariner. (From the published text of 1834)

the sailing ship. "Go on, go on!" she cried out involuntarily. "What happens next?"

Morris smiled before continuing. He had not been mistaken in this woman. Beneath the prim and proper disguise lay another person, passionate, caring, hating injustice of any kind. Fleetingly he saw her as a tiny caged bird, trapped within her social class.

> *"Day after day, day after day,*
> *We stuck, not breath nor motion;*
> *As idle as a painted ship*
> *Upon a painted ocean."*

Suddenly Morris sensed that Eva was far too anxious. He stopped his chanting, rushing forward to lift her small form easily from the boat. Swinging her to the deck, he enfolded her in his coat in an embrace. For a moment she was taken aback as she leant against his chest. Then gently he lifted her face to his, placing his hand at the back of her neck to steady her, kissing her very gently on the lips. It was only when he slowly released her that Eva realised that she had been standing on tiptoe. Now she stepped back, looking anxiously at him. Never before had she felt this way. Her heart pounded. She felt a deep strange unidentified longing for him. He was no longer smiling but looked serious and concerned.

"Eva, it's only a poem. A wonderful sea poem to be granted, but still only a poem. Don't take it too seriously,"

But darker thoughts were shadowing Eva's features. She remembered well what the deckhand had told her years ago about albatrosses and sailors. "What happened to the ancient mariner? Did he die?"

"No, just the opposite. He had to wander the earth for years and years as a penance, unable to die as all his shipmates had done, for the killing of the albatross brought them bad luck. Their ship was becalmed and they died of thirst. The ancient seaman was made to wander for eternity across the world. He could never die. He was forced to teach by his own example, love and reverence to all things that God made and loved." And to himself, he thought, that is right, is it not Eva? All human life must be treasured and cared for. Everyone and everything is precious. That's what you believe, isn't it?"

As if she could read his mind, Eva turned away, her eyes full of tears. But she hadn't read his thoughts. It was the description of the events of the poem that spoke to her. It spoke her language. She thought of her brother suffering through the isolation and lack of love in his mental prison. Then her sister and finally her remote and troubled mother came into her thoughts although she fought her dark memories.

"Am I never going to be free of this!" she voiced angrily, feeling her temper rising to the surface. She stared out over the black sea, as dark as her mood. She was far away. The transformation from the woman who had only moments before been the laughing princess of the sea was startling.

Morris gently touched her shoulder and without speaking, they made their way onto the upper deck. They sat for a very long time without speaking, letting the wind caress them. The beauty of the stars calmed Eva's racing mind. Finally Morris spoke gently and carefully to the still silent woman who sat next to him, but as far away as if she had been in New Zealand. But she was still sitting with him. She had let him lead her up here. She hadn't retreated to her cabin. She must still want to be near to him.

"Eva, I met you tonight through your laughter and your beauty. I want you to know that I would never ever harm you in any way. I know that you're deeply troubled. I think you may even be sad. I'm not asking you to talk about it. But I want you to realise that I care for you deeply even though I've only known you for a few hours." He paused before going on. "You're not like any other woman or indeed any other person that I've ever known. I would do anything,

anything to get the chance to know you better. I only hope that I haven't done anything to upset you, because if I have, then I'm more truly sorry than you can ever imagine." She still didn't respond, so he went on. "Even now after so short a time I couldn't bear to lose your friendship. How on earth you have slipped through thirty-three years of your life without someone falling in love with you I have no idea. How you have remained unmarried I can't even conceive, but I thank God for it."

Slowly Eva turned. Her tear stained face showed in the moonlight, her mouth downcast but determined. Finally, I've reached her, he thought. But this assumption was shattered as she started to speak.

"Morris," she said carefully and with precision, using his name for the first time, "how do you know that I'm thirty-three?"

He burst out laughing at her question. Any other woman would have responded quite differently. And suddenly he realised how strong was her sense of self-preservation. He stood up and sheepishly began, "I have something to confess. After we met earlier today, I was completely intrigued. And well, being a reporter, I just couldn't help myself. I looked on the passenger list. I know, I know. I should be ashamed of myself, but I'm confessing now! Anyway, I know a fair bit about you now. Well, at least the information that you gave. Of course it could all be lies," and he laughed as she frowned at him. "For instance, I know that you are a domestic. You lived in New Zealand for five years. You are going to the YWCA when you arrive in Vancouver. Also, that you are not penniless. Maybe I am seeking my fortune from a wealthy lady!"

Eva started to laugh. The tension was broken. The albatross had flown away. After all, she had rescued him and pushed him over the side of the ship all those years ago. She didn't have a penance to serve! Impulsively she jumped up and ran to him, putting her arms around him as he stood there waiting for her.

"I've never been with a man," she explained simply. "I don't even really know how to behave with one. All I know is that you make me happy and I want to laugh when I'm with you." And then she kissed him gently. "Let's not get so serious again," she said half as a question.

They sat down together again and stared out at the blackness of the ocean, neither speaking. Finally, Morris spoke very quietly to the woman at his side. "Eva, we will be friends. I think we have a lot in common. And we won't rush things. We have a wonderful voyage ahead of us, over two weeks sailing across the South Pacific. I want you to enjoy this journey. I think you deserve to. If your life has been what I suspect it has, then you've never had time to be yourself and have fun. In three days we'll reach Suva, which I know you'll love. We can go ashore for the few hours that we are in the port. You can enjoy a tropical island paradise and let the gentle nature of the people there capture your imagination."

She still didn't speak so he went on. "I don't want to make you feel like you have to be with me. Or that being with me is another chore, an imposition. I've spent time with many women in my job and through my travels. On the other hand, I suspect you haven't known many, if any men apart from through the people you've worked for. The last thing I want is to place a strain upon you. Let's face it, you may even find me tiresome and lock yourself in your cabin!"

Eva responded to this long speech by laughing. Very shyly she took his hand. "Thank you, Morris. It would be almost too easy for me to quickly become involved with you in this romantic setting, but it would not suit me. It's just not in my nature. I would be plagued by doubts and guilt. My family is thousands of miles away but in so many ways they are right here with me now. Their lives have helped to give me the strength and will to venture out into the world."

He met her eyes as she continued to gather her thoughts. "But just as how I always take my family with me, I will also always return to them to tell them the stories of places they'll never see and the things I've experienced there." She paused then. "It's a very difficult thing to be a single woman, without anyone to depend on, you know. But I decided that this was the path for me a long time ago. It might seem strange to the rest of the world, a woman choosing not to marry and have children. But I have my reasons, very personal reasons. Reasons that mustn't be asked about."

She leant against him, slid her arms beneath his jacket. "Morris, don't feel like you're pushing me. You haven't asked me for anything. But something's happened to us tonight. I've spent my whole life watching people, observing their lives from the edges. I'm a very good judge of people and I feel safe with you. You tell the truth." Looking up she could make his face out in the darkness. He was staring beyond her. He seemed not to be listening.

Eva's heart pounded. She wanted to belong with this man. But he would never push her. She knew what he wanted, but also sensed that the intimacy must come from her. His heart was beating quickly but he still didn't move or make a sound.

"Morris, I think we should say goodnight."

"Of course." Then, clearing his throat, "I'll walk you to your cabin."

They walked in silence to their cabins and once there, Morris took her hand and kissed the palm. "Thank you for this evening Eva." She squeezed his hand and said, almost in a whisper, "And thank you for your patience."

Eva then fumbled with her key, finally getting through the door and closing it behind her. Thank God the cabin was empty! Her heart was beating so hard and fast that she was sure anyone would be able to see it through her dress. Her knees felt weak. She knew that Morris had wanted to take her to his bed, but it was too hard for her. She'd sworn all her life that she wouldn't give in to a man, but this was the first time she'd really wanted to. She needed time to think. What if she'd lost him? Then he wasn't worth her trust. But what if he was as genuine as she thought he was? What possibilities might there be if he was? Was he married? She had to know.

She tried to dress for bed, but she couldn't concentrate enough even for that. The thought of him just on the other side of the wall almost drove her mad. Could a woman as level headed as Eva Madden fall in love in just one day? She couldn't believe it.

After barely any sleep, Eva arose and dressed for breakfast. What was she going to say to Morris? What if he wasn't there and was avoiding her? Her mind was racing. Still, she had to face the world again whatever the consequences. There were two weeks left of the voyage and she could hardly spend them in her cabin worrying about events of the first day! No, she would walk proudly into the dining room and take her seat with her head held high. Only when she reached the dining room, any confidence was a façade. She desperately sought him out, not knowing whether she wanted to see him or not. Her knees felt wobbly and she wasn't sure she'd be able to eat when she did get to her table. And then there he was, standing, smiling, gesturing for her to come and sit with him. And her world began turning again.

"Eva! Good morning," he said, his voice full of cheer. "I trust you slept well?"

"Not really. But I'm sure it was something I brought on myself."

"I wouldn't say that at all. I suspect it has something to do with the pressure of your new circumstances. But I'm sure there will be fun and entertainment enough today to make you laugh again."

Eva noted the twinkle in his eye and knew that things would be as they had been yesterday. The fact that he was going so far to protect her dignity only made him seem even dearer. By now the other diners at the table were completely confused. It seemed to be a conversation about nothing, as though it was between strangers. And yet they had all seen these two the night before and they were anything but strangers.

Together they ate in comfortable silence, stealing looks at each other and small secret smiles. Later over a cup of tea, they made plans for the rest of the day. It was wonderful to have Morris with her. Eva never imagined that she could talk so much. She described her childhood. She shared exciting moments of Brereton Hall. She told him about George, Edith, Tom and Augusta. Briefly she referred to her mother and father. But no mention was made of Ellen and Joe. She was not prepared to disclose that information. It would take a lot more than twenty-four hours and an infatuation to pry that secret loose.

Nevertheless, having someone to share each new experience with was exciting. Eva enjoyed the meal times when she could dress in her finest clothes, even being persuaded by Morris to enter a dancing competition. Together they won second prize for the old time waltz. Eva was able to wear a lovely dress she had bought in Wellington, one of the few treats she had allowed herself there as she focused on saving as much money as she could. At the time, she thought she might never have the occasion to wear it, but couldn't resist it anyway. It was a dainty frock of pale pink satin, with a skirt made of white tulle in rows of crisp ruffles falling to the floor, slightly revealing the pale pink slippers matching her outfit. She'd never worn anything so extravagant and she was pleased that she could wear it just for Morris.

"I don't believe it!" she gasped when their names were read out. But Morris confidently led her out in front of the clapping guests where she was presented with a box of sweets and him a tin of cigarettes. They laughed about this later on because Morris didn't smoke.

How much life had changed for Eva Madden.

Fiji Heat

On April 11th the ship approached Suva, the capital of the island nation of Fiji. Morris and Eva had spent almost every waking moment together since their breakfast discussion on the second morning aboard. And yet they hadn't exhausted the things they had to talk to each other about. They stood together now at the railing, as the ship sailed into port.

Many of the passengers crowded the decks. The air was filled with their excited chatter. They were enchanted by what they saw and leaned over the safety rails exclaiming at the hundreds of brightly coloured jellyfish clearly visible in the tropical waters. Then the focus shifted to several sharks that were spotted before a pod of playful dolphins seemed to welcome them to Fiji.

The *Niagara* sailed into the inner harbour, slipping smoothly through the channel in a reef that lay barely concealed just below the water line. The main source of interest was now the sight of the colonial town of Suva. Forty passengers were to disembark here and they were the most excited, crowding the area where the gangplank was to be attached. But their journey was of no concern to Eva and Morris, who cared only that the ship would not leave until 10pm, allowing the ongoing passengers time for a short journey into the town.

Eva stared down at the quay, fascinated by the early morning activity. Morris pointed out things of interest to her, naming the great crates of goods to be taken on board. Copra, trochus shell, sandalwood, mustard oil, pearl shell, maize and many tropical fruits were all stacked on the wharf. Native women in bright printed cotton dresses were smiling as they offered the contents of their plaited baskets for sale on the dockside.

They were soon down amongst this activity and noise. Morris guided Eva to a motor taxi, which was the only means of transport on the island other than walking and where he had planned was too far to walk. But they were here to sightsee and he wanted Eva to see as much of Suva as a single day would allow and so he instructed the driver to make the journey in as winding and circuitous a route as possible. Driving through the narrow streets, they had a good view of the buildings and people, very few of them white. Eva was far more interested in the many races rather than stores or buildings. Every now and again she turned to Morris for information, curious and childlike in her wonder.

Fijian men, wearing long white skirts, bushy haired and bare legged, moved in small groups. Indians of various castes jostled as they made their way to work at the numerous market stalls. Chinese were busy in the many bake houses and Morris pointed out the lighter skinned straight haired natives. He explained to Eva that they were pure Polynesian in race. The fuzzy haired Melanesian Fijians dominated the streets. They passed the fish market where hundreds of locals were bartering and buying. Eva laughed because there seemed to be far more people than fish. Tantalising Indian shops spilled out onto the streets, offering ornate necklaces, jingling bangles, anklets and nose rings. She longed to get out and walk amongst it all but time was short. Morris wanted her to see the Botanical Gardens he had described on the ship.

The motor taxi moved away from the market streets and passed by jungle and thick foliage through which she could get occasional glimpses of red roofs of bungalow homes. Finally they reached the Gardens. Leaving the taxi, they walked along a weeping fig avenue. Suddenly it seemed very quiet. After all the excitement leading up to the adventure and then the business of Suva, Eva felt relieved and grateful for the beauty and peace in this lovely place. Morris had been absolutely right to bring her here.

Suddenly she noticed that the smooth grass of the botanical gardens was honeycombed with rabbit burrows. "Look at all the rabbit burrows! It's just like walking through the Cheshire countryside."

Morris roared with laughter. "You would never guess what it is that lives down these burrows." Eva knelt down, about to put her hand inside one of the dark holes, but Morris quickly pulled her back. "You'll get bitten!" he warned. "Down those 'rabbit burrows' as you call them, are land crabs. They come out in the cool of night and eat the fruit that falls from the trees. So do the robber crabs. But they actually climb the coconut trees here for their dinner." Eva stared at him in amazement but she could see that he wasn't joking.

Walking ahead of her, he picked a hibiscus bloom from one of the many bushes where they covered the greenery with yellow, pink and salmon colours. Eva thought she had never seen anything so beautiful. "The hibiscus flower only lasts for twelve hours, even if you put it in water," he commented as he handed the blossom to her. The few hours in the gardens gave Eva such a sense of peace and happiness that she felt almost sad when they had to leave. Travelling back to the ship, they saw women carrying enormous bowls of hibiscus flowers with which to decorate shrines and tables.

"Isn't it amazing Morris, I started off thinking of myself as being British, then English, then a New Zealander. But here on this beautiful island I'm just a person. None of that seems to matter."

"These islands do tend to have that effect on you. I felt like that on my first visit here. There's a simplicity and beauty here that makes you think that hard work and drudgery couldn't possibly exist here, and yet the people are thriving. If we had time, which we don't, I would take you to my other favourite place, which is the cemetery!" She started to laugh, so he added, "You may smile Eva, but it's a really beautiful garden, with the greenest grass, magnificent trees and really bright foliage and flowers. The Indians call it the 'garden of the unforgotten'."

Before boarding, Morris and Eva drank tea at one of the small stalls where Morris bought *The South Pacific Weekly*. The newspaper not only gave him news of local goings on, but also printed cabled articles from across the world. Eva liked to watch him as he sat and read the newspaper, immersing himself in his world for a short while. It was nice to see him focussed and interested in something other than her because it gave her another window into whom he was. She smiled at the occasional 'hmmm' as he read one article after another.

Eventually, aware that he was being watched, he lowered the paper, peering over the top. "Oh, Eva, I'm sorry. It's rude of me. See? I'm putting it away now."

"I was rather enjoying the peace actually. I told you once before that I've been a watcher and observer all my life. I'm quite happy to sit here and watch my man and the world passing by. Soak up the scenery. So by all means, keep reading." And with that she leaned across the table and pulled the newspaper up over his face again. He pulled it down briefly again only long enough to smile and wink at her and then went back to reading while Eva took in all the sights and smells that surrounded them.

Far too soon, they were back on board along with the twenty-four new passengers. As darkness fell abruptly at seven o'clock, the ship started up her engines ready to leave the island. Eva placed her already fading hibiscus bloom in a cup of water in her cabin, hoping that it would not die. Certainly her memories of the island would stay with her forever. There was an element of make believe in the entire experience, half leading her to believe that the whole thing was unreal. But it hadn't been a dream or some elaborate fantasy. Just as she had fallen in love with a man in a day, now she had fallen in love with a place in a matter of hours. What was becoming of her? Where was the Eva of 'work before pleasure', of 'duty before freedom'? She was unrecognisable even to herself! And now she was heading for the South Seas and the threshold of that world, which had up until now simply been a name in her atlas, Hawaii!

In all her life Eva had never felt happier than at this moment. Somewhere on board, reading his newspaper was a man who loved her as she loved him. He enjoyed her company, sharing his intelligent and shrewd comments with her, sharing his knowledge and respecting her wishes. He shared his passion with her. Changing quickly, Eva prepared for dinner, carefully pinning the pale pink hibiscus onto her chiffon dress, and made her way to the dining room where she knew that Morris would be waiting for her. Together they exchanged views on the happy day, anticipating their next landing on yet another tropical island. Eva remarked on the amazement her brothers and sisters would feel when they knew about her travels. In return, Morris described his childhood with brothers and a sister.

"I have known a New Zealand highlander, a friend of my sister, who had spoken Gaelic[31] as a little child. Then he forgot all about his childhood language for fifty years. As he grew older, he reverted to his first language and had to be reminded to speak in English! It is a curious fact Eva, that our very earliest impressions are our deepest ones even though they may become covered up by the events of day-to-day living. But then they have a way of coming to the surface when we least expect it. Very strongly, as though it was yesterday. It is as if the mind wishes to reach back and keep the things that really mattered to us."

Eva thought of her own family and her ties to the dirty streets of Crewe that she both loved and loathed and could see his point. But before she could respond she was interrupted by several of the passengers who approached them. They had come aboard at Suva, missionaries returning to Canada where they were going to buy fresh medical supplies for the islands. Morris had sought them out earlier. In his usual charming manner he soon had them talking

---

[31] Celtic language, native to Scotland.

about their experiences among the natives on some of the very isolated islands.

Eva sat back to listen to tales of the South Seas, marvelling at the missionaries' bravery. But at the same time suspicious of their deep religious convictions. One young woman named Jean Douglas was no older than Evelyn. She had been born in England. A calling to serve abroad had eventually taken her to such far away places. She talked fondly of the natives, the remote villages on islands where no white people had ever set foot and the work she had achieved with small groups of natives who she believed regularly practised cannibalism. In a remote part of the island was the customary leper colony where several of Jean's friends worked among the diseased people, having no fear for their own safety. Eva felt humbled by their stories for until now she had felt that she was one of the few single women in the world who had ventured so far from home.

Meanwhile, Morris was deep in conversation with the leader of the group, discussing the dilution of the island's culture due to the colonial way of life. They talked about the American writer Jack London[32]. Eva had come across some of his scathing writing on the appalling condition of the London slums, but now it also seemed he had sailed the South Seas too, visiting many of these islands. Surely not. The name must just be the same. But then she thought she had heard of stories about the gold rush in Canada and in particular the Yukon. The same man couldn't have done all this. And if so, was she somehow following in his footsteps? She decided to save the question for a less public moment with Morris. The life and work of this author seemed amazing. He had achieved so much in his short lifetime. She took her chance later that same evening as they sat up on deck where she and Morris shared thoughts on their earlier conversations with the missionaries.

Morris confirmed that she was indeed following

---

[32] Novelist, journalist, short story writer and essayist (1876-1916), who wrote The People of the Abyss (1903) based on his experiences with the impoverished in London in 1902.

in the footsteps of Jack London and while she wasn't spending as much time in the South Seas as he had done, she was making the journey as a woman on her own, far more impressive. As they moved on to the rest of the dinner conversation Eva discovered his true feelings. She was astonished because he'd managed to hide it so well under his chatty conversation. He despised the paternalistic help, which came with the bribe of Christianity, laughing bitterly about some of his experiences during his reporting which had taken him to the islands on previous occasions.

"What kind of a God do we hold up to a native people? You become a Christian and in return we will educate you on the right and proper way to live. Become a Christian and you will learn your place in the world, second to any white man who chooses to walk your land. You must give up your heathen ways, cease the mothering of your children in the animal way that raises them to be fiercely loyal, and have a passion and love for their people. Learning belongs in books. You cannot learn from simply living in harmony with nature! It is heathen and punishable to find a God in the ocean or in any form of nature. Punishment meant fear of hell beyond this short human life!

These people, and many like them Eva, they want to force independence and freedom onto the natives at a huge cost. The cost is to wipe out who they are, savages and head hunters who have no law or morals. Instead we can give them a good clean inhospitable and remote God. And alcohol. They will not find the Christian God in the skies or the trees or the ocean. He will offer them no explanations. He will remove them as far away as possible from the earth to which they instinctively know they will return upon their death. In return for the cloak of Christianity, they can be sanitized, respectable, clean living and moral.

I have found more genuine morality among these natives than I ever found on the streets of London! If these islands are to change, then they must do it from within themselves. They must find their own ways to seek freedom and morality. These are values that cannot be painted onto them through a foreign religion.

If they don't join the modern world their own way they'll become showcases for travellers, an oddity to comment but recoil from. Visitors can go away, placated by what they have seen, happy to skip back to their world, thoroughly explored and industrialised. And with its extreme wealth and its extreme poverty. Do you know Eva that the square mile of London is the wealthiest place on earth and within that square mile also live some of the poorest and most dejected human beings on earth?"

Two Hearts as One

Eva sat silently and in shock at such an outburst. All her life she had questioned her mother's controlling Christian ways, the narrowness of her views, and her control over her family. The blame and denial within her had resulted in such terrible damage within each of her children! 'Be quiet, say nothing, keep it a secret, don't speak aloud or voice your opinion, let the good Lord solve all in his way for we are his servants.' Too much of what he was saying was all too true in her own life. Deep resolve began to grow in Eva and a tear rolled down her cheek. Morris looked at her. "Eva, I'm sorry. I didn't mean to scare you with my tirade."

"You don't understand, Morris. I've never questioned other people's way of life. Since I was thirteen years old I've served and waited on the rich. I've even spent my life living through them. I've observed them as a servant, but never asked even myself if they were right or wrong about how they lived their life, or even the opinions they held. But I realise now that poverty breeds poverty. Surely the natives on those remote islands are richer in so many ways than the sort of pathetic families I grew up with, crowded into the filthy homes of working class England. Living life knowing their only purpose was to create wealth they could have no share in." She clutched her hand to her breast, agitated by so much challenging thought and her fingers closed over the dead hibiscus.

Morris was as surprised by her outburst as she was. He spoke quietly, reassuringly. "You've well and truly left all that behind Eva. Not just in terms of distance, but in your heart and mind. You don't ever have to be a part of that system again if you don't want to. And even if you work as a domestic again, you can be free in your mind. Freedom,

Eva, is always in your mind. It's not about escaping some sort of prison. You can still do what people tell you to do, but you can do it because you want to. That is freedom. And I do believe you have all that and more!"

They were standing near the prow, the wind from the ship's passage blowing cold air across her skin. Involuntarily Eva shivered. Morris put his arms around her to warm her and she turned her face up to his for a kiss.

"Morris, are you married?" The words were spoken almost in a whisper, as was his answer. "Yes". Quietly, unemotionally, he explained his situation. He had lived away from his wife for years. Their marriage had ceased to mean anything. There were no children but the legal arrangement had drifted on. She lived in Seattle. His journey to Napier had combined work and a visit to his married sister. Eva was silent for a long time. She had asked for the truth. Now the decision was hers alone.

"I'm cold Morris. Take me down to your cabin." The words slipped out almost in a whisper but there was no doubt about their meaning.

He stood up, lifted Eva up high in his arms and held her there for a few seconds. She didn't laugh or call out. Tilting her head back, she saw the entire universe in a glance, the stars, a great full silver moon, and fast moving clouds. She heard the movement of a sea being parted by the boat, and as he slowly lowered her to the deck, she could hear his breathing. Bending towards her, Morris cupped her face in his hands, his strong fingers gentle on each side of her head. He kissed her silently, first with a very gentle kiss on her closed lips, then as he felt the response in Eva, her body moving close to his, harder, his mouth exploring hers. Eva briefly felt his hands move to her hair. Her hat was pushed off and Morris buried his face in her soft curls. His deep voice spoke in her ear, barely above a whisper.

"Eva, I want you. But are you sure?"

She didn't answer. Instead, she took his hand, leading him down the stairs to his cabin. Still with no words between them, he unlocked the door. He slowly slid the pink wrap from her shoulders, placing it on the bed. He unbuttoned the sequinned grey dress, gently removing it and placing it on top of the wrap. He looked at little Eva, standing in her thin petticoat, her hair falling from the silver hairpin. She was shaking and nervous but she trusted him and she met his eyes, her gaze steady. He undressed but she did not look away. Finally he sat her on the edge of the bed, lifting each buckled shoe. Very gently he slid each one off her feet, placing them neatly together on the floor. Eva rolled down her stockings and he kissed the top of each small foot.

Naked, vulnerable, he knelt before her. She looked down at his thick brown curls. Saw the birthmark on his chest, a tiny crescent shaped blur. Realising that all the terror she thought she would experience in this situation was now gone, she placed her hands gently on his broad shoulders.

"Morris, I love you. That is all that matters to me". Without answering, he stood up and looked down at her. Have I said the wrong thing? She asked herself. But then as though answering her, he gathered her to her feet, holding her against his body before gently removing her petticoat. Once again he searched for her mouth. Answer enough, Eva thought, feeling reassured and finally able to give herself to the experience completely. Through the porthole came a sliver of moonlight enabling them to see each other. They needed no other light as she responded to his gentle, then passionate touch.

Making love to her, Morris slowly explored her body with gentle kisses. With his forefinger he traced the outline of her lips, ran his fingers through her now tumbled hair, and discovered her ears, which he whispered into. In response, Eva shyly touched his body, his chest and over his shoulders. Looking up at him, she could make out a slow smile as he caressed her. She repeated his movements, running her hands down his back, exploring him as she would a new land.

For his part, Morris thought briefly about what she

was giving him, breaking a set of rules she had decided to live by half her life ago. Her inexperience, but willingness was a gift without compare. He did not want to enter her at this point, merely to lie with her, love her, touch and stroke her skin and make her understand what their bodies could do together. He felt the urgency, but knew that he needed to be as gentle and reassuring as he could for her and that her hands and the friction or their bodies touching would be all that he would need for now.

Later, folded in his arms she slept. For the first time in a long time, a deep and untroubled sleep took her far away. Morris lay very still. He could feel her heart beat against his chest and he didn't want her to stir, in case he lost that connection. Later that night she awoke with a knowing certainty that he was there. She looked at him sleeping, gently searched his body and awakened him. As she saw his eyes open she leaned over him and whispered, "You lied to me."

"Hmmm. What?"

"I said you lied to me."

"When? Eva I've never lied to you!"

"The day we met you told me you snore dreadfully. You lied. You're actually one of the most peaceful sleepers I could imagine."

He laughed, relief plain in his voice. "Eva, that was a nasty trick to play on a naked man! You had me wracking my brain for a moment there." He paused for a moment before adding, "allright then, I booked a cabin to myself because I knew I would meet the woman of my dreams on the ship and wanted a private room to have my way with her."

"Now who's being mean? But now you're properly awake again."

They kissed each other all over again, caressed and stroked each other's skin until he knew she was ready for the ultimate intimacy and entered her. Slowly at first, never going further until he knew she was ready, responding to her every movement, sound, gesture and touch. Afterwards they lay together, their bodies shiny with sweat and enjoying the play of the cool breeze through the open porthole as it touched and caressed their skin.

Again and again throughout the night they sought each other. There seemed no end to their hunger. Barely any words were spoken as they explored each other's bodies and dozed contentedly in each other arms. Several times Eva cried out, relieving all the pent up emotion in her heart and soul. On any other night she would have worried about adjoining rooms, but on this night there was nowhere else but this bed. No one else, but the two of them. Once she wept as Morris entered her. But far from worrying Morris, they both knew it was with joy, rather than pain or regret. Only a couple of hours before dawn, they finally rested and they lay in each other's arms.

"Morris?"

"Mmm ... Hmm. What is it, darling?"

"When we were making love I didn't know if I was you or you were me. Do you know what I mean?"

"Yes, my darling," his voice all warm and drowsy. "I know exactly what you mean. You're a wonder you know. Inside you is the warmest, most beautiful place I have ever known."

"But Morris, I've never done it before. I didn't even know if I was doing it right! Was I a disappointment to you?"

He burst out laughing, propping himself up on one elbow so that he could look down at her troubled face. "Perhaps I need to show you again how disappointed I am in you Miss Eva." They'd thought they were spent, but they made love once more and then they slept wrapped around each other until the grey dawn lit up the cabin.

Eva slipped from their bed, smiling as she looked down at Morris sleeping. Very tenderly she bent and kissed his curls. Then gathering up her clothes she quickly dressed. It was easy to slip next door to her cabin. But she didn't sleep again. Instead she lay thinking about last night. She

The Price

was resolute not to analyse the meaning of it all. She gently laid the hibiscus flower in between the pages of the Bible her mother had given to her all those years ago. It would remind her in years to come of this night when she gave herself permission to break free from the constraining boundaries of the life she'd always known.

Later that morning, after resting and changing, she went for breakfast. Morris was waiting for her. Kissing her gently on the cheek, he seated her at the table and ordered their food. He sat staring at Eva until she flushed.

"Eva, do that again. You look so pretty when you blush," he laughed.

And that night, when she joined Morris in his cabin, they lay and talked about the inescapable influence of childhood on their lives. Morris described his own childhood whilst Eva lay still and safe in his arms listening, but at the same time trying to come to terms with her own family.

Now she lived in this world, the world where Morris was the centre, her family seemed less real somehow. The only way she could think to describe it was that she was finally living in light and her family was somehow willingly living in the dark. She couldn't imagine living in the dark again. Two days out of Suva she suddenly realised that it had been a whole day since she'd thought of Ellen or Joe and the secrets she had to keep and was overwhelmed with the relief of not feeling guilty.

The following few days were spent peacefully as Eva wandered the decks of the ship with Morris, often in companionable silence, reflecting on all that had taken place within a handful of days. Great changes were taking place within her. She was unfolding, relinquishing a lifetime of instilled moral authority, inhibitions and secrets. She already knew that at some point in the future she would tell all her secrets to Morris. Only then would she have the kind of freedom he'd described to her. In turn Morris waited for her, wise and sensitive to her inhibitions. He knew that later she would want more details of his marriage. But she had not referred to it since he had told her. It was as if the entire world existed for them alone.

He guessed a little of what was going on inside her, but he knew that he couldn't take any part in it, as it was Eva's journey and something she needed to work out for herself. Instead he gave her friendship. He watched in approval as she joined in more and more in the dining table conversations that she would have previously avoided and began to become the woman that was always within her bursting to get out. He smiled to himself as he thought about how he couldn't wait to see it all unfold.

Aloha

The Niagara was at last drawing close to Honolulu. Eva and Morris stood at the rail and watched the approach. From a distance all they could see were steep mountains covered with the varied green of Hawaiian forests. But it became clearer as the ship approached the harbour until the passengers could see individual features and get a feel for the place at which they were about to arrive. With great amazement they saw that the harbour was dotted with swimmers who were diving to retrieve coins the passengers threw to them.

Then small tugboats approached the ship. On board were groups of natives, their arms full of exotic flowers made into necklaces and garlands. The passengers and ship were soon covered with the flowers and the air was full of their heavy perfume. Morris watched as Eva laughed with delight, as did everyone else, men and women alike.

"Morris! Isn't this incredible!" Eva exclaimed. "Look at everybody! They're all so beautiful!"

Morris looked at her, smiling. He thought, Look at everybody? I can't look at anybody else but you. And marvelling at how such a simple gesture could lift the quiet and reflective mood of the past few days. He wrapped his arm around her and kissed the top of her head. The mood on board was infectious and he was as happy, excited and in love as any man.

"Morris, I could make a film of this and nobody in Crewe would be able to understand any of it. How could I ever capture the sounds of everyone laughing or the seagulls flying around us? And they wouldn't understand the smells of the sea and the flowers. Or all the colour. I don't even know how to put it in a letter!"

"It is certainly impressive."

"I remember when I first saw Panama and how colourful it was, I realised what a shame it was that I had nobody I loved to share it with. This time I'm glad I have you."

Morris smiled as he continued looking out at the harbour. Then turning to Eva he said, "I know what you mean. I've been to Honolulu before, but it's never looked as good as today. Because I've always seen it by myself."

Eva gazed in excitement at the city of Honolulu curved along the shore. Behind the harbour rose steep mountains covered with the thick tropical forests they had seen from a distance. Eva had read in information available on board that the hill she could see behind the town was the cone of an extinct volcano now named *Punchbowl Hill* and that it had once been a place where human sacrifices were made. She'd shivered when she read it, but it looked so majestic now that she couldn't help but love it.

At the water's edge in the centre of the row of piers, stood the pointed obelisk of *Aloha Tower*, with its clock faces and its legend engraved in bold block lettering: ALOHA, literally meaning LOVE. In the following few hours Eva would hear that word many times, the sweet word being spoken to her by the natives and translated meaning: 'my love be with you'.

The passengers left the *Niagara* for several hours, to explore an expanding town. Morris pointed out the old Hawaii that could still be seen in corners of the new city. It seemed to be modernising and expanding at a rapid rate, leaving old Hawaii behind.

Down to their left Morris pointed out the first harbour. It was filled with gigantic freighters, loading up with their cargos: pineapples for the United States of America, coffee from the Kona coast, bananas, honey, canned tuna, guava jelly and many more exotic foods. He also told her that in the past, sailing vessels, fur traders, whalers, guano ships, sandalwood carriers, explorers and missionaries had

The Price

used those same docks.

There was almost too much activity for Eva to take in. Her eyes were wide like a child and her voice slightly breathless as she directed Morris to look in every direction. "Look at those boats over there! The blue ones with the red stripes! There are hundreds of them! And they're tiny. What do you think they're used for?"

Morris patiently explained. "Probably tuna fish. They're incredible little boats. They're very light and they can be pulled right up to the shore because they have such a shallow draft. But the natives sail them sometimes thirty miles off shore. You'd never get me so far from land in a boat like that, but they do the job and the people who sail in them don't seem to worry about it."

But Eva could barely listen to his explanation. She had never experienced so much activity, laughter, shouting, colour and movement, not even at Crewe station on its busiest days. She was giddy with it all and she steadied herself, holding onto Morris's arm. He guided her away from the quay and into the town itself. Here they sat for a while outside a small food shop.

Calming down and settling into a more civilised pace away from the dockside, they were served a delicious breakfast of papaya on which they squeezed lime juice and followed it with fragrant coffee. After breakfast they headed for the outskirts of town where the air was soft and warm and filled with foreign noises. They could hear the incessant chatter of the mynah birds in the forests, the sound of falling fruit and the swish and fall of the palm fronds in the gentle breeze. It was certainly a change after days of the constant background sounds of a ship at sea.

The morning was cool and they decided to keep walking. They made their way around the edge of the town and past hibiscus hedges, covered in flowers in every rich colour imaginable. It seemed so peaceful that they were tempted to walk in bare feet like the natives. Finally Eva took her shoes and stockings off, much to Morris's amusement but only after he assured her that there were no snakes on the island. Barely five minutes later, Eva shrieked as a huge bat like insect flew close to her. "Ahhh! Bat!"

"That," laughed Morris, "is a flying cockroach. It only looks like a bat. They breed in the banana leaves in their thousands. But they won't hurt you."

No sooner had he reassured her than Eva shrieked once again, pointing speechlessly at an enormous spider, which was sitting harmlessly on a wall.

"And that," laughed Morris, "is a local spider known as the *Doorknob*. It's completely harmless but I wouldn't touch it!"

"It might be beautiful, but it's nerve-wracking here. I'd better put my shoes on in case I need a hasty escape!" And checking a log very carefully for creepy crawlies before sitting down, her stockings and shoes went back on, which resulted in further gentle teasing from Morris.

"Women! You go for a quiet walk in nature and look what it turns into!"

Eva opened her mouth to answer back, saw the smile on Morris's face and bit her tongue. "Oooh! How can I get mad at you? We'll put you on the scary streets of Crewe one day and see how you get on!"

"Nothing frightens me Eva after seeing you lose your temper."

"Truce! Truce!" Eva laughed out loud. "I think we'd better stop now before one of us goes too far!"

She stood up then and Morris put his arm around her shoulders and said with a hint of a smile in his voice, "I don't think you could ever go too far with me Eva Madden."

All too soon the time on shore had come to an end. The *Niagara* prepared to sail. Evening brought refreshing cool winds as she steamed away into the blackness. The harbour lights of Honolulu winked on and off as Eva leaned against the ship's rails. She could see the rows of portholes casting light onto the water below, the fading masts of a schooner yacht and the torches of the fishermen. Out at sea, far beyond the swells, she could spot the lonely little lamps of the tiny boats she'd seen when they first entered the harbour.

The steamer slipped along through a moonlit ocean on its way to Victoria, the capital of British Columbia. Not a sound broke the stillness but the swish of the waves and the steady throb of the engines. Eva and Morris were once more in conversation, discussing the events of that day. They were both reluctant to discuss their futures beyond the next port of call. They were completely happy in the moment and for them the *Niagara* was their entire world, as though the pressures of their lives away from the ship simply didn't exist.

Eva realised that she'd never felt so disconnected from hardship, grief and loneliness before. In that moment she was completely happy with Morris. For his part, Morris had already decided that Eva must always have a place in his life.

The warm winds and calm seas began to change and within two days of leaving Honolulu there was an icy wind blowing. Most passengers stayed in the passenger saloons but Eva loved to walk the deck even though the seas began to pound the ship. One morning she and Morris spotted several whales and many seals. During the evening they finally sighted what looked like land. Eva's heart sank a little because she knew that their adventure was almost at an end, that things would change and the real world would soon intrude.

Morris sensed what thoughts resulted in her quiet mood. "That's Vancouver Island and we'll soon reach the capital of Victoria, maybe even in the morning," he told her. Eva continued to stare apprehensively into the distance, wondering what this new land would hold for her.

"Don't worry Eva, I know what you are thinking. There are no bears roaming around and no Indians to chase you off. And no flying cockroaches or doorknob spiders!" That brought a smile to her face. It wasn't what she was

Aloha

thinking about at all, and Morris knew it. But, as always, he wanted to cheer her up.

He continued. "Actually the coastal Indians who used to inhabit the island had an interesting religion. It was in the form of animism. They saw and worshipped spirits in living things and objects. That wouldn't be a difficult thing to do in this part of the world. Just inland, it is very wild and beautiful. Imagine it before it was settled, a paradise of a different kind from the Pacific Islands. Incredibly lush and green. In some parts of the island the trees are so big and the forests so dense it's hard to imagine how the Indians used to find space to live there."

That night Eva found it difficult to sleep, partly through anxiety and partly through excitement. Several of the passengers at their dining table lived in Vancouver and they talked excitedly about returning home. For Eva it was the beginning of yet another huge change in her life in a country so vast that it could fit most of Europe into it. The pink Canada in her atlas was suddenly more comforting than the reality of finally landing there. She comforted herself that she had Morris with her. Also a letter from George would hopefully be waiting at the hostel. It seemed like another lifetime since she'd heard from her family.

As a grey light showed beyond the porthole, Eva was up and dressed. She returned to her cabin to say goodbye to the roommate she had seen so little of during the voyage. She knew that Catherine would leave the ship in Vancouver to make her way by train to her family in the United States. The two women had exchanged addresses over dinner the previous night. Although she did not attempt to pry into Eva's business, Catherine did comment very favourably on Morris, knowing full well that Eva had not slept in her cabin since Fiji.

"I wish I'd met a man like him, Eva and I wish you both the best. I've watched you dancing with Morris you know. And I couldn't help but wonder if one day a man will look at me like Morris looks at you. I'm really happy for you

The Price

both."

Eva blushed. She'd been living in a cocoon, knowing what she was feeling, but to hear it from an observer was another story altogether. Imagine her, Eva Madden, a plain servant girl from Crewe finding love with a man like Morris Miller. Was it too good to be true? Suddenly she was filled with doubts again. He was married yet she didn't care. That was the strange thing. If he wasn't meant to be with her then she could still look after herself she decided. She thanked Catherine and wished her luck before leaving her to seek out Morris again.

As she came up on deck, the icy wind took her breath away for a moment. Holding her head down, she struggled to the safety rails and looked up. Victoria was stunning even from a distance. The forests were so dense, covering the hills as they rolled into the distance. Mountains, still dusted with the last of winter's snow on the peaks lay beyond. She saw Morris and went and stood next to him. He put his arm around her, offering her warmth.

Eva spoke first. "Those mountains. They're so huge. Bigger than anything I've seen before."

"Those mountains? They're barely hills. Wait till you see the Rockies."

It was far more impressive and wilder than Auckland. Would there be a place for her in this vast country?

"Here we are then, perched right on the edge of the Pacific."

She was grateful for Morris's quiet voice in her ear as his arms enfolded her. She suddenly felt much better. The awful moment of loneliness and doubt had passed. But still, she knew from experience that it was entirely up to her to make something of her life. She could never rely on anyone, even Morris. She had fought too hard for her independence.

The *Niagara* slipped through the straits to dock for a few hours at the busy port so that the transfer of mail, goods and fruit could take place. Passengers leaving the ship disembarked full of cheerful chatter and goodbyes.

Eva could only look at a distance at the magnificent Houses of Parliament, a slice of England on the other side of the world. And the buildings and cobbled streets she could catch glimpses of from the ship reminded her of fairytales about old Europe. It was somewhere Eva would like to visit, but not when she was so close to where she knew her future waited.

Then the *Niagara* was sailing again, expertly navigating her way to her final destination past many small inlets and islands, balls of green rising out of the freezing deep grey water.

Vancouver

Their first sighting of Vancouver from the ocean was spectacular. The air was clear and they could see for miles. Mountains, still with a faint dusting of snow, could be spotted in the distance through crew member binoculars to the north and long deserted beaches to the west.

'Wait till you see the Rockies.' "Now I understand what you meant."

"Oh, they're only the foothills to the Rockies," Morris whispered in reply. "One day I'll show them to you up close and they'll take your breath away."

In English Bay many cargo vessels had dropped anchor in readiness for the small pilot boats to guide them into the docks. Workers were busy transporting goods into the various warehouses along the quay.

Eva felt the challenge that came with facing the unknown. She knew that just a handful of years ago people had sailed here, gaining a slim foothold on a primeval land. They had battled the unknown, building cabins, facing long winters and even travelling north to the Yukon in search of gold. She was, after all, only following in the footsteps of other women who had pioneered this land, so she had no reason to feel nervous.

Hearing a noise she looked up to see a 'V' formation of wild geese flying high overhead. They never hesitated as they honed in over the sea, heading for the mountain range. She remembered the geese that marked another turning point in her life, her farewell to Brereton Hall. Her emotions welled even closer to the surface and she asked herself how she could be so filled with the wonder of the new and yet still have strange little flashes of the past. Perhaps it is human nature to look for the familiar when things are most unfamiliar, she thought to herself.

Suddenly the journey was over. Passengers jostled one another as they left the ship, smiling and chattering, amongst them Eva and Morris. Her luggage would be sent on to the hostel separately. They had decided to spend one night away from each other. He must report to his newspaper office and it wouldn't be a bad idea for Eva to settle in at the YWCA on her own to take some time to think. Here she was in Vancouver already and she hadn't made any plans about what she would do next.

Morris found a taxi for her and gave the driver precise directions to her destination. He put his arms around her for the last time before putting her in the cab and kissing her. He closed the door and Eva looked out at his comforting presence then up at the *Niagara*. She felt upset at leaving him but it would not be for long.

Everything in her life had changed aboard the ship and she felt a fondness for it, wondering how other lives had changed during its many voyages. She briefly remembered the young couple who had met and become engaged on the journey to New Zealand aboard the *Suffolk*. How strange it had seemed then and Eva had never imagined that the same thing would happen to her. Lifting her hand, she gave a wave to Morris. Then they were off, driving from the port and away across a city with wide straight roads that criss-crossed in a rectangular pattern.

'Organised' and 'clean' were the two words that kept coming to mind as she looked eagerly out of the window at the city town speeding by. The taxi driver commenced chattering, speaking in a pleasant Canadian accent, giving her the history of the place as he had done so many times before.

"So, you're English?"

"Yes, I'm from …"

"Thought so from your accent and very nice too," he interrupted. "I love the English accent. We all do here. Leaving your man behind are you? Expect you'll see him

The Price

soon. Do you know that this city, well hardly more than a town, is only forty-four years old? Even more amazing, it has as its first citizen an Englishman by the name of Jack Morton, a native of Yorkshire, England. Do you know of the family? Do you come from Yorkshire?" There was a pause at last.

"No, I'm from Cheshire but it isn't too far from Yorkshire."

"Well anyway, this man whose family came from near to your home, he built a log cabin in the shadows of the forests, near to a place called Burrard Inlet. All on his own he was. Will you be staying on your own?" No answer. Eva was silent. He paid no attention to her lack of reply and merely continued with his history of Vancouver.

"A real pioneer, real loner he was. Not for long though. Other settlers soon built near to him. Heard about the good soil and the mildness of the climate. Course, he didn't know how shallow the soil is and how much it shakes, but it was a good spot."

"There are earthquakes?" Eva interrupted tentatively, thinking of the destruction in New Zealand.

"Oh, yes. But no big ones in my time. Just little tremblers really. Not so you can even really feel 'em. Now, where was I? The early folks loved the weather here, not too cold and not too much snow. You have to love rain though if you want to be happy in old Vancouver. You see, many of them first settlers came south from the Yukon during the winter. Some of them froze to death up there too, but that's another story. Half frozen to death, they loved this place. They built log cabins and soon there were a 1000 people living there. My grandfather was one of them. This place was a paradise after the frozen north. This early settlement they named Granville. By 1886 the Canadian Pacific Railway reached the coast, bringing work and more people. All started off by an Englishman, from up the street from you!"

Eva opened her mouth, ready to correct him, but

thought better of it. In any case, he was off again with more information.

"The two main streets were Granville Street and Hastings Street. The place has grown and grown since then. And here we are Miss!"

Triumphantly he screeched to a halt outside a well-established building with YWCA printed in the stonework above its door. Eva started to laugh, so much entertaining information in such a little time and told so cheerfully. She was happy to tip the 'historian' as Morris had instructed her to do.

"Thank you Ma'am and good luck," and with a big grin, he drove off.

Eva hurried inside to book in to the hostel for one night. Her earlier letter from New Zealand had secured accommodation, but no news from England was waiting for her. Disappointed, she was assured that there had been a delay with all mail from England. Feeling a bit sad and let down, she unpacked a few of her things and decided to explore a little of Vancouver. It was already strange not to be able to turn and talk with Morris. It was a different kind of loneliness for her.

Setting out she soon discovered that the city was undulating. Little hills now covered in roads and stores made up the centre. The smell of pinewood was everywhere. Down the main street Eva again caught glimpses of the vast snow covered peaks of the Rockies in the distance. She found herself shivering with excitement, sensing that this was a wild unexplored land. Much of it was still untamed. The sadness she'd felt as she'd arrived at the hostel was evaporating. What a place to be!

Walking as far as the corner of Granville and Robson Street, she saw the Hudson Bay Company. It reminded her of those long journeys north to the Yukon not so many years ago that she'd read about. She would probably work in a large house where winters could be managed without risk of injury and death. A cold wind swept down from the mountains already covered in cloud, reminding her that it was time to return to the warmth of the hostel, where she found company and laughter.

Many of the women at the hostel were seeking work of all kinds. They passed information to others about places to go and places to avoid. Employers who required domestic service came to the YWCA to seek women of a reputable nature, often leaving behind their addresses, requirements and times for interviews. Eva studied a map of Vancouver, anxious to learn about the wealthier areas where she would find work as a domestic.

"You should be looking for work in Shaughnessy," said one of the staff, looking at the maps and lists Eva was juggling. "It's not too far from downtown, only about twenty minutes in a motor and there's plenty there in their grand houses that can afford to pay for domestic help."

"Thank you. You've probably saved me hours of poring over all this and trying to make sense of it all. I really don't know north from south yet and here I am trying to get around and find a job."

"Oh, you'll like Shaughnessy. Built for the bosses of the Canadian Pacific. The railway. Also to try and get some other nobs to come and settle here and invest their money. No point in building the railway if there's nobody to buy anything at one end, right?"

Eva took a tram ride to the area the following morning. Certainly these weren't the 'grand houses' she had imagined from the girl at the YWCA. They had little in common with what would be described as a 'grand house' in England, but they were huge houses nonetheless. Many of them were built in the Tudor style and they might have only been built mainly of timber, but were the castles of the rich. People who had made their fortune in British Columbia's timber, mining and other lucrative industries owned them. These people loved to show off their wealth and status, employing numerous domestic servants to run their grand homes. The streets of Shaughnessy were wide. Chestnut trees and maples lined the edges, the mansions set back discreetly within their own grounds behind high fences and hedges. Each one was a different design but all of them were made of wood.

Morris had phoned to say that he would be at the hostel that evening. He knew that Eva would be out looking for work. Her nature would convince her that she must be financially independent. He loved her for it, but knew that taking work in one of the houses in Shaughnessy would mean long hours with only one day a week when they would be able to see each other. But there would be no changing her mind not even to stop for a week and live off her savings, while she actually planned something. They would see each other when she had a day off and perhaps he could take her out occasionally in the evening. That would have to be enough. For now, he just looked forward to hearing all about her adventure across Vancouver by tram.

When she returned to the hostel that afternoon, Eva was thrilled to hear the news that there may be a job for her already. An experienced domestic was required at a large house in Granville Street and an interview was arranged for the following day.

"Thank you, thank you, thank you! This means so much to me!"

"Well seemed to me any fancy house would be glad of someone who's such a lady as you. Besides, the lady of the house seemed awful fussy. Couldn't see any of the others here that are looking for work being good for the job."

"All the same. Thank you doesn't begin to express my gratitude."

Morris was delighted when he heard the news. He had been right. She had been looking for a job and already had a good chance of getting one. He had no doubts that Eva would get it. They hugged each other, Eva clinging so tightly to him that he mockingly chastised her.

"Eva, you would think I'd been away for weeks!"

"Seems like you have. We've barely been apart for

more than a few minutes in two weeks. A whole day is an eternity! I need to wean myself off you in little doses!" Then more quietly, "I'm booked in at the hostel for another night but I want to be with you," she begged.

"Ahhh, then I'm a mind reader. I've already made arrangements so you can stay with me. Even though I live down in Seattle with my sister, at my office here in town there's a small room where I often stay overnight when I'm working on a long story or waiting for a cable. It's no luxury, but it's my home away from home and at least we can be together in private."

They made love in the small room where he had written so many of his stories. Eva dreamily touched his clothes. Many of them had been hanging there while he'd been away in New Zealand. She was discovering the man before he knew her. Puzzled, he asked her what she was doing burying her nose in his jackets and shirts.

"I'm smelling you Morris. I love the smell of your body. It's here again on your clothes, part of you."

"Hope you're not telling me that I need to bathe more often!"

"No, no!" she laughed. "But you have a special smell. I love it. Surely you've noticed that Morris. About people I mean."

"Can't say I have. But I will from now on. Come here. Time to test your theory. Now I want to smell the perfume called Eva."

She laughed. She knew it was just silly lover's talk, but she didn't mind. That night they were so happy, just to be together again, to reach out and rediscover each other. The past no longer seemed to matter, her family, and the marriage. What was happening to Eva was far more powerful and real than anything she had ever experienced.

The next morning Morris drove Eva to Shaughnessy, waiting for her to return to him with the good news she hoped for. He felt regret in one way. Eva could be with him most of the time. He could keep her, but she would have hated that. She was not a mistress. He knew her well enough not to even suggest it for her pride and independence gave her no choices. It was far too soon to suggest that she stop working.

A Mr Dalton was the owner of the house situated on the southeast corner of 34th and Granville. Eva had impeccable references and so Morris had told her she should not be in any doubt that she would win the position. He could see her confidence as she walked through the gate in the high hedge. He smiled as she turned once to wave at him. He looked at the house. The design was interesting. Three storeys high with open stairs going up the side of the house to the third floor. It was built of wood with a black and white trim, and would be quite unlike any house that Eva had worked in before, Morris thought to himself. He watched as she looked up at it from the bottom of the steps with all its angles and strange gables. It seemed to loom over her tiny frame. Then she appeared to take a deep breath before walking up the steps to the front door.

She was gone for at least an hour. Morris knew that despite the long interview, it would be clear from both Eva's appearance and her references that she would be ideal for the position. Staff with Eva's background came along too rarely in Vancouver and Morris knew that if Mr Dalton didn't hire her on the spot, someone else would within days.

Finally she rushed out to tell him the good news. She had been appointed general housekeeper and lady's maid. In a tumble of words she told him that the staff included a cook, a nanny for the two children, a gardener and a scullery maid. But only Eva and the nanny would live in. She would see to the general running of the house, commencing immediately.

She was delighted as this was a senior position with excellent pay. But Morris had never imagined that she would start immediately. He thought that they would at least have the afternoon together before she started work. But that was Eva. She amazed him. Most women in her position would by now be planning not to work at all, to have him support her. Certainly any other woman that he'd ever been involved with. But not his Eva.

They made arrangements to see each other at the weekend. A little reluctantly, Morris said a brief goodbye, hoping to delay their parting by the need to go and collect her luggage from the hostel, but Mr Dalton had even taken care of that.

"I think he's really serious Eva. This Mr Dalton doesn't want to give you even the slightest chance of changing your mind. Sure I can't change it just for this afternoon, maybe tonight?"

She laughed at that. "If we can't wait for the weekend, then there's something wrong with us! I love you and I'll see you then!" Then more quietly, "but I won't go to sleep at night without thinking about how nice it would be to have you next to me."

"Then that will have to be enough. I love you for who you are Eva, and your independence is part of that. The weekend it is. See you then." And he bent down and kissed her before getting back in the car and driving back to his lonely office.

There were to be no secret liaisons in her relationship, no secrecy, no hiding their relationship she decided. This was the part she loved most of all. The normality of her love for each other was essential to her. The trust and love between them was something very precious and now they could and would build on it for a future. There were such things as divorce and his legal wife was far away. But if Eva had barely managed a night without him, how would she manage waiting until the weekend?

She occupied herself by sending a post card to England with her work address. Her parents would be worried by now. And then she prepared to throw herself into her work to distract her from the agonising wait until she saw Morris again.

On the first night at the Dalton house she looked out of her back bedroom window over massive chestnut trees and bright green gardens. Spring was showing itself in blossoming trees and daffodils, which were also blooming bright yellow even in the dusk. She was reminded of an English spring.

A New Life Unfolds

Eva met Morris on her first free day. He planned to take her to Stanley Park, a huge reserve he told her was called 'the heart of Vancouver', and they would go by car. He talked of little else as they walked, describing all the things she would find there, the smells and how the park felt after rain. He kept telling her what a special day it would be, but she had no idea of how special. They both had so very little time off from work and the park would soon be one of their favourite places to go. But this was their first visit and it would imprint itself upon Eva's memory like few other days in her life.

Morris had greeted Mr and Mrs Dalton when he collected Eva and they looked on with approval as Eva left for her day out. Officially summer was nearly upon them, but Eva still felt chilly, even though bright sunshine promised a warmer afternoon. Dressed in blue, her favourite colour, and not wearing a hat, she looked like the lady of the house. At least that was what Morris told her and they both laughed about it.

She couldn't stop talking and Morris was pleased. She had lost none of the vivacity and confidence she had discovered on the voyage. Did he know that she was the housekeeper, not a mere domestic? She now earned a good salary, having won the job over fifteen other women! Finally, they were ready for the drive north. Settling back in the car she asked Morris about his work.

He had been extremely busy, submitting a number of articles, and reporting various incidents across Vancouver including economic findings relating to Canada. They talked about the possibility of settling in Canada. As they talked, the scenery changed from city buildings to suburbs.

A New Life Unfolds

Finally they were driving along Georgia Street towards the Causeway Approach to Stanley Park. Looking down, Eva could see spectacular views of Lost Lagoon to her left before they entered the park itself. Giant cedars, Douglas fir spruce trees, and beautiful native maples closed them in. A mass of ferns with bright green foliage hemmed the road through the forest. Her face wore the same sense of wonder it had in Fiji and Hawaii and he loved seeing familiar places through her eyes. Morris smiled to himself. He had known that she would love the great trees, centuries old.

"This would have been how the entire West Coast of Canada would have looked before sailors discovered it."

"How big is this place? Could we get lost?" Eva finally enquired, for in that moment this land looked stranger than anywhere else she'd been.

"Only if we want to!" laughed Morris. "It's a thousand acres and thirty odd miles of trails. Unique actually to have a park this big as part of a city. Today I'll only drive around the edge of the park. Next time we come we can stop the car and take a long walk in the park itself. I'm at your command, Madam."

"Or am I at your mercy?" she teased.

"No, no," he laughed. "You decide. There's an animal enclosure here that we could look at if you like. We can see buffalo, elk, deer and goats. I think there are also sheep and some animals from other countries. There are even some big bears."

Eva looked at him sharply at this last piece of information.

"Don't panic, in a bear pit! I'm beginning to realise that bears are not your favourite animals!" And he laughed. "Seriously. You won't come across any wild bears in Vancouver and if you did, they'd have to eat me before they could get to you." He knew Eva's worst fear and it would not be too difficult to imagine a huge grizzly coming out of this forest!

They stopped the car and walked a little way into

the park itself, treading softly on the thick carpet of pine needles. There was an eerie silence. Not even the sound of a single bird could be heard. It was dim and everywhere was the smell of cool wet timber and leaves on the ground. Eva looked up but could only see the giant cedar climbing to the sky. She leant against its ancient trunk, could feel the snows of winter covering her, the isolation and loneliness of the pioneers and the hardness of the land. These great trees had witnessed it all. Feeling dizzy, she shut her eyes. When she opened them, Morris had vanished! She called his name but there was only an echo. Suddenly she felt a panic rising in her chest and then the old anger came to the surface to defend her.

"Morris, stop playing silly games! Where are you?"

The circumference of the giant tree must have been at least fifty feet. Against her body it felt strong and reassuring. Slowly she edged her way around the giant trunk, stretching her fingertips as far as they could go. She wasn't afraid any more, simply in awe of something so ancient and yet living. Suddenly she jumped and squealed as her fingertips touched Morris's outstretched hand. He emerged from further around the tree, laughing loudly.

"Before you shout at me, I did that so that you could feel just for a second or two what it would be like to be here entirely on your own, to know that feeling of isolation. That was how the pioneers of this land must have felt not so many years ago."

He gently took her hand and started to lead her back to the car. "The first time I saw this tree, one of the people I was with said that he and his friends had tried to measure it around one day. He said it took fifteen men reaching their arms out to completely surround it. Have you ever imagined a tree so big? Can you see what this place would have been like when it was all like that?"

Eva remained silent until they were back in the car. "I had no idea, Morris. No idea about Canada and it's all there in that big ancient tree."

They parked near to the picnic grounds that looked out over English Bay. Second Beach was very popular for swimming during the short summer months. Here at the tearooms, Morris bought tea and cakes before they walked as far as the Picnic Grounds, passing the Ladies Bath House.

"Maybe in the summer we can swim here."

"I can't swim," laughed Eva at the very thought of it. "When would a servant girl from Crewe have ever learned to swim? But I'd be happy to paddle!"

As they made an exit from the Park by way of Beach Avenue, Eva sighed. She'd had a wonderful day. She couldn't help but think that if she'd had somewhere, and someone, in New Zealand for days like this, then maybe she wouldn't have suffered from so many illnesses. She'd waited so long, maybe even wasted many years thinking that all there should be to her life was work and security. But maybe she'd just been waiting for this moment. In which case not a day of what had come before had been a waste if it led her to here.

Her thoughts returned to the giant tree. What would the untamed parts of Canada look like? Would she ever see them and more importantly, would they ever be tamed? She looked up at the distant mountains as they drove through Shaughnessy, deciding that it would be impossible to ruin such a wilderness.

Work at the Dalton household was pleasant. Although they patterned their lifestyle around British traditions, formality such as that found at Brereton Hall did not exist. There was even time for laughter amongst the staff. She left the cook entirely to her own devices, for she was efficient and economical. Meals consisted of traditional dishes. Rarely was lamb used, which was a big difference from what she was used to in New Zealand. Perhaps with all their forests, there just wasn't the room in Canada to graze sheep. A great amount of chicken and turkey was served up along with fresh vegetables. There were many apple dishes but the favourite of the family was pumpkin pie, which Eva thought was an acquired taste, but grew to like.

The cook proudly showed her a slab of Anchor butter, which had newly been imported from New Zealand, prompting Eva to talk a little about her experiences. Even Emily the scullery maid joined in their conversations from time to time. She offered scraps of information to 'Miss Madden', whom she admired tremendously. She compared the subtle differences in language with Eva, asking her for the English words for drapes[33] and fall[34]. She requested information on England and the royal family and she wanted to know the working conditions of scullery maids when Eva first started.

Eva recalled her time with her sisters and brothers. She told stories about Brereton Hall to a wide-eyed little girl of fourteen who had only ever known a few streets in Vancouver. In that respect, Eva could definitely identify with Emily. And Eva gave hope to Emily that one day she could travel the world and wear beautiful clothes like 'Miss Madden'. In return Emily would search for jokes, making Eva smile. She loved to see her laugh, her wide brown eyes lighting up even before she smiled.

One day she bounded into the kitchen, coming in from a visit to her family home. Eva happened to be talking to the cook. They both turned, smiling to see the happy girl wrapping herself into the large white pinafore.

"Guess what Miss Madden, I've got a joke you'll really like," she said, waiting for permission to tell it to the adult audience.

"Well go on then," the cook smiled, "and let's hope it is suitable!"

"Well, there's this girl who comes from the employment agency and she says to the lady of the house, 'They said you wanted a servant.' 'But I do all the work myself,' replied the lady of the house. 'Then this place will just suit me fine.'"

---

[33] American and Canadian word for curtains.
[34] American and Canadian word for autumn.

A New Life Unfolds

Emily waited for the laughter and approval from Miss Madden before rushing off to do her duties. She learnt a great deal from the English lady, and not just housework. Eva showed her how to act in company, when to speak and when to be silent, how to walk and look smart. She taught her table manners, how to hold her knife and fork and eat properly even when she was hungry and wanted to stick all the food into her mouth in one go. Eva explained small details of housekeeping, providing all the tools for Emily to become an excellent lady's maid some time in the future.

"Remember Emily, it's the details of your work that count. Hats should be placed upon shelves, not on bedposts! Shoes should be put straight on to trees[35] from warm feet. Gloves should be treated with respect, pulled out and folded."

Emily remembered all of these things although she could hardly imagine that one day she would not be peeling potatoes and forever washing up. She wanted to end up looking and being like Miss Madden.

Eva decided in her time off she would sew some dresses for Emily and teach her dressmaking. She invariably made her own clothes using the pattern books she always carried in her case wherever she went. It was not that she couldn't afford to buy clothes, but why would she spend the money when she had the means and the time to make them herself? She did splash out and buy some ribbon for Emily's hair, which was in the process of being tamed from a wild mass of red frizz. Soon the little girl had learnt to fasten it up neatly for work.

This was a very happy time in Eva's life. She was relaxed and sociable with everyone around her, confident in her own abilities. And she was again saving carefully, depositing most of every pay in the post office. She wrote to her friends in New Zealand with glowing reports of Canada, knowing now that she had made the right choice. She and

---

[35] Wooden inserts for shoes

Morris were growing closer, sharing much of their life together. Yet something inside Eva told her it still wasn't the time to fully confide in him about her family. She was waiting to hear if he planned a divorce.

George's letter arrived at last acknowledging the postcard. She showed the enclosed newspaper cutting to Morris who commented on the handsome couple. Laughingly he asked Eva if she came from a family of film stars! In the privacy of her room Eva read the letter from George once again, committed it to memory then destroyed it.

Crewe, May 1930

Dear Eva,

By now you would be settled in Vancouver. I am sure that you will have much to tell us in your next
letter. Sailing through the Pacific Islands must have been a wonderful experience for you.
You left behind a very dry country. A friend of mine who works on the railways has a brother who has recently immigrated to the North Island. His brother wrote to tell him of the drought, which has been the worst one experienced in 50 years! He says that unless rain arrives soon the milk production will suffer badly.
We don't have that trouble here in Cheshire. It has been non-stop rain for days but never mind, spring is on its way.
Winter has seemed long and cold here in Crewe. At last Edie and me are out and about on my Ariel motorbike. You will note the folded newspaper cutting enclosed with this letter. Look carefully at the photographs and you will see yours truly with Edie, both in our leathers and out for a spin on a spring day!
It was taken in Coventry on the last Saturday in April. A reporter from the Midland Daily Telegram spotted us when

we stopped off. He took a photograph to be included on the front page as part of the 'All Sports Day' the town was holding.

The newspaper kindly sent us the photograph and two copies of the paper so I thought you would like one of a couple of film stars! Soon the aerial bike will be sold, as I need to put the money into the buying of our new home. I don't intend to have a mortgage for long if I can help so it's also lots of overtime for me.

Mother and Father are well and happy that spring is on its way at last. The daffodils have almost gone now and the bluebells are visible in the woods. You know how much I love spring. I get out and about quite a bit with my Sealyham dog. We are soon in the countryside from here and it's only a short walk to Gresty from this end of Crewe.

Tom is courting a very nice girl. They may become engaged and he is seriously considering buying a house. Gussy and Tom are thinking of buying a house close to Mother.

I have good news for you about Ellen. She is far more settled in her mind and may soon be well enough to take up employment as a seamstress. She is keen to move to Chester where there is more employment in that line. Mother thinks she should wait a while. But you know Ellen. She will do what she chooses to do in the end and Father will back her up!

I have heard nothing more from Chester so I assume that Joe remains unchanged. We never discuss it in the family and I have warned Edie not to mention it to Mother and Father either.

As you know, her Mother lives just up the street. She already strongly disapproves of her lovely daughter riding behind me on the back of a motor- bike!

As soon as you are settled, write to me again if only to say that you are safe. I know very little about Canada except that the great Canadian Railway runs from the East to the West Coast ending up in Vancouver. What a run that would be!

Take care of yourself Eva and I look forward to hearing from you. The airmail to Canada is still uncertain but I hope this letter reaches you soon.

Best wishes,
Your brother, George.

During her next day off, Morris planned to take her to a supper in Stanley Park Pavilion where there was a dance and a jazz band. Knowing how much Eva would want to plan for an event like that, he told her in good time, calling for her on a warm evening in July.

Emily and the cook watched on fondly as Eva happily left the big house dressed in a handsome gown of cinnamon georgette and carrying a feather fan. Morris was dressed appropriately and as the two of them drove away the cook sighed, poking Emily with her arm and declaring them the 'perfect couple'. When Eva saw the very pretty dresses worn by other Vancouver ladies, she was glad that she had used a little of her by now considerable savings to buy her gown. The lights in the ballroom were shaded in orange and many coloured lights extending to the sides of the lawn lit up the verandahs.

Supper was laid on tables on the lawn where matting had been placed to prevent the ladies from getting their shoes soiled. Jazz music was playing and several people were already dancing.

Morris escorted Eva to a group of people standing together near the supper table. "Miss Eva Madden, I'd like you to meet my Editor, Mr Paul Williams."

Eva glanced at Morris before shyly extending her hand for the man to shake. "It's lovely to meet you Mr Williams."

"And you Miss Madden. Where has Morris been hiding you all these months?"

"There's been no hiding, Paul. But sometimes it is wise to keep your cards close to your chest," interrupted

Morris, continuing the joking tone of his boss. The men all laughed at this as Morris went around the group introducing Eva. More than one of the men and their partners made comments about her being Morris's mystery woman.

"No wonder he's been so much easier to get along with since he got back from his last trip to New Zealand," remarked one, while another suggested that she had saved his marriage by keeping Morris from dragging him off to the theatre or out for a drink after work.

Mr Williams stepped back into the conversation at that point. "Perhaps now he has you to keep him here Miss Madden, he'll settle here properly and stop these overseas trips to New Zealand to see his sister, and to London for the theatre. Either the man is secretly heir to a large fortune, or I pay him too much for the time he's here. I tell you he spends more on travel than any man I know."

"Well, you know what they say; it's made round to go round." Another peal of laughter rose up into the warm night air.

For a moment Eva was distracted. How different Morris was from her after all, she thought to herself. She was determined to save all her money in case she was ever in a position where she was unable to earn it and Morris apparently spent his as soon as he earned it. If they were so different, could there really be a long-term future for them? But the doubts were quickly swept away as she felt his reassuring arm on her back, gently directing her toward other acquaintances. Her attention now returned to the social niceties, Eva quickly got over her nerves at meeting Morris's colleagues. After all, she'd watched how people behaved in these sorts of situations all her life and none of these people knew she was a domestic and not born to the situation she now found herself in.

The evening grew very warm with thunder rumbling over the mountains but there was no sign of rain as they made their way to the dance floor. Eva remembered the first night that she had danced with Morris aboard the *Niagara*,

The Price

the memories of that eventful voyage flooding back to her, calming her and allowing herself to fully enjoy the evening.

All doubts gone again, she could now only think how right she had been about Morris! How lucky she was to have met him. Here was a generous, affectionate man who treated her like a lady and who was respected and liked by the people he worked with. Yet caution held her back from fully committing herself to him. She wasn't sure why. It wasn't that he was spender and she a saver, but something inside told her to hold something back. Morris sensed her apprehension, encouraging her to enjoy herself and just let go and live in the moment.

The music and supper completed a wonderful time, and for the rest of her life Eva would recall the lights, the dancing, the laughter and joy of being with the man she loved in his native environment. Suddenly their relationship didn't just exist on the Niagara any more, where all that counted was what went on between each other. It had fully emerged and they were a public couple. It was a strange feeling and one that made her a little nervous, but she no longer had any fears about Morris's intentions. He had made them clear before all the people who mattered to him. She felt his integrity wouldn't let him do that if she was just a passing fancy.

As the magical evening drew to a close Eva realised she wanted to visit the other end of the park once again and even find the big tree from her first visit.

"I want to see my tree."

"What?"

"My tree. At the other end of the park. Can we, Morris? Can we go there before you drive me back to Shaughnessy?'

"In the dark? I'm not even sure we'll be able to find it without even moonlight."

Her face dropped and then he broke down. "How can I resist that face? Come on then, we'll make an adventure of it, but if we get lost Eva Madden, you'll be sleeping in the car till morning!"

He may have tried to look stern, but Eva could see the smile in his eyes and could tell he was as keen on the adventure as she was. So they bid goodnight to Morris's friends and headed for the car before driving away from the bright lights and towards the dark forest, silent and primeval. Yet Eva felt no fear of the dark, of getting lost, or even of bears, the constant silly fear she had whenever she was away from city streets in Vancouver. The same fear that Morris teased her about so mercilessly.

Finally stopping the car, they walked arm in arm over deep layers of old leaves, moss and bracken and into the forest itself. With the lack of light it was a place of shadows and the tree trunks resembled a great army, each with a memory, each with a life of its own. At last she found the great giant she was looking for and leant on its massive trunk.

"Don't laugh at me Morris, but this tree helps me make sense of my whole existence. It makes me seem very small and unimportant. Whenever I feel overwhelmed by my worries I just think of how this tree has endured and I realise that the things that seem too big for me are not so significant. Now, what is it my brother always says? 'We are only stepping stones of thought.' That's right, isn't it Morris. That's all we are."

Sometimes Morris had no answer when Eva talked like this. In any case, he sensed that she didn't need him to answer. He knew that she'd had a wonderful time tonight, but that something inside her had also shifted, that she'd learned something about herself. He'd probably put her in a new situation tonight, but it was only what he knew she could cope with. So he was silent, just standing back and admiring her strength and determination and ability to adapt to the changes in her life.

Their quiet thoughts were rudely interrupted by a flash and ear shattering bang as high above the forest, born in the mountains and spreading rapidly, came a storm so vicious and unrelenting that it caught them both by surprise.

The rain hadn't reached them yet, giving them time to run for the car. The trees, which only a few moments before had seemed so peaceful, were lit up by forked lightning and began to thrash in the rising wind.

The branches began to crack ominously, causing them to run even harder, Maurice holding Eva's hand, trying to help her as she struggled on the uneven ground in her formal dress and evening slippers. They managed to reach the car just as the rain hit. Huge, fat drops that were so loud on the roof of the car made conversation almost impossible. They could barely see through the windscreen and Eva was frightened.

"Morris, maybe we ought to stay here until the rain clears a bit," she shouted.

"We can't! We need to get back to the city. This rain could set in and we'd never get the car out. Besides, we need to get away from these trees in case any of them catch fire in the lightening or fall on the car. I'll go slow I promise," he shouted back.

As carefully as he could, Morris made his way into the city to meet a scene of utter devastation. The roads were already flooded. Everyone was hurrying to the safety of their homes.

"Morris, is this normal? Does it happen often, like once a year or so?"

"Eva, this is a once in a lifetime storm. I've never seen anything like it. In fact, I doubt anyone living here would. I need to get you home and then head in to the office. Hopefully we can still get cables in and out, but this is big."

"Morris, I'm scared and I want to go with you."

"Eva, you'll just be watching me work. You'll be safe at home. The Dalton's is on a sloping block and Shaughnessy is hilly enough that there won't be any flooding there. And your room is far enough from trees that you don't have to worry about trees falling on the house or anything. You're much better off there and I won't have to worry about you. Think Eva, I know you understand."

Of course she did. She'd spent her life putting work and duty first. What had she been thinking? "Of course you're right. I'm sorry, I should have thought."

"Don't be sorry, my lovely girl. I'm sorry our evening had to end like this. I had planned to take you back to the office, you know. But now this has happened, well plans change."

Once Eva was safely back at the Daltons, Morris made his way to his office, carefully weaving through the storm damaged streets. The more he saw of it, the more he realised that it was an exceptional storm and he needed to record its progress. His article was the first to be read in the newspaper the following day. Overnight he had received cables from across Canada and America reporting the loss of fifty lives, injury to many people and property damage costing thousands of dollars.

The Vancouver summer passed quickly into autumn. Or 'fall', as Emily was quick to correct Eva. Shaughnessy was a blaze of colour, the pavements coloured for days by the falling leaves. Morris had long planned to make up for the evening that had been ruined by the great storm. And as Eva reminded him more than once, she had seen little outside the city. He would have liked to take her for a week away on Vancouver Island or up to the mountains, but after taking so much time off for his last trip to New Zealand, more modest plans would have to be the order of the day.

One of his friends at the office owned a small fishing cabin on the shores of Browning Lake about an hour's drive north from Vancouver. From here Morris and his friend had trekked through the mountains on several occasions in the past before the snow and ice of winter made the area impassable. The cabin was well stocked with tinned and powdered food, the supply of firewood had already been chopped and laid up against the house and a small boat was pulled up just in front. It was rustic, but he knew that Eva would enjoy a few days alone, and the fresh air with nothing in particular to do would be good for her. He managed to keep his plans secret until the last few days while he made careful preparations for the trip. When he finally announced the details, Eva clapped her hands like a child.

"Morris, do you think it will be too cold for walks and maybe a picnic by the lake? Or could we even visit Shannon Falls? The Daltons told me all about it and I've been dreaming of seeing them. What do you think, can we?"

"Hold on Eva, we have four days left before we leave, four days in which to make plans." Then he added in a whisper, "Besides, we might get there and you may not want to get out of bed!"

That made her smile. Visits to the office had been few and too far between recently.

"I'll pick you up early on Friday and we'll drive back at our leisure on Monday. By the way, I've already asked Mr Dalton if you can have this time."

"You've already talked to him? You have put some planning into this! Who else knows?"

"Only the cook. And probably the scullery maid. You know those two are as thick as thieves! Then there's the nanny. Who probably told the gardener!" His shoulders were shaking by now and the laughter was evident in his voice. "Seriously, I would have liked a full week but I just can't take that much time off. Everyone would miss me too much. I'm popular you see!" He laughed when he saw the look of dismay on Eva's face. "Eva Madden! When will you learn when I'm joking? But seriously, we do have until Monday for our holiday and we shall just have to fill our hours so that our four days feel like a week!"

Eva found her excitement hard to contain for the next few days and when Friday finally arrived she was more than ready and packed the car with warm clothes, knitted woollen hats and scarves and strong shoes, all essentials with winter closing in. By the third week in October days were short and mornings icy cold.

As they drove north, Eva exclaimed at the first

dustings of snow on the mountains. Soon they were beyond Vancouver and heading for Britannia Beach. The roadside showed signs of landslides but the scenery was breathtaking as their route wound along Howe Sound and past small inland lakes and streams too numerous to count. They entered Murrin Provincial Park, reaching the waters of Browning Lake, which almost lapped the roadside. Morris stopped the car and studied his friend's directions while Eva stared at the incredible scenery and then back at Morris.

Reaching out, she touched his face. "Thank you, thank you Morris. When I first left the *Niagara* this is what I imagined lay beyond Vancouver. I don't actually have words to describe a place as beautiful as this."

Morris turned to look at Eva. He was alarmed for a moment to see there were tears on her cheeks, then realised what was going on. She was, after all, a girl from Crewe, an industrial town in Northern England. He handed Eva his handkerchief. "I love you Eva. I understand why you're crying. It's this place, it's all so much more than us and makes you feel tiny and insignificant. Whenever I've been here I've felt like I should whisper. Like there is no space here for human voices. I'm not religious but if there is a God ..." His voice trailed away. Hugging Eva tightly to his chest, he kissed the top of her head and then her cold nose. "Well, we're as close as the car is going to get us. Now I'm afraid we have a short walk to our little log cabin."

Eva silently trudged after him down the path that led alongside the still lake. In the few days since Morris had told her where they were going, she'd taken the time to find out as much as she could about Browning Lake. She was amazed because everything she'd read in the Dalton's library had said it was just a shallow lake, but as she looked at the water, she couldn't believe that. It looked so dark and deep and as infinite and old as everything else around her. Finally, in a clearing she saw the log cabin set back amongst the trees, with its door opening onto the water and the small rowing boat moored to a log on the edge of the lake.

The Price

"Well Eva, what do you think? Not quite the usual houses you live in, but do you think you can stand it for four days?"

Eva ran forward, opening the door to their first 'home'. She couldn't help laughing with delight as she peered inside to see the open fireplace, the wooden bed and the rough table.

"Stop, Eva Madden! Stop right there!"

Morris dropped the bags and coats, ran forward and lifted Eva into the air. He whirled her round several times, then cradled her in his arms and carried her into the gloom of the cabin. Standing in front of him, pale faced and solemn, Eva said the strangest thing.

"Morris, I am the *Lady of the Lake* you know. I am the *Lady of Shalot*. This is my lake. Tomorrow you must row me out and we can look back at our little house, knowing that I will return to it with you. Then I'll tell you the whole story. But believe me, this is my lake!"

That night the cabin walls danced with shadows cast from the log fire. Eva lay sleeping as Morris slipped from their bed to put another log on the fire. From the fireplace he turned and looked at her. One small hand lay on the folded coat she was using as a pillow, the palm open and relaxed. He crept closer to examine her face. Her mouth was slightly open and she breathed very softly. Small curls rested on her temples.

"Who is she? I really know so little about this woman I love," he said softly to himself. Then he got up, wrapped a blanket around himself and stepped outside. A full moon lit up the clearing. Nothing moved. The lake was a piece of glass and the stars were reflected in the water. The rowing boat was just an outline.

Creeping inside he slipped into bed with Eva, awakening her with kisses. No words were spoken during their lovemaking but afterwards Morris leant over her. "Eva, I love you completely." She smiled, snuggling up to him and they slept.

Rising late the next morning, they went about their day at leisure, finally taking the boat out on the lake for three hours. Morris rowed near to the banks, not risking the deeper ice-cold waters. Occasionally they saw a fish and Morris thought how different this trip was because of Eva. If he'd been here with men, the fish wouldn't have stood a chance and it would have been rowdy and somehow insulting to the surroundings. But today the silence was palpable.

Then he remembered the strange *Lady of the Lake* business from the afternoon before. "So, we're out on the lake now. How about you tell me why you're the *Lady of the Lake*. I mean, looking at you here now, you're quite probably the only lady anywhere near the lake, but there's more to this story. And who is the *Lady of Shalott?*"

"The *Lady of Shalott* lived in Betley Mere, in the grounds of Betley Hall. Our Dad used to take us there on Sunday afternoons. Mostly to get us out of the house because Mam was pregnant and needed a break, but for us it was the best time of the week. We were outdoors with our Dad and he talked to us about the animals and birds, even all the plants. Now I look back and realise how hard it must have been for someone who loved nature as much as him to work on the railways. Coming here reminds me of him somewhat and I think that's part of why I've been a bit emotional about this place."

Morris pulled in the oars and let the boat drift as he listened silently to Eva's story. It was the first time she'd ever said anything of significance about her childhood and he wasn't about to interrupt.

"Dad made up magical stories about everything we saw. Anyway, our favourite place to go was Betley Mere. Our Dad taught us how to skim stones there. And we'd run and skip and sing until our little legs only had enough strength to carry us home and up to bed." Morris smiled, encouraging her to go on. "One day he told us a story about the *Lady of Shalot*, the *Lady of the Lake*. He said that the flowers waving in the breeze were like magical flags waving to welcome her home. He also told us that if we touched as much of ourselves as a toe in the mere, we'd never see her, which we all desperately wanted to do. Our Dad said that she was so beautiful that men fainted at the sight of her!"

"Well, if the *Lady of the Lake* is a renowned beauty and you are the *Lady of the Lake*, then I agree completely." And then he pretended to faint in the boat, closing his eyes, clutching his hand to his chest and slumping backwards.

Eva laughed. "Morris Miller, don't tease me! Or you shall also discover that the *Lady of Shalot* has quite a temper! Besides, unless you recover yourself, we'll be stuck out here forever, because the *Lady of the Lake* rows for no one!"

With that he opened one eye and laughed. "You are indeed my *Lady of the Lake*. Now, I want a kiss before I row us back."

"Oh, but there's more! When I was a child I always thought I was the *Lady of Shalot*, and then when I got to Panama on the way to New Zealand I noticed a lake and a road called Madden. There, I finally had proof. My friend's son, who I'd told the story to, declared me to be the *Lady of the Lake*."

"Your own a lake in Panama? Now that is impressive. I'm not sure there would be a Miller Lake anywhere to match it."

"Morris, they were some of the happiest days I had as a child. Things were never as good again. But on those afternoons, I couldn't imagine life any other way. Dad taught us the Lady's song and we'd skip around the edge of the water singing it." Then her voice sounded quietly across the still water. *'When day is done, and gone the sun, remember me.'*

"Eva that's lovely. I'm glad you told me. And now, Browning Lake, even though its name is hardly as romantic as Betley Mere, will be our lake and you shall be the Lady of this Lake."

"Completely. Now do as the song says and

remember. Remember me, remember us, remember today. Keep it in your memory like a photograph. Because this is truly the happiest I've ever been since those Sunday afternoons at Betley Mere and you made it happen Morris. To make someone else this happy is truly a precious gift."

"Only when compared with the gift of happiness that has been given to me Eva. I spend all my days working with words and I don't know what else to say. You make me happy. Thank you for the story." And with that he put the oars back in the water and began rowing again.

As the shadows lengthened they returned to the cabin, once again lighting a fire, as the nights were chilly. They prepared a meal together and then exhausted, they slept without even making love. The following morning they drove to Shannon Falls. The roar of the waterfall was heard as soon as the car's engine stopped and well before they trekked along the rough boardwalk to where they could properly see the falls.

Eva was nervous as she stared upwards at the smooth granite walls over which the water tumbled, making a mighty roar. They were more than fifty feet from the base and the fine spray filled the air and covered the rocks. "Look at the rocks Morris. Completely smoothed from the water. And have you ever seen such a beautiful brown?"

"They're almost as beautiful a brown as your eyes," he replied and hugged her close to him. It was a silly thing to say she knew. But she loved him for it all the same, and smiled. "They might only be a few yards wide, but they're over a thousand feet from top to bottom. And I know the Niagara Falls are more famous, but how can you compare with standing here in a forest and looking up at that falling from the sky?"

"It's beautiful Morris. I can't imagine a more beautiful place."

"Let's see if we can get closer."

There was a rough trail, but it was slippery and they were clinging to each other and almost soaked to the bone before long. Finally the cold forced them to leave. Eva had endured snow in Cheshire winters, but she'd never felt so cold and icy. Clinging together in the car to keep warm, Eva rubbed her hands together.

"Eva, you're freezing."

"Morris, what I need is a winter warmer"

"A what?"

"You know … a winter warmer."

They both burst out laughing.

"I'm your winter warmer Eva, surely." Then he hesitated. "All right, I give up! What is a winter warmer for goodness sake?"

"You don't know?" Morris shook his head and Eva grew serious. "All right, I'll explain. My father first showed me a winter warmer. He gathered up some of the solid Cheshire clay and he made one for us children." Morris now knew to be quiet. Eva rarely spoke of her childhood and this was the second childhood story in two days. He was intrigued.

"Yes." Eva screwed up her eyes remembering the winter day at Betley. It seemed so many years ago. "He made an oblong shape about this big," showing Morris with her hands. "It was about a foot long. Then in the clay, from one end he hollowed out a tunnel half way along the oblong brick. And half way across the flat top he poked a hole into the roof and we gathered small sticks. Then Dad pulled an oily rag from his pocket. Remember, he worked on the railway so he often had things like that in his pockets. Used to drive Mam mad when she'd try to do the washing!" She paused, remembering little Joe and inquisitive Ellen pushing closer to look at the strange object.

"Now, where was I? Ah, the rag. Well, he stuffed the rag and twigs down the chimney and lit it. Then he held it up in the air and ran along the bank with his back to us. Then he turned, running back to us." Instinctively Eva smiled with delight at the memory. "It was glowing dark red from inside and smoke was puffing out through its chimney. He let each of us hold it Morris, and warm our hands on it until my sister dropped it onto the grass and it broke into two halves."

"What happened then?"

"Apart from her bursting into tears? Nothing much. Dad explained that for it to last it had to be baked in an oven or bonfire. Then we could run along the streets holding the winter warmer above our heads."

"I can just imagine you as a little girl running down the street with a flaming pot over your head," he said with a smile she could hear in his voice. "Did you ever make any?"

"Oh yes, I made three, carving them out of clay I got from the soft embankment of Betley Mere. I carried them home. We were covered in mud, all three of us. The winter warmers ended up in the back yard. Mam wouldn't allow them in the house. But it wasn't all bad. My sister had filled her pockets with conkers from underneath the horse chestnut trees. Mother relented, allowing her to bake them in the oven because we were all crying over the destruction of the winter warmers."

Eva grew silent. She realised she'd skirted around the Ellen issue again, referring to her simply as her sister. Such an outburst and recall of memories was very unusual for her and perhaps soon she would be able to tell all about her family. Morris made no further comment and asked no more questions. But later that night he gently teased Eva, asking her if he could be her 'winter warmer'. He grew even closer to her during those few special days. Eva made him promise to return with her to the cabin in the spring.

All too soon their little holiday was over and it was back to town for both of them. And just in time because suddenly the frost arrived and with it a long cold winter which would last for months. The temperature rarely fell below freezing, unlike the remainder of Canada, which froze over for months. Eva was unprepared for such changes as the climate was far more extreme than in New Zealand. Here it seemed to rain without end, even more than she remembered in England. However, she was well and happy and much of her work was indoors.

Making up for the long weekend away, she saw less of Morris for the next couple of weeks and took the opportunity to write to George now she was well and truly settled. Her relationship with Morris was still too special a thing to share, but she knew her brother would be interested in the opportunities in Vancouver and her parents would want to know that she was safe and well.

October 1930, Vancouver

Dear George,

Finally I am settled and in good employment with the Dalton family as I mentioned in my postcard to you. Mr and Mrs Dalton really are excellent employers and have made me housekeeper. That means I supervise the work of the cook, scullery maid, nanny and gardener and the pay is excellent. I have already sent money to New Zealand to be deposited in my account at the post office in Wellington. The Daltons give me plenty of time off and I have used it to explore the city and countryside nearby.
I have become particularly fond of Stanley Park, a very large park of some 1,000 acres in the city. I have also ventured a couple of hours north to Britannia Beach and saw Shannon Falls. I visited Browning Lake recently. George, you would love it. It is peaceful like Betley Mere and reminded me of Sunday afternoons there with Father.
I hope Mother and Father are well and Mother is keeping strong so she does not become ill over winter again. I had intended only staying in Vancouver a short time before resuming my journey across Canada and then home to England, but I am happy here and health problems I had in New Zealand have not shown themselves. So I am going to stay for a while, perhaps a year before resuming my journey. The Canadian Australasian Line say that I can hold my ticket for the rest of the journey almost indefinitely with just

a small annual retainer, so I shan't be wasting the money I paid for the fare.
Give my love to all at home and please let me know of any news regarding Joe and Ellen.
Your loving sister,
Eva

Life was passing happily. She and Morris saw each other when they could. He invented unusual outings around the Vancouver area that delighted her, and they continued to use the bedroom at his office to allow for more private moments. For the first time since she could remember, she felt released from her past and the burden of her family's problems. Nevertheless, she was delighted to receive another letter from George, which kept her in touch with her family so far away, even though it had been posted months before.

August 1930, Crewe.

Dear Eva,

We were all relieved to receive your postcard and to know that you are safe and sound in Vancouver. It looks like a beautiful place. Mother and Father have asked about you so many times. It made them very happy to hear from you. Mother is pleased to hear that you are in full employment.
The family is much the same here. Joseph remains unchanged. It seems that he will remain permanently in hospital.
Ellen has finally decided to move to rented accommodation in Chester where she will be employed as a seamstress. You will be glad to know that she has not suffered a nervous attack for months so we feel less worried about her leaving Crewe.
Tom is going ahead and buying a house. He will marry later this year. Augusta is well settled.
Edith and me are still getting about, but I haven't sold the Aerial yet.

We are experiencing the hottest August days since 1911! It has been 92° today. Men everywhere are without waistcoats and wearing tennis shirts. Girls are without stockings and in Manchester they are working in bathing suits! Unfortunately, I have to wear my overalls for work and by the way, I am now officially a fireman on the steam trains. I've done my apprenticeship as a cleaner. Next step, engine driver.

When we do a double trip to London (and that means we take a passenger train to the city, have time off and then bring another steam train back to Crewe), I spend my few hours off resting in the barracks.

Then to waste some time before the return journey I take a walk around London. Last week I had a meal in a café recommended by some of my work mates. It must be the cheapest place to eat in London. Hundreds of people eat there, a pint of ale, a meat pie, a packet of Woodbines and change out of a sixpence! Is there anywhere in Vancouver that can beat that?

I met up with the Hollis family the other day. They send their best wishes to you. Their uncle and his family have settled somewhere near to a town named Napier so no wonder you couldn't find them at Wellington.

How long are you thinking of staying in Vancouver? You appear to have settled down well but I think you were wise to leave your savings in their original investment in New Zealand.

We know that you are very busy and work long hours but we all look forward to hearing from you,

Best wishes,

Your brother, George.

A Bigger Storm to Weather

Christmas time in Canada was very special, for there was no shortage of Christmas trees. When the young firs and spruce were no longer available, cedar, hemlock, juniper and pine replaced them in peoples' homes. Wherever Eva walked she could spot a tree in every window. Christmas had never been celebrated so grandly in Crewe and it had never seemed quite right in the summer of New Zealand. Eva felt like she was really experiencing it properly for the first time. Listening to the radio in the warmth of the kitchen, Eva thought how lucky she was to have arrived when she did. If she'd waited any longer and not sailed on the *Niagara*, she would never have met Morris. Maybe she would have changed her mind and returned to England without stopping off in Canada. She thought of her last employer in New Zealand, Mrs Abraham who convinced her that Canada was a land of opportunity. She must find time to write to her.

Morris had to visit Victoria to report on a shipping incident whilst Eva had been very preoccupied in her job. It was the first Christmas with the Daltons, which was very important to her, as she wanted the house to run smoothly. Now with Christmas over, it was time to have some time off. Morris returned from Victoria, arranging to meet her. Eva was as excited as a young girl because she sensed that this would be the start of their new life together. But as soon as he arrived, Eva knew that something was terribly wrong. He was downcast and sad, hurrying her to the car and driving away from the house before he spoke.

"Eva my dear. Oh, how do I say this? All day long I work with words and now I have none!"

Eva said nothing, just looked at his stricken face. Finally he began to speak again, his voice filled with emotion.

"Eva, I'm afraid that I need to go away for at least three months. My sister in Hastings has suffered a terrible family tragedy."

"Oh Morris! What's happened?"

"Her husband has been killed in a motorcar accident. She wants to sell up her property and come home with the two children. I need to go and help her. I'm her big brother and the man of the family and she's begged me to help. I hate the thought of leaving you even for such a short time but this is something I have to do."

Eva had a feeling of dread. She loved him. Now she would lose him. She was sure of it. But she had to let him go without feeling guilty. "Morris," she spoke firmly, "of course you have to go. Your family is very important to you. I would do the same for any one of my brothers or my sister. I'll be here waiting for you when you get back in the spring. Maybe I can even travel to Victoria and meet the ship."

She desperately longed to tell him how she really felt. She would go with him. She would return to New Zealand. She would refuse to leave him. But she said none of these things. He needed her to be strong right now and she knew all about duty and doing what was right for others. She loved him and she would support him in what he needed to do. Besides, at a time of such grief, what would his sister think if he suddenly arrived with a stranger? His family needed all his attention and she would let him give it.

That day they drove to the park they both loved. In silence they strolled on the beach at English Bay, silent and empty of holidaymakers. Eva walked along the water's edge, remembering her efforts to paddle up to her knees in the summer time. Looking down, she spotted two white irregular stones at her feet and picked them up. She held them in her hand, rubbing them against each other, just looking at them, seemingly lost in thought. Morris stood at a distance, silently watching her.

Suddenly she looked up and ran over to him. "Let's

go to the big tree! We haven't been there since the storm last July." They returned to the park in silence. Finally reaching their tree, she leaned on the huge trunk and looked up at him.

"Eva, we will miss each other but it may be a comfort to know that whilst I am there I can tie up the ends of my divorce. It is possible that I could return a free man".

"I know Morris. I know what you want to say and the answer is yes. Just come back safely to me and that must be a promise. Don't make any other promises today. They can all wait. Just promise you'll come back safe."

She rolled the two stones in her hand. Then she said the most surprising thing.

"Think of these stones as our hearts. Put them together in the tree as high up as you can reach. Find a little hole in the bark and press them in tightly so that they can never be found."

Morris looked at her quizzically, but didn't speak. He just gently took the stones from her hand and reaching up, did as she had asked. He never questioned why, he knew that would be unwise. Eva never did anything without a reason and he didn't try to analyse her motives.

From his pocket he took a little red box. He handed it to Eva. "Wear this and remember our love, Eva. Always. It's simple. It cost very little but I want you to have it now."

Shyly she snapped the box open. The little silver Celtic ring fitted perfectly onto her wedding finger. Then he lifted her hand and kissed it.

"Wait for me. I'll be back very soon and then we'll think of more fancy rings. You are the most important person in the world to me, Eva. We will spend the rest of our lives together. So don't cry. We have something together that the world must envy. We just have to wait a little longer."

"I know Morris. I know what we have is rare and very precious. But, oh God!" The tears started to well up in her eyes. "I'm going to miss you so much," she managed to get out before a sob caught in her throat.

Morris looked down at her, knowing the vulnerability, which came with loving someone. "Eva, I must go. I have to leave soon". His voice had changed. Emotions were being hidden by practical details. This was a Morris she hadn't seen until now but like her, he had found ways with which to cope with difficult decisions.

Within two weeks he was gone, his passage booked on the *Niagara*, comforting Eva in some strange way. During those last few days they grew a little distant from each other for necessity's sake, each making the temporary parting easier to bear.

As she saw the ship off, she thought how he would walk the same decks where they had walked. Everywhere he would be surrounded by their memories. More than that, she would be able to trace his journey in her mind, and imagine what he would be seeing, imagine him reading his newspaper in Suva, leading the conversation at dinner, rocking to sleep in his cabin. Determined not to grow miserable, she returned home to work hard and wait.

Her sickness started suddenly and without warning. As she tried to stifle the noise of her vomiting when she woke each morning, she couldn't help but feel great joy. She knew that she was pregnant. Morris's child, their child, would be born in that year, and he would be so happy, she just knew it. She told no one but paid to see a doctor. As she travelled back from the appointment she no longer felt lonely. Within her was the seed of their passion, their love. How could this be?

She'd decided so long ago to never have children that it was hard to comprehend. She just hadn't included children into her daydreams about her future. She'd always worried that they'd be like Ellen or Joe, but how could any child conceived out of the sort of love she and Morris shared possibly be like that? She allowed herself to dream of a perfect future for the first time in her life.

She was convinced that Morris would know of their

child. She knew that he was thinking of her, missing her, longing to be back with her. Like a child, she imagined that if she thought hard enough about the baby, or even other things they'd shared, that maybe Morris would know what she was thinking. Every time she found herself floating off on one of these fantasies, she pulled herself back, thinking about how ridiculous she was. Then a few minutes later she'd be telling herself to just let go of the practical for once in her life and just enjoy what was magical.

Every day she waited for a letter, knowing that mail from the islands would be slow. She grew more anxious as the days went by, scanning the newspapers for any information on New Zealand. Even snippets about the weather made her feel closer to him.

On the 7th February she saw on the billboard outside the general store the startling headlines. Her heart lurched and she felt weak all over. Somehow she managed to find the strength to run into the store and buy a paper but the report was very brief.

'The catastrophe is the greatest calamity that the Dominion has ever experienced. Napier flattened, hundreds dead.'

Eva tried to calm herself, reasoning that Morris was staying in Hastings at least twelve miles away where it was perfectly flat. Surely it hadn't affected Hastings?

Reaching the Dalton house, she rushed to the kitchen and turned on the radio. Once again there was very little mention of the disaster. The news simply gave out facts. Eva listened, feeling sick but remaining hopeful. Nothing could take away their happiness now. She felt certain of it. Or was that just wishful thinking? She remembered how she felt when Morris first told her that he was going back to New Zealand that she was going to lose him. Then she'd decide that she was panicking and that Morris would find a way to get a cable to his office and they'd call the house with a cheery message for her.

The next news broadcast had more information:

> 'No one is allowed to visit Napier. The Salvation Army is supplying fresh vegetables, sugar and flour. In Park Island cemetery a huge pit for a mass grave had to be blown out with explosives, as the ground was too hard to dig. Fifty-two coffins were lowered in. Communication to the outside world had taken four days as all lines had been cut. The tremors are still continuing.'

Still no mention of Hastings. That was good wasn't it? Eva turned off the radio, slumping onto a chair at the kitchen table. That is how the cook found her. Soon the entire household was alerted to the tragedy, Mr Dalton ringing around to his contacts to see if there was new information. Eva called the newspaper office to see what they knew, if Morris had been able to get a message out.

"All we know is what's printed in the paper, Eva. We've had no news from him and reporters can't get in there. The only news is coming from some of the army and Salvation Army people who have delivered relief supplies. No names of the dead have been released by the government officially and they're not even sure all of the dead have been found yet. But I will get a message to you as soon as I hear anything."

The news was terrifying to Eva. More news came through the next day:

> '... Even the land along the edge of the sea has risen from between three and eight feet. Further tremors continue to shake the entire area, levelling many of the old wooden buildings, shops and offices. The Nurses' Home, Technical College, Public Library are all gone. Scientists estimate that the floor of the ocean has risen eighteen feet three miles offshore. Witnesses described huge mushroom shaped clouds that appeared over Napier and Hastings as the earthquake destroyed buildings.'

She paced the kitchen, unable to rest or eat. Where was Morris? A hideous nightmare began to build inside Eva's head. Was he trapped, pinioned or choked? Was he somewhere bleeding to death? Was he caught under a girder? She heard news of one man. He had been found wandering miles away from Napier, having lost his memory. He wasn't Morris. She contacted his newspaper office each day, sometimes twice. But there was no news. It appeared that the whole world was now aware of the disaster, but knew little of the specifics about the fate of the people caught in the disaster zone. Condolences and help poured into New Zealand.

For days Eva heard nothing. And then weeks without word. Even the newspaper had been unable to find him. The editor, Mr Williams hadn't the heart to tell her that they'd given up hope and had even held an office wake for him. He would tell Eva nothing until Morris was officially confirmed among the dead.

Finally, Mr Williams himself appeared without notice at the front door of the Dalton's house. As soon as she saw his face Eva knew what he brought. She found it difficult to reach out and take the envelope from his hand, feeling as though it contained poison. She put on her most professional manner, learned from years of exposure to the seemingly emotionless British upper class, as she found her voice to invite Mr Williams in for refreshment in the kitchen.

But he could hear Eva's voice quiver and knew the invitation for what it was. His voice was full of concern. "I can't be staying Miss Madden." He paused a moment before adding, "But will you be all right? Is there someone here so you're not alone?"

He couldn't understand that being alone was a state of being for Eva. She could be forever be surrounded by people, but still essentially be alone. The secrets she'd been forced to keep since childhood kept her locked in her loneliness, a condition only briefly broken by Morris. No,

The Price

she needed to read this letter in solitude.

She cleared her throat a little before speaking again. "Thank you Mr Williams, but I shall be fine. And thank you for taking the time to bring the letter yourself. I know you are a very busy man."

Their terrible business now at an end, neither knew what to say to the other and there was a moment of awkward silence before Eva remembered her training and said, "Goodbye Mr Williams. Thank you again." And she closed the door and walked away from its glass panes until she could lean upon the wall for a moment and catch her breath before beginning the walk upstairs to her room.

Mr Williams meanwhile stood motionless on the step for a few moments not knowing what else he could do. His relationship with this woman consisted of one meeting and a few phone calls over the past couple of weeks and yet Morris Miller had been his friend and he knew that he had intended to marry Eva Madden as soon as possible after returning from New Zealand. He should do something, but was at a loss to imagine what, so he slowly turned and walked the short path to the front gate and drove away, leaving Eva alone in her grief.

Eva reached her room and sat on her bed, her hands shaking as she turned the letter over and over in her hands. It was addressed simply to *Miss Eva Madden, c/- The Daltons, Shaughnessy*, Vancouver. There was no stamp but Eva supposed that it had been mailed inside a larger envelope, probably to Mr Williams at the paper. She looked at it for maybe half an hour, thinking irrationally while there was no written proof, that perhaps Morris wasn't dead. Finally she carefully tore open the edge and slowly pulled the letter from the envelope.

5 February 1931, Hastings.

My Dear Eva,

Forgive me for addressing you in such a familiar way, but that is how my brother Morris always spoke of you, 'My little Eva' or 'My dear Eva'. How often he talked about you and your future life together. Now it is left to me to tell you the terrible news. There is no easy way, though surely by the time this letter reaches you, you will already have heard what I feel it is my duty to tell you.

My brother went in my car to the main street in Hastings at 10am on that awful morning, the 3rd February, to collect some groceries. When the earthquake struck, he was coming out of the store to reach his car. The pavement caved in and the front wall of the store collapsed into the street.

He was trapped among the debris. Shock after shock occurred. Many people were entombed under the buildings. As I write, his body is not yet recovered, but there is no question that he died.

As you can imagine, I am grief stricken here alone with my two children. I have lost my beloved brother only a few months after my husband. I brought Morris out here to his death and my grief threatens to overwhelm me, so I will soon be making plans to return to my parents in Seattle and leave behind this country that has taken two such precious things from me.

Eva, I want you to know that I have never seen my brother so happy as when he came over. We have all been aware of his unhappy marriage for a number of years and happy for my dear brother for finally he had found someone very special. You were the most special person in the world to him my dear. Having lost my husband so recently, I truly understand how you feel and my heart and prayers go out to you. It is a very difficult thing to come to terms with, but we must all try one way or another. I intend to tell my parents and brothers about you Eva. They would want to know how happy you made him. I have enclosed my parents' address in Seattle, should you wish to get in touch with them. It is only a short journey from Vancouver and we should all very much like to meet you.

I hope you don't mind me writing to you care of the newspaper, but I didn't know how else to contact you and didn't want you, who Morris loved so much, to receive the news via a telegram or messenger boy from the paper.

Take care my dear. Morris loved you so much that you must surely be a very special person. You changed his life.

Yours,
Margaret Bowden.

Eva folded the letter, storing it away at the bottom of her trunk. It was an unreal situation. She felt numb. There were no tears. But as the hours went on, she felt the pain in her stomach grow, almost as though someone had ripped out her innards and replaced them with a huge weight that seemed to get harder and heavier with each passing hour.

She would never contact Morris's relatives or mention him again she decided. The way that she could cope would be by hiding her memories away along with those of Joe and Ellen. She knew how to do that and it would be the only way. It was strange. She'd been so busy spending all her spare time with Morris that the letter she'd been intending to write to George about him, but never had time, would now never have to be written. She'd never be able to explain what he meant to her, so better not to say anything at all.

For days Eva remained in a state of shock. It manifested itself in long bouts of total silence. She ate nothing and seemed to sustain herself with endless cups of tea. The heaviness she now felt in her stomach prevented her from eating. A huge weight loss and a sadness about her was visible to the few friends she had in Vancouver. She received a letter from Paul Williams, Morris's editor, but couldn't even open it. She put it away at the bottom of her trunk with the letter from Morris's sister and tried to put it out of her mind.

She could not come to terms with Morris's death, expecting him to return, telephone the house or even simply turn up. Then she was angry at everything and everyone around her. She questioned the unfairness of it all. She had found another human being to share her thoughts and passion with, to eventually live the remainder of their lives together and all that had been taken away. She had nothing, she was nothing, empty and meaningless and not understood.

With Morris's help, she had stepped out of her isolation, ceasing to be an observer. He'd shown her the world and that she had a place in it. Now, how could she go back to being subservient little Eva? The way forward was a mystery to her. She'd invested all her plans in Morris's return and living her life beside him. What would she possibly do with her life now?

A partial answer lay as usual in her work. Household duties and routine gave her the sanity and distraction that she craved. She felt at times that she was one step away from the madness she feared so much. In her soul she joined those dark unravelled thoughts that tightened around her sister Ellen and had choked her brother Joe. She could not escape her fate. For a brief moment she was shown real happiness. Now it had been taken away forever. He could not be replaced.

Four weeks after the letter that changed her life arrived from New Zealand, she awoke with her bed soaked with blood. The baby, their baby, was leaving her. "How could it have lived with her sadness?" she thought. She'd barely given it a passing thought as she'd grieved for Morris, and she'd given it no nourishment to sustain it.

Nevertheless, its departure was acknowledged with tears. Eva accepted its death as part of her enormous loss. First one, and now the other. She wanted to follow. She could not remember spring or summer. She rarely left the house and retired to her room at every opportunity. The household felt her numbness and pain. The wall of privacy she built around her and maintained at all times forbade them to ask how she was. Often she found herself talking to him, sometimes aloud. The domestic staff commented among themselves as they heard her muttering. They were far too fond of her to ask her about her grief, but watched over her carefully.

The cook considered writing to her family. But then they all realised with dismay that none of them actually knew of any family details regarding Eva, except that she had a brother who occasionally wrote to her. Nobody even knew his address. So they kept their distance, hoping that she would eventually recover.

With relief, Mr Dalton finally handed her a letter from England. He hoped this might be a catalyst. Maybe it would trigger off a release of the emotions that had been kept in check with such iron discipline. He was finally retiring from the export business, but impressed upon Eva the continued need for a housekeeper. Her sense of duty and work ethic were rare. He was anxious not to lose her, unless it was to return home to the sanctuary of her family.

She read the letter in disbelief. What had she been thinking of? She had a family in England and she had cut herself off completely from them. She had ceased to think of them. She had remembered no one as the depression within her had deepened.

June 1931, Crewe.

Dear Eva,
It seems so long since we heard from you. We can only imagine that you are busy, involved in your new work looking after the Dalton family.
We are all fine, apart from Joseph. He grows steadily worse. None of us have visited. I know this is a terrible thing but appearances by family could precipitate another stupor and

doctors have advised us not to visit.

Of course, I have been to Chester and checked with the doctor. There is no change for the better. I am resigned to the fact that Joe will remain in the asylum for the rest of his life. We were all shocked to hear about the terrible earthquake back in New Zealand and so relieved that you were well away from the place. There was much talk of it here. Several people that you know stopped me in the street and asked where you were. It is such a relief to know that you are in Canada.

I will try and give you some of the news since I last wrote to you. Imagine our surprise when we experienced an earth tremor here in England! It was unbelievable and frightened a good many people.

It happened on June 8th at around 1:30am lasting for over half an hour. It was felt over most of England and Scotland! People rushed out into the streets yelling and screaming. In parts of Crewe, as in other towns and cities, chimneys and walls came crashing down. According to the latest bulletin it was the worst shock ever experienced in the history of the British Isles. Did you hear anything of this in Vancouver?

Back in March, I was reminded of the dangers associated with the railways although I have never experienced a rail crash myself. Sadly I lost a good friend when the 'Royal Scot' left the rails at Leighton during a blizzard. There were six killed and many injured. On the railway we are proud of our safety record and this has been a blow to all of us.

March was a very cold month and we experienced the heaviest snowfall this last winter. Traffic was held up owing to ice and snow in parts of Cheshire and Yorkshire. There were six-foot snowdrifts.

On a more cheerful note, I was at Paddington in February waiting for a run back to Crewe when I heard that Charlie Chaplin would be arriving on the next train! I stayed with the crowds and managed to see him from a distance. It was quite a moment.

The working class of this country love him. I think they see

little bits of themselves in his films. The grinding poverty shown in his films has been experienced by a large number of them, particularly in the twenties.
Edie says to tell you that the latest fashion here is the wearing of longer skirts. She says it reflects Victorian fashions. She wants to know if you wear furs in Vancouver. She still has her hair in a bob even though I prefer it to be a little longer. Mother is well again now but this last winter she suffered another bout of bronchitis, which laid her up for two months. Write and tell us how you are getting along. I hope your savings are growing. I heard a good quote the other day; 'The best way to spend money now is to save it'.

Hopefully, we will see you soon.
Best wishes,
George.

Now it ended, the loss finally acknowledged with tears, longing and such sadness, but at least she would be able to contact her family once again, telling them nothing of the events, for they knew nothing. There was no need to share such awful grief. She stayed in her room for hours, the tears finally coming in floods, the household leaving her alone until she felt ready to rejoin them. She made several attempts at writing the letter, hardly able to disguise her feelings. At last she managed to put together some of her thoughts.

September 1931, Vancouver.

Dear George,

At last I have had the will power to sit down and write to you. I have been so busy adapting to my new life here and so selfish in not replying to your last letter.
I am fine and well, enjoying life here in Canada. Spring and summer have come and gone so quickly.

Now it is autumn as it will be with you in England. It is called 'the fall' here. You can see why when you walk along the tree lined streets. The trees are ablaze with reds, yellows and oranges. Everywhere the leaves are falling in advance of a long cold winter.
I was very interested to hear about the earthquake in England as I received no news of this beforehand. I was preoccupied with the news of the terrible quake in New Zealand. Several of my friends from Auckland wrote to me about it. We just never know when the entire pattern of our life can change, do we?
Your winter sounded terrible and also the train accident. Our winters here are not too bad. We don't usually get the very heavy snow experienced inland but we do have very thick fog, which rolls in from the Pacific. Then we hear the foghorn, a melancholy sound that warns all the shipping.
We are presently enjoying tinned fruit that has been imported from Australia. For the first time, we're tasting peaches and apricots, ¾ million of tins of it have come into Canada according to the cook. She is having a wonderful time inventing new recipes!
Unfortunately, Canada will stop the airmail service in Western Canada. It will resume when conditions are different and methods more advanced.
I think it is the same the world over. As you said George in one of your previous letters, once airplanes can make the longer journeys, this will not be a problem. None of us will feel far away.
Send my best wishes to everyone.
I have not yet decided how long I will remain in Canada. I do not envisage a time longer than five years but do not tell mother of this as I am still not sure of my plans. I think everything at home will be much changed when I return.

With best wishes,
Eva.

There, she thought to herself. That's what they want to

The Price

hear. Happy stories about how good my life is abroad. That life is not a struggle away from the dirty, close little streets of Crewe.

Picking up the Pieces

Winter came in early that year. By November, the Yukon[36] River had stopped running and would remain frozen until the following May, but Eva barely seemed to notice as she went about her duties. She returned to her old habit of working and saving, taking very little time off. Even then she only walked a little way from the house. Nagging at the back of her mind was the place she knew she had to visit, but the time was not yet right. The truth was that she just couldn't bring herself to go anywhere that had been a part of her life with Morris. She was barely functioning by keeping up a façade. She couldn't risk it cracking even slightly.

Christmas of 1931 passed by in a flurry of activity. Last year Christmas had delighted her, but this year Eva took no part. She was the observer, looking in on the lighted windows as she returned from her walks. She battled loneliness but this time it was worse than ever before because it was in contrast to the deep happiness she had felt briefly and would never feel again. She was guilt ridden. On many occasions she cursed God for his indifference to her suffering. Then she cursed herself for her weakness and intolerance.

In March 1932, smallpox broke out in Vancouver resulting in seven deaths and twenty-two more cases notified. Citizens were called upon to be vaccinated at once. Eva read in the paper that the Niagara, expected in Auckland within a week, was late due to strict scrutiny. Painfully, she recalled the times aboard the ship during her voyage to Canada. Now everything had changed and she felt no joy when she thought about her own journey on the ship.

She seriously considered not bothering to attend

---
[36] Flows through Alaska, Yukon and British Columbia.

the town hall for the vaccination program. Mr Dalton anticipated this and put her in charge of Emily, who was terrified of the entire procedure. In order to convince the little girl that she was not about to catch the disease through the needle, Eva went ahead of her for the vaccination. Then she held Emily's hand as she received hers. She explained the importance of this step to the young girl, pointing out that one day there would be a way of immunising people against many diseases. They should be thankful for the advancement of medical science, providing protection against such terrible diseases as smallpox and diphtheria.

Emily knew only too well the horrors of such diseases as her youngest brother had died of diphtheria. She trusted Eva, proud to be out in the city with her. Seizing the opportunity to talk in confidence, Emily questioned Eva on many things, including the existence of God. What did Eva think about such things? She emphasised to the wide-eyed Emily that it was really up to every individual to believe as they wished, despite the strong guidance of the church. She did not feel guilty about influencing the girl. She knew that Emily had a sharp mind and would eventually find her own way in life.

Emily had already decided to travel, and her first adventure would be in England where she proudly told Eva she hoped to find work in Cheshire. She begged Eva to talk once again about her childhood in Crewe. Soon they were back in Shaughnessy, the vaccination long forgotten and both cheerful in each other's company.

Eva's depression had slowly begun to lift. Memories of Morris were guarded and treasured but the remainder of her time in Canada was not so painful. She had realised that no matter what she did in her life, she would have to live with her past, taking the good with the bad. She'd tried to stop time when she grieved so desperately for Morris and it hadn't worked. Just like trying to ignore her family and their problems. It couldn't be done. She couldn't shut the world out. She needed to come to terms with it and move forward.

Picking up the Pieces

She would never leave behind those grim meal times, the hollow feeling of hopelessness when she visited her sister in the lunatic asylum or the look on Joe's face when she told him that she was leaving for New Zealand. But there were also the half remembered memories of her mother and father in their bedroom when Joe was born and the candle flickering in the bedroom window as she lay awake at dawn with her arms protectively wrapped around Ellen. These good memories would also remain with her forever, keeping balance with the bad ones.

She would always carry with her Morris's love. She wouldn't ever completely get over his loss, but the good memories could sustain her. All her memories were treasured, even Joe's. It was an enormous and intricate pattern where no part could be lifted out or changed. It was her fate. She had no choice but to move forward and accept it. She knew that she was living a life of restlessness. Her journey home would reveal to her whether or not she was displaced. She would find out whether she could live out the remainder of her life in Cheshire or continue to travel. She longed to be settled, but maybe it wasn't for her.

Her brother's letter arrived just two days before Eva's 36th birthday, bringing welcome news of her family in Crewe.

August 2nd, 1932

Dear Eva,

Sorry about the long time in writing but we all get caught up in our day-to-day living. Mother has repeatedly asked after you. I am ashamed to say that you are owed a letter from me! The family is all well apart from Joe whose condition remains unchanged. Ellen is working in Chester. She makes monthly visits home much to our parents' relief.
You will find a very different homeland. The motorcar has had a big effect on this country. Even the gypsies who settle

on the spare land just outside Betley village have abandoned their horses for battered old cars!

I am thinking of buying a car myself but will probably join forces with Tom and go halves. He is very good at the mechanics of the engine. We have discussed the idea at length.

There is much saving to do. First we hope to buy a small piece of land, where we can build a garage, turning the rest of it into two allotments. So much for my farm!

Times are still hard in Britain. I work with many young men who remain unmarried because they cannot support wives. There are more than two million unemployed people in this country now. Young men are finding it hard to look after themselves. I think they are sensible. Nothing is worse than the terrible poverty endured in family life. The effects are very long reaching. It is terrible to think that there are thousands of men even older than me who have never done a day's work in their lives.

Father says to tell you that he was speaking to the gamekeeper Mr Charlesworth a few weeks back. He asked to be remembered to you. He wondered if you knew of any domestics who worked at Oulton Hall in Cheshire? I only saw the hall once when I went over there with Father. It was situated near Tarporley and was the ancestral home of Sir Philip Grey Egerton. Unfortunately, he had lent it to a Manchester ironmaster[37] and left for France. Shortly afterwards the entire place caught fire.

Treasured artwork was in danger. Two domestics ran to the upper rooms to try and save some of the valuables. The floor gave way and fell to the burning debris below. Both maids were burnt to death. Altogether four people died in the fire including a volunteer fireman.

Of course the old halls are real tinderboxes being made of wood. I often used to think of Brereton Hall catching on fire during the winter months when so many fires were lit. I never voiced my fears to you of course. Mr Charlesworth

---

[37] The master of a foundry or ironworks, a manufacturer of iron.

was really shaken up about it, as he knew the hall well. It stood in 350 acres of magnificent deer park.

In England there are the beginnings of real social changes. Old religious beliefs are being questioned and old social habits are losing their hold. There is much doubt about things our immediate ancestors took for granted. In many ways this is good as the ordinary folk are beginning to think for themselves. Of course there is still that old fear of walking on a lord's land without permission. The law of the aristocracy still holds sway but its hold on the common people is beginning to weaken.

We know that the English middle class revere the aristocracy but I personally feel that snobbery plays an enormous motivation in the lives of the English. You of all people Eva must understand the aristocratic English culture and the enormous power they have over the working class. Yet I feel that you have managed to escape from that world into one where those values although copied are diluted. On the other hand, if it were not for the aristocracy, who would keep such acres of beautiful English countryside from being destroyed?

When I find time to watch a fox hunt across the Cheshire plain, I am reminded of the upkeep of the horses, the survival of tradition and even the fox himself. At least he is given a chance to outrun the hounds rather than die of poison or traps.

By the way, Crewe is now on the world map! Cheshire cheese has been tinned and sent overseas for the first time. It was sent to Calcutta where it was a great success.

Let me know of your plans in your next letter. As always I will keep you informed of events here at home. Everyone sends their love.

Your loving brother,
George

The Price

Eva read the letter several times, delighted with the news from 'the old country'. She was particularly intrigued by her brother's comments on the social changes in Britain, looking forward to the time when she could sit and talk to him. She shuddered at the thought of the old hall burning down, recalling the many small fires that had occurred during her time at Brereton Hall. She always had a fear that the old place could catch ablaze.

How well she understood the sense of duty that had cost the two domestics their lives. She knew that she would have done the same thing if she'd been in their position. Once in service, the great wealth contained in such places becomes everyone's responsibility, servants included. There was no question of disloyalty or second thoughts about putting the lives of the aristocracy before your own. She shivered thinking how easily it could have been her. Protecting the estate was your duty. Eva began to wonder how much of that dedication and unquestioning servitude still remained in her. She certainly knew that she had changed since leaving England. But if she went back to work in one of the great English Halls, would the class system put her back in her old place? Perhaps she'd changed so much that she'd never be able to work somewhere like that again. Eva knew exactly how lucky she was to be in secure employment and continued to save. On two occasions she sent her money back to the post office at Wellington, where it provided a nest egg for her, giving her the financial security she needed.

Ironically, it was to be the most difficult winter she'd experienced in Canada. The new year of 1933 brought icy weather and blizzards and on February 8th the worst blizzard for twenty five years swept across the Canadian Prairies. The mountains of British Columbia were thick with snow and many roads were blocked. Eva had been used to the milder winters in Vancouver, with little snow but this winter she barely left the house except on necessary business for the household. As the bad weather started at the same time as the anniversary of the loss of Morris, Eva

Picking up the Pieces

couldn't help but wonder if the world was somehow wilder and less forgiving without him in it.

There were many days when she longed for the warm summers of New Zealand. The same summers when she had so often thought she couldn't possibly survive! Her chest ached and she had a continuous cough, which kept her indoors for weeks, even when the weather allowed opportunities to venture out. Finally, when she almost despaired of the icy conditions, spring slowly crept in, first by the melting of the snow, followed by a softening of the earth and the first signs of the daffodil bulbs. The great western maple trees, widespread in Vancouver, began to break into leaf and pale yellow flowers appeared in the gardens. She knew that she would never see another winter like this one and she was glad of it.

One more letter came from Crewe before she left in May. George wrote of the influenza epidemic in the British Isles, which had swept the country, killing over a thousand people. Perhaps the Vancouver winter had not been so bad after all. Her mother had been very ill but had recovered. George put it down to her determination to see her eldest child again. She had shown amazing willpower to survive, but no one in the family who knew her well was surprised. Martha was a formidable woman. George assured Eva that the family was fine and glad that the winter was finally over.

Reading between the lines, it seemed to Eva that the ordinary people of England somehow had to endure the terrible weather whilst the rich simply left the country for southern Europe, only to return with the swallows in May. And she was going to do the exact same thing, arrive home with all the swallows nesting and the wildflowers in the fields.

For twelve days Eva once again became a traveller. Wrapped in her fur, well dressed and fashionable, she could converse with anyone but withdraw politely from people if she chose to do so. Her employer gave her an extra £25 plus her wages for a month, quietly telling her she must accept it as his household had run smoothly under her guidance. Goodbyes from the household were brief with many things best unsaid.

Mr Dalton drove her to the train station where she boarded one of the sleek silver coloured coaches. He made sure that Eva's luggage was stored and that she was in the seat he had reserved for her. He pointed out the panelled observation domes from where Eva would view the impressive scenery as she crossed the vast country, a journey of almost three thousand miles. Finally, Mr Dalton said his goodbyes assuring her that employment was always available if she chose to return. The long train steamed out of the station into heavy low-lying cloud and thick white mist.

Eva settled back in her seat, lost in her own thoughts. The leaving of any place always brought sadness with it but this was even harder as she felt that she was leaving so much of herself behind in Vancouver. She thought back to her final farewell to Canada and to Morris. It seemed a long time ago but in reality it was only just over a year. She had taken a cab to Stanley Park, making her way to the great tree where she and Morris had last stood at Christmas 1930.

Eva had looked up to the place where he had pushed the stone hearts deep into the tree's bark. Her feet sank into the thick bracken and moss. Taking out the little red box, she'd held it in her hand, and then slowly opening it she had taken out the little Celtic ring. 'A ring for my Celtic woman.' She had buried the box containing the ring deep in the soft soil. Peeling a small piece of bark from the trunk, she had slipped it into her coat pocket and left. Morris and Canada were now in her past. It was time to move on.

She examined a map of her route, smiling to herself as she realised her love of maps was probably rather eccentric. This fascination was something from her childhood for they had provided a key to a world she could only imagine. Now, even as a traveller, maps held a special fascination. Long after the journey she could touch a map and remember smells, sounds and images. She loved looking at the names of places, wondering how and why they had been invented. She recalled the name of the lake on her journey through the Panama Canal, and thought back to her first journey across New Zealand.

Now she saw other names, which hinted at a country that once belonged to the North American Indians, *Salmon Arm*, *Medicine Hat*, *Swift Current*, and *Chalk Fiver*. She observed the ravaged forest ranges and miles of logging which left the land tortured and bruised. Great pools of water lay in hollows where once great trees had stood. Skeins of wild geese flew inland heading instinctively towards the wilderness beyond.

She experienced twelve days in which she felt an overwhelming sense of peace. She looked out on a landscape so huge that she realised she was no more than a grain of sand in the rivers that helped shape this immense place. Here where the spirits of the many Indian tribes lay, part of the river, the snow and the mountains, she found peace, the first of the Madden women travelling in order to unravel the mysteries and unanswered questions in her life.

One day there would be an end to the grieving for Ellen, Joe and Morris. Like her brother George she was taking her strength and finding answers through nature.

Part 4 – Home to Crewe (1933-1934)

Crewe Again

Eva stood on the icy deck, watching the retreating coastline of Canada, wondering what lay ahead for her in Cheshire. It had been 1925 when she left home. She had travelled so far, and changed so much from the girl who left, coming to terms with the powerful influences of the Christian religion, which had so dominated her family life. She had also come to terms with the strange madness that afflicted her brother and sister. Yet it was to her brother George that she returned, to confide in him her thoughts about her environment as a child and just how much of it she still carried within her.

She loved her parents, but knew that she must face the unrelenting gaze of her mother. Her views on morality would never change. Heaven only knew what she would think of her thirty-six year old daughter still unmarried and childless. But Eva didn't really care. She had found a newfound confidence from being loved by Morris and from the journeys she'd made, both in herself and across the globe. Nevertheless, there was some trepidation. She also knew she must face the prospect of a visit to Chester to see her brother Joe, consider the future dilemmas of her sister Ellen and be of comfort to her ageing parents. She must learn to be more patient with her mother, more forgiving, she thought.

Passengers were gathering on the deck to exclaim at the icebergs, some of them a quarter of a mile long, drifting several miles off the Newfoundland Grand Banks. Shelving under the icy waters, only partly visible, they indicated the end of winter as the Northern Summers developed. Their appearance in the shipping lanes resulted in an immediate call from the crow's nest occupied by a shift of sailors on danger watch for the next few days and nights.

As the ship finally reached Liverpool, Eva quietly gathered her belongings, the butterflies only partially quieted by such routine. Then, wrapped up well against the cold, she waited silently along with the other chattering passengers for disembarkation and the customs check. At last she began to look at the people on the quay, excited relatives, children in arms, anxious faces looking for their loved ones. Would George be there? She had written to him but had not received a reply before she left Vancouver. She desperately wanted him to meet her, but her more practical side prepared herself for an unaccompanied train journey to Crewe.

Looking at the sea of faces, she suddenly saw him smiling and waving at her. Her heart skipped a beat as she ran through the crowd towards him and into his arms. Holding her at arm's length, her brother examined her critically, noting the tiny lines around her eyes and her anxiety as she fought back tears. Stroking her gently on the head, he comforted her. No words were spoken for several minutes as they clung together. Then she stood back in admiration of her handsome brother, smiling reassuringly at his eldest sister for whom he had waited for so long.

"Eva, you look wonderful. A real lady. Edie will be envious of you."

Eva spoke slowly, measuring her words. She was filled with all the emotions that she never normally allowed to surface unless she was alone.

"George, we look alike. I've never thought about it before but we do! Well, apart from your incredible teeth. I can't boast of that. In fact I can't boast of front teeth at all if you remember how Edith and I made our fateful visit to the dentist."

George listened carefully to Eva's changed accent. Gone was the singsong voice of a working class girl from Crewe. In her place was a woman well travelled and confident, using trivial conversation to mask the real feelings of love for him that he could see bubbling away just below the surface.

"Come on Eva, let's get your luggage and head for the train. Everyone at home is waiting for you. I think the entire street is anxious to see you, lovely sister."

Lifting her into the air, he twirled her round, refusing to let her feet touch the ground. Around them the crowd laughed, but when he finally placed Eva unsteadily onto the dockside, he noticed with concern the tears that spilled down her now white cheeks. Saying nothing, he briskly organised luggage to be taken to the train and they set off arm in arm, George covering up the unexpected show of emotion.

The train journey through the English countryside was almost ignored, as they talked incessantly of family news. Occasionally Eva glanced through the steamy windows to catch glimpses of wild daffodils, green fields and hawthorn hedges spilling with snow blossoms. She was home at last and glad of it!

At Crewe station her father was waiting for them, aged now and not wearing work overalls. It was strange, but Eva realised that whenever she had thought of her father in all those years working at Brereton Hall and then in foreign lands, the picture she'd carried of him in her mind always had him wearing overalls. She was almost overwhelmed with love for the old rascal. He broke down and cried at the sight of Eva, his eldest child, alighting from the train after what seemed a lifetime away. Finally, he felt as though he'd only lost two of his children again and not three as he'd imagined the whole time Eva had been away.

They took a cab from the station even though it was only a very short distance to their home, Joseph making jokes about her heavy luggage all the way.

"No doubt full of clothes," he joked as she hugged him. "Too thin by far Evelyn, nothing on you girl. We'll have to feed her up, won't we George?" he added as his son paid off the cabbie, an extravagance Martha would never have allowed in Eva's childhood, but had no say in now her adult children made all the decisions. But if Martha felt like

Eva did today, she knew her mother wouldn't begrudge the small extra expense.

Neighbours stood on their doorsteps waving at Eva, although several of them hardly remembered the young woman who had left the street all those years before. Now they saw a fur coated lady, smiling and assured, entering the small terraced house. No one waited at the family door. Closing the door carefully, Joseph's voice changed to a whisper. "Your mother isn't too well. Been a long winter and she's had the usual bad chest but she'll come down in a minute. Nothing to worry about," he reassured Eva, as they moved quietly into the front room to continue talking.

Eva noted the lack of warmth. No fire burning in the grate. The chairs and curtains she remembered from when she left in 1925. The only photographs were one of her taken in London for immigration purposes, George, Tom and Augusta. There were, of course, no pictures of Ellen or Joe. It was as if they had never existed. Eva couldn't help but wonder if her own photograph, or Gussie, George or Tom's pictures would disappear if they met some calamity and had to be somehow erased from her mother's life. But this was not the time for being judgemental or even sad. So she turned away from the mantle and back to her father and brother.

Her eyes drifted instinctively to the velvet-covered table. The Bible was closed but marked ready for the next reading. George followed her gaze, knowing exactly what she was thinking. Laughingly, he turned and whispered, "Shall we put *On the Origin of Species*[38] in its place Eva?" With relief, Eva looked at him and he winked! What a relief to have a brother who understood her.

A laugh threatened to burst out of her but "Oh George! Mam would have you burning for that!" was all she could get out before her father came back into the room, followed by her mother.

For a few seconds, mother and daughter stared at

---

[38] Charles Darwin (1859)

each other, one from the new world, one from the old, before inhibitions broke down. Eva moved forward to hold her, feeling her vulnerability, until Martha broke free to shyly acknowledge her daughter.

"God has brought you back safely to us, my dear Eva. I have prayed for this moment for so long." Her voice broke, tears falling onto her worn, sick face.

In that moment, Eva forgave her the fierce indoctrination that had influenced their young lives, remembering the rigid enforcement of her mother's rules. She knew that these rules had been essential to Martha to keep her from danger. The times when she and her brothers and sisters stayed for hours in their rooms, punished for shuffling through a Bible reading or for not attending church whilst the street rang with the laughter of playing children were in the past. Gone were those moments when the door slammed as her father left the house to escape. All she knew, was how much she loved her mother. That was all that mattered.

Standing behind her, George smiled to himself. He knew all that was going through her mind and felt that this change of heart would be the case. Eva would see the lines on her mother's face and realise how much she suffered inwardly about the fate of two of her children and how pride and her belief in God gave her the strength that separated her from the frailties of others.

Joseph smiled at his two children. He hoped at last that as adults, they would understand his devotion to Martha, despite his frustration and sadness at how she isolated herself from the community and the world at large. "Well, let's get the kettle on. Augusta and Percy will be here in a moment Mother. We have our daughter back. Let's be happy and not be having any more of those tears and standing around."

Martha straightened her apron, retreating into the remote figure that Eva remembered. She went into the back kitchen to organise tea. Joseph lit the already prepared fire and conversation continued until nightfall, interrupted only by her younger sister and adoring husband who came in to welcome Eva home.

This was the first time Eva had met Percy and for a moment she could see how she and Morris would have looked to other people. Augusta was completely secure in the love of her adoring husband and Eva was happy for her.

That night Eva slept as if in her old bedroom in Monks Coppenhall, falling asleep with memories of Ellen climbing all over her to reach the candle. She remembered the first cry of baby Joe and once again saw her father sitting at the side of her mother, following her brother's birth. For a while she lay awake listening to the sound of the trains, sniffing the old smells of worn furniture, knowing that the now banked up coal fire would trail its thick smoke up through the chimney where it joined another thousand polluted spires, coating Crewe in fogs which would last into the month of June.

Despite the poverty evident in the house, she was surprised at something she hadn't experienced almost longer than she could remember, the security of home. Her loneliness eased and she realised that for the first time in months the heaviness she'd felt in her stomach since the loss of Morris was gone. Not just lifting, but gone and she was at peace. He wasn't forgotten and he was missed, but she could cope. Unexpectedly, her family was healing her.

She awakened early to the loud dawn chorus of the birds, listening to her mother's rituals as she crept about downstairs. The bible marker would have moved on slightly, the fires would be laid in the back room and kitchen. Eva's small amount of washing would be soaking in the dolly tub, ready for a pounding. Smiling to herself she washed in cold water and made her way to the back kitchen to rescue her more fragile clothes from the inevitable beating. She followed her mother but was not allowed to help with any household duties.

"Eva, put that down. You won't be doing my housework for me. You've travelled across the world after spending your life waiting on other people. Now you can be waited on."

"Mam, I don't mind, really. I don't know what to do with myself if I'm not busy."

"I won't hear of it. Sit down, or just follow and talk to me like you're doing now. Or go and spend some time with Edith or Gussie. But I won't have you doing what's properly mine to do."

"Then at least let me do my own washing," which was only a tactic to rescue her clothes from Martha's usual washing treatment.

"You will not set foot in my washhouse Evelyn Madden. Not today anyway. Not until you've had a decent rest."

Martha was no less a formidable rule maker now that she was older, so Eva relented. Instead she continued to follow her mother, chatting in a way she'd never done with her before. But she never discussed her brothers and sisters, keeping the conversation to locals and friends. She asked about the rent, intrigued to hear that it was paid to a family of gypsies who owned at least six houses.

"They still live out on the edge of town themselves, mind. Buying all those houses you'd think they'd want to live in at least one of them! But they seem nice enough and leave us on our own to get on with things."

"They probably all get together and buy a house and then share in the rent. I suppose all the rent they collect helps them to live the way they want to."

Martha interrupted, "Eva, it's still strange if you ask me. For who am I to judge people for wanting to do things their own way?"

"Mam, what do you mean by that?"

"Oh, I know what the neighbours thought of me, Eva. I never had many friends in the neighbourhood because I was determined to have some standards. And before you get all sad, I don't regret a minute of it. I'd rather have my standards and my dignity than almost anything else in the world. Well except God's grace of course." And that was the last word as usual with Martha Madden. But the two words that were so important to Martha struck a cord in Eva, 'standards and dignity'. Without her even knowing it, Martha's values had become the core of Eva's own.

In the absence of any real gossip about the neighbours being forthcoming from Martha, Eva found herself stepping from the back kitchen into the small yard. She narrowed her eyes to look upward at the identical chimney pots of the dark, closely built, terraced dwellings. Tightly cramped against one another, the identical brickwork merged from one house into the next. Black smoke poured from every chimney into the still morning air. A neighbour coughed as he came out to use the lavatory. The earth closets were cleaned out at night by the soil men under cover of darkness.

To reach the back of the houses, occupants entered a communal tunnel. The grim entrances to the backs of the houses were spaced at regular intervals, by dark, concrete pathways leading to the rear of the houses. There were no gardens. High walls separated neighbours who shouted greetings to one another from their yards. Nothing had changed here since she had left to work at Brereton all those years ago. So this was where her parents would spend the remainder of their days, following a lifetime of work for the railway. Eva suddenly felt anger, knowing full well how many lived a brighter existence.

She came in to sit by the fire, listening to her mother's comments on various changes in the neighbourhood. Then she talked of George and Tom, her voice softening slightly. "He's a good son, George is. Never misses calling and Edith is a dutiful wife. Augusta and Percy too, living only a few doors from here. And doesn't Augusta have a look of you? Although she is taller. You girls, always very fashionable and fond of dressing up. Well, you didn't get that from me!"

But Eva remembered a young Martha, knowing they had inherited their looks from their mother. Even if they'd never seen Martha with fashionable or extravagant clothes, they nevertheless all resembled her. That George had married someone like his sisters was no accident in Eva's mind.

Never once during her stay in Crewe did her mother acknowledge the existence of Joe or Ellen. It was a Madden secret kept by all of them. Even the neighbours knew better than to ask. Augusta refused to be bound in secrecy, speaking passionately about Joe.

"I tell you, there's nothing wrong with him! He's as gentle as he ever was and he shouldn't be in there. I don't care what George says. I visit Joe whenever I can get to Chester and take him a food parcel. You know Eva, he's always trying to escape but then he wants to come home doesn't he?"

Then she added very quietly, "They've signed forms you know," nodding towards the back kitchen where George was busy discussing something with his mother.

"Oh yes, they've signed papers and now he is a prisoner in there." Her eyes filled with tears.

Eva felt bewildered about the conflicting opinions concerning her brother, determined to question George on the matter. For now she remained silent, unsure of the situation but trusting George implicitly. Meeting up with Edith dispelled the gloom as the two good friends shopped in town, exchanged gossip and compared notes on living both in Crewe and the colonies.

Summer Months

The summer months passed quickly in a whirl of activity. Eva proved to be quite the celebrity in her hometown, even giving short talks to interested and would be immigrants. Praising New Zealand and Canada as both lands of opportunity, she was quick to point out the advantages for women who could leave for new opportunities in the colonies. They could travel safely, earn their own keep and experience adventures well beyond the English shores.

But Eva also pointed out the dangers of immigration. Never think that it was possible to travel thousands of miles with as little as £10 as some young women had done. Never rely on charity or the church to rescue you from an awkward situation. Never imagine that you might find your prince charming on such a journey. Learn to make your own clothes, be practical and save money. When in service, as many young women would be, keep to your own well trained English standards of etiquette even though there was a far more relaxed attitude in the colonies. If nothing else, it would make you more employable.

Several young women attended a number of Eva's information evenings, asking her personal questions. Had she ever fallen in love with her employer? Did she want to marry over there? Eva kept her distance and gave nothing away. She had her own Madden secret to keep now. George wondered about the obvious changes in her but he never asked.

Many evenings were spent at George and Edith's new house, where they would sit for long hours catching up on local news. The conversations took place at night when Edith went off to bed. She knew they needed time to be together and she was not interested in politics. And politics seemed to be the core of what the two of them liked to talk about for hours on end.

Did Eva know that the Nazis were now in control of Germany? Did she know that German students in Berlin and other cities in Germany had now begun a round up of Jewish books and other non-German books, which were burnt on bonfires in the public squares? Or that new laws had been passed in July imposing the death penalty for various political offences including anti-Nazi writings?

Eva admitted that she had been a little out of touch for the previous year or so. She didn't have time to follow the news she told George. When the reality was that she had been grieving like a widow for Morris. But George would hear only the happy version. And most important of all to the two Maddens was the news that the German Nazi government had drafted a law for the compulsory sterilisation of the unfit. This included incurable drunkards, sexual criminals, lunatics and sufferers from incurable diseases. If the College of Doctors decided that an operation was necessary for the welfare of the nation, it would be carried out regardless of family opinion. The idea had already been rejected in Britain, but there was nevertheless much interest in some quarters and it had even been raised in Parliament.

Eva argued this point with George, insisting that the state could not overrule the individual in such personal family matters. After all, had they not got a brother locked up and classed as a lunatic? Should this happen to him, how would the family feel? How far would it be then for the government to decide that if one or two of the six Madden children were incurable lunatics, then perhaps all of the Madden children should be sterilised? Eva knew that George and Edith were still of a mind never to have children, but her own mind had changed once she had fallen pregnant, what if the same were to happen to them? But all she said was that if George and Edith were someday to want to have children of their own, how would they feel if the government had taken that choice away?

And what if many of the so-called lunatics simply required a different treatment and change in environment? How great a part did poverty play in the incarceration of such people? Joe was put into the Nantwich workhouse and then placed permanently in an asylum as his family was poor. He couldn't be offered alternative treatment. Institutionalisation would deprive him of any real progress. She also argued that predisposition was an important factor in insanity.

George supported the Darwinian theories that only the fittest in society could survive. There was no medical answer for Joe, maybe in the future, but not now. Ultimately he had to stay in the asylum for his own sake and for others. Sometimes their talks lasted until dawn. At times, Eva was astounded by her brother's self discipline. She knew he got the strength from his mother, but he was still such a young man. The family decisions must be a great responsibility to him. He seemed able, like her, to approach many situations in a controlled and objective way, but at what personal cost she wondered? He was face to face with the decision making everyday, but how would he be over the coming years?

He protested over the words of Herr Hitler, the dictator of Germany, who when addressing thousands of athletes at the Stuttgart Festival praised muscle before brain declaring that the intellectuals threatened the nation with decay. 'Strong men,' Hitler asserted, 'are our protectors, not strong philosophers.'

George hardly needed to argue this point with his sister. Both of them knew the power of an educated mind and believed fervently in education, even if they'd had very little of it themselves. But they had the love of books and learning that their mother had instilled in Eva before she even started school and which encouraged them both to read whatever they could.

It was with relief that they heard over the wireless that England was proud to offer Professor Einstein, generally admitted as the world's most eminent man of science, shelter at Oxford under the Nationality of Jews Bill to protect him

The Price

from persecution in Germany. England would not go down the insane path being travelled in Germany.

Intellectually, brother and sister were equal. They revelled in their time spent together. Europe was on the boil and both sensed the deeper implications, fearing that another World War could develop. They would all be affected. For her part, Edith organised outings to nearby Beeston Castle[39] where they would picnic together. The three of them enjoyed the incredible views over the Cheshire Plains and beyond to the misty mountains of North Wales. They travelled by train, then walked the short distance up to the castle. Standing on the rocky crags, looking out across the land, George turned to Eva, offering a hand in order that she might climb up beside him. Together they stood in silence before George spoke.

"Did you know that the history of Beeston stretches back over four thousand years? It was a Bronze Age hill fort back then. And down there," he said, pointing far below to a big Tudor farmhouse, "Tom and I fish the pool near to it. It's on Lord Tollmache's[40] land. I know the long-standing tenant of that farm. He told me the other day that down in the cellar, but cleverly bricked up, is the entrance to a tunnel that leads all the way to the castle. Everyone who knows about it says that a treasure of precious jewels lies hidden in there." Eva looked at him sceptically.

"Michael has never told anyone about the secret tunnel. Says he doesn't want people swarming all over his land. Strange thing that, thinking of the land as his own, because one day maybe in fifty years time, the lease will run out. He will get kicked out to the day and the house and all of it will go back to the aristocracy again. This country will always be the same Eva, one rule for the rich and one for the poor, laid down for generations."

Eva knew immediately that this was her opportunity to mention Joe. "George, is there any way, any way at all

---
[39] Built in the 1220s, one of the most dramatic ruins in the English landscape.
[40] The holder of the ancestral land at that time.

that we could bring Joe home? Maybe if I sent money from New Zealand?"

Her brother turned, looking at her sharply. "So, you are thinking of going back. You're going to leave us yet again." He sighed. "As for Joe, the doctors believe he's incurable. And we have to go along with informed opinion, not guesswork. Believe me Eva, he is safe from himself where he is."

Climbing down, he lifted her into the air and swung her round. "No heavier despite all the feeding up!"

Edith called them over for a picnic spread out on a tablecloth. A primus stove was boiling water for the tea, a precious tin of salmon had been opened and Edith proudly showed them the bunch of bananas, which she had managed to buy at the market. Clearly the conversation about Joe was over, but Eva still had hope that maybe Joe could be released.

Another of their favourite places was Betley, a small village a few miles from Crewe, which George often visited 'for memory's sake' he would say laughingly and Edith would chastise him, joking that he had a lady friend there.

By the end of September, red, amber and green lights appeared mysteriously in Crewe, attached to walls near to the main roads. Many people over-ran them as often they were obscured and in some places they were death traps.

George came into the house laughing. "Those new traffic lights are smashed again. The ones on the wall can't be seen. They've finally caused a van to run into a horse and cart. The driver and the vegetable man with the cart joined forces. They broke the lights into little pieces in front of a cheering crowd." Eva and Edith burst out laughing.

"What's happening now?" asked Eva.

"It's still going on. The police are trying to sort it out. They're death traps, those lights."

Edith interrupted. "I think they're stupid. We were all right before. There are so few cars on the road. Why do we need lights?"

"I agree," added Eva. "Who can afford a car round here? It's difficult enough to run a home."

"Change," George said thoughtfully. "We must anticipate change. The lights are an experiment, but one day," he added prophetically, "they'll be essential." Edith and Eva shook their heads in disbelief.

A Visit

Augusta planned a visit to Chester to see Ellen who refused to travel to Crewe. Eva longed to see her. Leaving the railway station at Chester, they made their way to the factory where Ellen worked. Eva felt nervous and excited to see Ellen once again. Augusta pointed her out as she came through the factory gates. Eva was shocked to see her wandering out slowly with the other workers. A little woman bloated from medication, she scurried along, head down. Suddenly she spotted her two elegant sisters, and broke into a run. She hugged and kissed Eva whilst Augusta stood back, proud that she had finally reunited the two of them.

"Eva, I can't believe it! Tell me all about yourself. You look like a princess. Remember the stories? Remember you and me on dad's allotment? Remember our bedroom? And our walks over Betley woods? Sing it with me. When day is done and sun is gone, Remember me". On and on she chattered, living in the past where most of her vibrant memories lay.

They arrived at her lodgings and over tea they continued, Ellen interrupting at every opportunity as Eva told her about New Zealand and Canada. She spoke lovingly of George and Edith, Tom and Joe. There was no mention of insanity and yet there was no secret either.

"Tell me again about Brereton Hall. Do you like it there?"

Eva gently reminded her that she had travelled on from Brereton, looking questioningly at Augusta. So this is what the treatment at the asylum had resulted in. All rebellion and spirit had gone from Ellen. She was left with just enough mental ability to fit in with a small part

The Price

of society, and to do a repetitive job at a factory. There was no more raging, no more laughter or self-opinionated talk. But there was also no more questing for information, just a confused mixture of memories. No more Ellen as Eva had known her.

Eva turned away, tears in her eyes. Years before George had described her as a unique white crow that would be destroyed by all the black ones. Now the white crow had vanished. Where did Ellen fit now, she wondered. Augusta touched her arm.

"I know," she said quietly. "Just accept what we can't change."

Eva turned to look at her. Suddenly she realised how wrong she had been. She had always thought her sister was selfish and demanding. Augusta was as powerful as George in her own way. She had great compassion. She could see beyond the walls of the asylum.

"No more tears. You'll frighten Ellen." Augusta was in charge, not Eva.

"Come along you two. Why don't we see if there's a chance of visiting Joe?" Eva looked at her in astonishment. "Can we? I didn't think we could."

"Of course we can. We just don't tell George. And he never thinks to ask anyway. We've been several times, haven't we Ellen?"

Ellen looked up from unwrapping the presents Eva had brought her. "Yes. We love Joe, don't we Gussie? He likes the cakes and biscuits we take for him. He talks about you a lot Eva. We tell him all about you. We tell him the news from your letters. But we don't tell him about volcanoes and earthquakes, do we Gussie?"

"Certainly not." Her sister smiled.

"No, we told him once and it made him cry. So we tell him lovely things about you. Do you know Eva, he remembers everything about Brereton Hall, even about the bear. Except that sometimes he gets headaches and bad moods. He starts shouting. I don't like that so we have to leave." She frowned and hung her head.

"Come on, put on your new cardigan. Get ready Ellen and we'll see if he is well enough for a visit."

On the way they bought food, but when they arrived at the asylum they were refused a visit. Joe had been very unsettled and seeing his sister after years of absence might disturb him even more. Dejected they left the food, returning to Ellen's lodgings where they said goodbye, Eva promising to visit again. Making their way to the train station, the two sisters were silent, knowing they were powerless to help. Joe no longer belonged to the Madden family. He remained locked up, just a number on a medical register, someone who ceased to exist.

"Oh Eva," Augusta finally broke her silence as the train sped towards Crewe, "isn't it so miserable, our own brother trapped inside that awful building? Every time I go to see him I come away so upset that I can barely think about anything else for days. Imagine what it would be like living there. It's no place to cure Joe's sadness, surely."

"I don't know Gussie. I just don't know. It seems awful, 'but what else is there?' George says."

Augusta interrupted suddenly. "We mustn't say anything to George, absolutely nothing or I'll be to blame. He's already warned me not to excite Ellen now she's doing well since her illness. She copes far better when she's away from Mother, but this would have done her no good at all, not at all."

"Of course. Our secret. Gussie, what do you think this madness is?" asked Eva, longing to talk about the family secret.

Augusta looked at her in astonishment. "What madness? I don't believe in any of that. Ellen and Joe just got lost, that's all. You went away when you were thirteen. Don't feel bad about it, but they missed you so much Eva. You gave them the love Mam couldn't give them."

"Because she was giving it all to God?"

"Exactly. Then when Ellen got lost, Joe was isolated

even more. Then you went away to New Zealand. He thought of it like you'd died and he blamed us I think for not making you stay. Then he somehow decided you'd left because of something he'd done or because he just wasn't worth loving."

She paused for a moment and then spoke quietly. "He never spoke to any of us again until that awful day."

"What do you mean?" Eva had a feeling of dread.

"As if the not talking wasn't enough, it all came to a head one day. He was living with Mam and Dad. One day he came in, shut himself in his room and refused to come out. He didn't eat for three days. Finally Dad broke in and there he was sitting on his bed, head down. Wouldn't look at any of us. Wouldn't wash. Wouldn't speak. There were other things too but I don't want to talk about that. So Mam got the doctor and they took him to Nantwich. When he was in there he cut himself with a razor. He ..." and then the words trailed away. The pain was too great. The sisters sat close together in silence.

Augusta finally spoke. "I call it loneliness. They needed love, both of them. They were different. They needed to be understood. And there was no one to reach them. It was all too late."

Again there was silence between them, finally broken by Augusta in a quiet voice. "Well, I shall go on seeing both of them wherever they are. I won't have George telling me what I can or can't do."

No Consent

Christmas approached. Edith and Eva planned festivities for the Madden family. Eva had confided in her best friend, describing the visit to Chester. Edith begged her not to let George know for he handled Joe's illness in the only way he knew how, by telling no-one and bearing the sadness of it by himself. Eva was surprised to hear that he rarely mentioned Joe even to Edith.

Edith came from a home where the special days were celebrated in traditional ways. She had always known a Christmas tree, a family dinner and presents. Eva wanted this for her parents so they planned together. After much arguing, Martha agreed to let Eva buy all of the food, but insisted that she cook the meal. The family would be reunited, differences put to one side for Eva's sake. No drink was allowed in the house but at George and Edith's home the three of them celebrated with glasses of sherry. George was in a festive mood, whirling Edith about and calling the sherry 'dancing juice'.

The following day he disappeared 'on business' as he called it, leaving his sister and wife wrapping presents. By teatime he had still not arrived but time passed quickly as they chatted and laughed after their dinner. It was after eight o'clock before George came in to find his wife and sister laughing together. He frowned, hating to end it all, but there was nothing for it. He stepped into the room and the women could see from the look on his face that there was something wrong.

Edith rose slowly from her chair. "George?"

"I have some unfortunate news. Not unexpected, but bad news anyway." He paused, moving to Edith's side and looked across the table at Eva.

The Price

"Last week Joe escaped. He had got it into his head that Eva was here in Crewe and was determined to see her."

Eva's mouth went dry. Who had told him? she wondered.

"Well, anyway, he was caught and put in a high security cell for his own safety."

He looked tired, sitting down despondently. The two women waited, realising there was more to come.

"The doctors have made a decision. They feel that they have to do something to settle his rages and dangerous behaviour. They want to perform an operation." His voice faltered.

Eva suddenly felt herself on the edge of hysteria. "What George? What are you telling us?"

"I've already agreed to it Eva. There isn't any other way."

"Agreed to what? For God's sake will you stop talking in riddles!"

"I've told them they can operate on his brain. They said it will pacify him and give him peace of mind." He turned away, not able to look at Eva.

"No." Her voice was quiet, but it was clear that Eva was angry. "I refuse to allow this to happen. It's not natural, George."

"Eva, you don't have the legal power to stop this. I am the one acting for Mam and Dad. I need the consent of one other family member. You have been out of the country and may leave again. So it won't be you."

"Who?" Edith stared in horror at him. This was a nightmare for her.

"Augusta will have to sign. Mam and Dad have asked me to deal with all of this. It would kill them to involve them at this stage. Tom doesn't even know about Joe. We never told him. He thinks he's working away and doesn't bother to contact us. No, it has to be Augusta."

All three discussed the implications of the operation but Eva did not argue with her brother for Edith's sake.

She knew it would be a waste of time. She left the house, calling in on Augusta to tell her the news. Once again she was amazed by the strength of her sister.

"Never! I will never sign the papers. I'm not going to be responsible for turning my brother into a cabbage!" There wasn't a tear. Her voice never wavered. For the first time, it struck Eva how much Augusta was like Martha. "Let him come here and ask. He'll get my answer. Some Christmas this will be! But at least it'll be an honest one. Don't distress yourself Eva. It will never happen. Not while I have any power over the situation."

That night Eva sat with her unsuspecting parents answering their many questions about her travels. But she wasn't really paying attention, her mind was wandering, thinking about her stubborn brother and sister and how it would end. The following day Edith met her in town to tell her that George and Augusta had had a huge row. Augusta had ordered him out of her house. George had vowed never to speak to her again. The operation would not take place. Augusta went one step further. She visited the family doctor to protest, asking him to write immediately to the asylum on her behalf.

Christmas came and went, a sad affair amongst a divided family. George took more shift work away from home whilst Eva visited the domestics' agency in Manchester to check for jobs in New Zealand. She was now a New Zealand citizen and would be given preference.

Travelling back to Crewe, she thought about the long journey back to New Zealand. It was no longer a foreign land to her. She wasn't a new immigrant and yet she remembered the lack of wisdom in taking out the nightingales in an effort to make them sing on foreign soil. Was she doing the right thing? Would she ever feel settled there or would she always long for this railway town on the other side of the world that held her memories of childhood. For that matter, would she ever feel settled anywhere while she felt such absence of Morris and Ellen and Joe? On the other hand she couldn't do anything about her losses. Morris was gone forever and she could do nothing to help Joe and Ellen. Poverty would stalk her here no matter how careful she was with her savings. By returning, she could at least earn a living and even send money back to her parents. Times in England were now very hard with the recession resulting in many out of work.

With no intention of ever marrying, she had grown too independent for a single woman living in Crewe. She wanted more than a restricted life lived out in the back streets that all the other Crewe women seemed to have. And maybe the feeling of helplessness about Joe and Ellen would ease with distance. Her anger towards George would fade, surely. Her admiration for Augusta's bravery and determination had brought her very close to her sister in a way she'd never expected would happen before she went away. Her new relationship with Gussie and her friendship with Edith might be the only things that could keep her here. But they weren't enough.

Over the last few weeks she had experienced the beginning of a deep sadness. It was a sadness completely different from the grief she'd felt for Morris and secretly she'd wondered if she might fall into melancholy, an almost overwhelming fear given what had happened to Joe and Ellen. She wondered if there was any place for her; she hadn't been happy in New Zealand and she wasn't happy here. She often dreamed of Morris, wondering what he'd tell her to do. She knew in her heart that he would encourage her to go, that she had more chance of finding something for herself in New Zealand than she did here in Crewe where she didn't fit with the town, and her family was always consumed by their secrets. By the time the train from Manchester had pulled in at Crewe station she had her answer. She would return to New Zealand.

The Christmas of 1933 turned out to be a poignant time for the Madden family who now knew that Eva would leave for New Zealand in the New Year. She had already booked a ticket on a ship sailing from Southampton to arrive in Auckland on April 30th 1934. The decision to go or to stay had been very difficult for Eva. She had been so very excited to come home, but in doing so, she'd only realised that all the reasons she'd left the first time were still there. She loved her family and friends, despite her anger over George's treatment of Joe she dreaded leaving him behind and she would grow homesick for England and the Cheshire countryside, which she loved. She knew full well the sad lack of wisdom in taking nightingales out to New Zealand in a vain attempt to ease that dreadful feeling of loss when leaving a home country, but like the nightingale that sang after being believed dead, she would survive there too. But there was no life here for her. No, it was time to make future plans and she could never return to Canada. Her memories would go forward with her. She had considerable savings in New Zealand so could spend time with friends over there and seek employment at a later date.

As she posted Christmas cards to the Dalton family and to Emily in Canada and several to her friends in New Zealand, she confirmed her thoughts by telling them of her decision. Finally she talked to her parents. They privately and separately wept for the loss of their eldest child yet again, but encouraged her to go, feeling that there was little to keep her in Crewe.

George tried hard to cheer his sister up, knowing that the decision had been a difficult one. "Well Eva," he joked, "you'll be in good company when you return. I heard on the wireless today that the writer George Bernard Shaw[41] and his wife are going to New Zealand on February 8th. I believe they're visiting the North Island. Maybe you'll get a chance to see him!" But nothing seemed to cheer his sister.

What a difficult thing immigration is, she thought, you work hard to settle in the country you have chosen to live in but all the time your heart is back in the homeland.

---

[41] British playwright, critic and political activist (1856-1950).
Wished to be called Bernard Shaw. Writer of Pygmalion among other well-known works.
Rated second only to Shakespeare among British dramatists.

"Never mind, you can come back in a year if you miss us all so much," laughed George. "You're not bound by the rules of immigration any more. You've done your time. And anyway, who would want to stay in Crewe if they had a chance to visit the places you have described? Who knows, maybe one day Edith and I can come out and visit you!"

"Oh would you? Say you will!" Eva begged and George spoke convincingly of a future visit, which cheered Eva and enabled her to pack her belongings and prepare for the long journey.

Part 5 – Return to New Zealand (1934-1935)

Return to New Zealand

Goodbyes were brief, promises made and departure for Southampton by train was soon underway. Martha appeared briefly and the last Eva saw of her was the small figure of her mother standing proudly on the doorstep as the taxi drew away. For the first two hours of the train journey very little was spoken between brother and sister. The fields were under snow and an icy wind swept across the landscape as the train travelled south.

Later, they began to talk, each promising the other to keep in touch and Eva would return immediately if her parents became ill. For his part George promised his sister that he would look after the family and that if she needed him in any kind of crisis, he would come out to New Zealand. On the subject of Joe, Eva told him that she supported any treatment that he decided was best, for George was carrying the responsibility of his brother's welfare. It was her way of saying that even though they had argued about Joe's treatment, that she conceded George's right to make decisions without her. Augusta's confidences were kept though, and George never knew that they'd tried to visit him at the asylum.

The *Tainui* was to call at Jamaica and Pitcairn. She was a fine ship, fitted out well for travellers. Eva was travelling third class at a cost of £67 for the thirty-three day sea voyage, which she thought was reasonable given that she had paid barely any less for the journey from New Zealand and that was several years before. Like the first time she'd travelled to New Zealand, the route was via the Panama Canal, but this time the passage had been slightly altered so that they could call at Port Royal, Jamaica for bunkers, which gave an added attraction to the passenger service.

The Price

George came aboard to inspect the ship before she sailed and he checked out Eva's cabin, which was very adequate. He asked one of the crew about the name of the ship and was fascinated to hear that the *Tainui* carried the legendary name for one of the principal canoes that had carried the Maoris to New Zealand in the fourteenth century migration. There was a fleet of canoes, the Maori sailor told him, the *Tainui, Kurahaupo, Takitumu, Aotea, Tokomaru, Matatua* and *Arawa* war canoes.

"Now I've seen all this, quite frankly Eva, I wish I was coming with you. There is so much to learn and travel is a way to do it."

But Eva didn't answer. She knew that no matter how much George might dream of something similar to her travels he could never do it. He'd become the parent to all the Madden family. He wore the responsibility cheerfully, but every now and again Eva could catch a glimpse of the life he would like to have if he was free like her. It made her love him all the more and even more determined to make the most of the opportunities that her ability to travel gave her and to treasure each of them for George's sake.

Visitors were asked to leave the ship as she prepared to sail and George said his farewell, holding his sister tightly in his arms, and made his way ashore with barely a word. They had both agreed that he should return to the station immediately as a final goodbye from the quay would have been too painful for both of them. For her part, Eva went straight to her cabin, sure she didn't want to watch all the other families saying their goodbyes.

Then, as a wintry sun, set over England, the *Tainui* sailed, carrying Eva yet again to New Zealand. She lay in her cabin until the ship was well underway, recalling the wonderful few months she had spent with her family. Using all the resilience that she could summon up, she went up on deck to see the fading lights of England before making her way to the dining room for dinner.

The ship docked at Auckland on the 1st May,

passengers quickly making their way to trains or waiting relatives after clearing immigration. Eva readied herself to organise a taxi to take her and her luggage to the hostel. Just then she was astonished to hear her name shouted from the docks. It was the Bruces! She couldn't believe it. And her little Tommy ,now a strapping young man, suntanned and tall. Mary Bruce, never one to hold back, hugged Eva as both of them laughed with tears rolling down their faces.

"I can't believe this! But what are you doing here?"

"What are you doing here, Miss Eva?" laughed Tommy. "Thought you'd got away from New Zealand and all of us, did you?"

Finally, Edwin spoke, his Scottish accent still broad, "It was young Tom's idea, Eva. When you wrote to say you'd be coming back on the Tainui, it was easy to find out when she was getting in and make sure you had a friendly face here to meet you. There's nothing needing harvesting right this minute and young Arthur can look after the sheep for a day or two, so we thought we all deserved a little break in Auckland."

"I'm so pleased to see you all. You can't imagine! What a homecoming!" Her voice was filled with emotion.

"Now, have you arranged a place to stay Eva?" asked Edwin.

"I booked a room in a hostel in Queen Street before I left England."

"Well, we can only stay the day now with the ship being a bit late, but if you're not too tired, we'd like to take you to a hotel for a good meal and to hear about all your adventures."

"And I want to hear if you managed to see that lake and highway called Madden this time through the Canal," added Tom. Eva was astonished that he'd remembered, because she'd quite forgotten.

"Young Tom here still tells stories about the trip out here and especially the Canal, don't you love?" Mary said as

The Price

Tom started to blush.

"So! Food?" asked Tom impatiently.

"Ah, it's all these boys of mine ever talk about, Eva. Consider yourself lucky to not have raised any rascals like mine. From the time they were twelve they became eating machines. I swear it was a race between the boys and the farm horse as to who could eat the most some days! Oh, where are my manners? What are we still doing standing on the quay here? Will you be coming with us for a bite and a natter Eva?"

"Are you joking? Of course I'll come! You can have no idea how lovely and unexpected it is to see you here. I thought I'd just be picking up my luggage, heading to the hostel and starting my hunt for a job."

"You don't have one lined up?" asked Edwin.

"Not yet, but I have a couple of leads and I don't expect it will take me long. I still can't believe you're here!"

"Edwin, Tom, see to Eva's luggage and we'll get out of here for somewhere where we can sit and have a proper talk."

Edwin arranged for Eva's luggage to be taken to the Queen Street hostel and they all headed off to a place nearby that Tom had found the previous day. Over cups of tea they discussed the hard times evident in England and all agreed that they were better off in New Zealand, even though things were difficult there too.

"I went home because I missed my family and imagined I'd settle back there, but there's no place for a woman like me in Crewe. I don't think I could have gone back to work in the stifling atmosphere of one of the great halls after living and working in New Zealand and Canada. I think I've seen too much of the world for that. Besides, I can live better in New Zealand as someone's servant than I can in Crewe as someone's wife."

"So that's why you're still a single woman, Eva," Edwin said with a hint of a smile in his voice.

Carrying on in the same vein, and not wanting to

let on about Morris, Eva replied, "It's my high standards, Edwin. That and the fact that I never met a man I could marry."

That wasn't a lie, she thought to herself. I would have married Morris if I could have. "And then there's the fact that Tommy was far too young for me!" And with that comment everyone laughed out loud and Eva could move the topic of conversation away from her romantic life or lack of it.

"So Eva, tell us about all the places you saw on your journey home," prompted Tom.

Relieved to have something she could talk about easily, she told them that if they were ever to return to Scotland for a visit they must go via Canada, so that they could see Suva and Honolulu for themselves. She described the mountains of western Canada and the great grass plains where any farmer could surely make a solid living.

Tom couldn't help but listen in admiration for his friend, this woman who had travelled the world by herself, doing things on her own that most men he knew would think twice about before trying. He'd only known her through letters and photographs through most of his life, but she was nevertheless a dear friend, who had always been thoughtful of him, never forgotten a birthday or Christmas and was as close to family as he could have in this land where almost everyone seemed to have come from somewhere else.

Before they knew it, the sky was beginning to darken and the time had come for them to take their leave of each other.

"I'd best be checking in at the hostel," apologised Eva.

"And we'd better get ourselves back home before Arthur thinks he's been orphaned," joked Mary Bruce.

"I still can't describe how thoughtful it was for you to come and meet me. It has been a wonderful afternoon and I'm so glad to see you all!"

Mary replied, with just a hint of a tear in her voice,

"You're family Eva. Oh, I know we're not related, but out here you're as close as we have. I wish we could just sit here for hours catching up. But Father here has a farm to look after and there's chores to be done."

Tom smiled and hugged Eva, "Write and let us know where you end up. And Ma's right, you're part of our little New Zealand family. Take care, Eva."

"I'll walk you to your hostel, Eva. Tom lad, you look after your mother and I'll catch you up."

Eva and Edwin walked slowly away into the gathering gloom. The talk between Edwin and Eva revolved around the hard economic times in Britain, with Eva, telling him that it wasn't any better in Canada nor the United States from the American newspapers she'd managed to get hold of when she was in Canada. Through the hard years Edwin had put in establishing his farm, he'd often wondered if he'd made the right decision to emigrate. He'd had to take his two bright sons out of school early to help on the farm and there had been times that he'd felt guilty. Eva's description of the cities in Britain put his mind at rest, bringing his family to New Zealand had been the best thing to do. If nothing else, the hard work would pay off for the next generation and his sons and their families would benefit in more prosperous times. Finally they reached the hostel and Edwin turned to Eva to say his goodbyes.

"Look after yourself Eva. You've not said anything, but I think the last few years have not been as kind to you as they should. You're still our Eva, but something's changed."

"Edwin."

"Don't be interrupting me, just listen. Well, New Zealand has also changed in the past few years too. It will be tough for a single woman like you, a woman of means, to look after herself. There are many poor men on the roads here, out of work and they look for easy targets to help make ends meet. So you just be careful."

"I'll be careful, Edwin. Of course I will. I've been

careful enough to get by on my own for all these years. I'll not let any shiftless drifter take advantage of me. Now, give my love to Arthur, although I'm sure he won't know who I am!"

"Och, he's not such a baby that he can't remember a certain elephant ride once on a visit to Wellington! But I'll pass along your regards to the lad. And once again, look after yourself and stay in touch."

"Thank you Edwin, for today especially. I'll send you a new address as soon as I leave the hostel. Goodnight."

"Goodnight lass."

Eva headed into the hostel and checked into her room, thinking about the day, all the things they'd talked about and all the things she hadn't mentioned. Why could she still not talk about Morris? It was more than the thought that she would break down if she forced herself to talk about it, or the inevitable sympathy that would flow so strongly that it would overwhelm any other conversation. Maybe it was that it was special and she wanted to keep it for herself.

She rose early the next morning and scanned the vacancy board at the hostel, looking for employment. The demand for experienced housemaids and housekeepers was not great, although scullery maids were wanted in great numbers, causing Eva to smile to herself as she recalled her own experiences as a girl. Perhaps she should write to Emily and tell her, she thought to herself.

Knowing that she had sufficient money to live on, Eva spent the next three months helping out at the hostel, encouraging young English girls to think wisely about their placements and even accompanying several to interviews held in Auckland. In exchange, her accommodation was free of charge, helping her savings stretch even farther. She also took the opportunity to catch up with old friends and Tom Bruce managed to come to town several times to catch up for tea or to see a film with Eva. She could imagine what the gossips in Wellington or Crewe might say about the two of them, but she didn't care. They were friends and that was all there was to it.

They were happy months for Eva as she enjoyed friendships forged through previous immigration. She felt loved and cared for, writing back regularly to George who in return sent her cheerful letters concerning the family. He and her brother Tom had successfully organised a fishing club, which met every month to present prizes for the fresh water fish they caught. One letter included a fascinating photograph of both brothers along with a group of fishermen, some of whom had been presented with fishing rods for catching the largest of carp from the lake at Bolesworth Castle.[42]

Scrutinising the photograph, Eva wrongly identified her brother George but realised that it was in fact Tom. She felt proud of her two handsome brothers who had climbed beyond the searing poverty of their childhood to become two intelligent and caring young men. She could also see the family resemblance between herself and her brothers and sisters, the strong high cheekbones from her Irish father combined with the sensitive thoughtful eyes of their mother, and she felt proud that despite the family tragedy of a brother and sister affected by an illness which no one appeared to fully understand, she came from a powerful and creative family.

By August she was giving serious thought to future employment, looking carefully for suitable positions that would acknowledge her experience as a domestic. And then it happened. She read the notice several times before going back to her room to give it serious thought. She recalled the last time she had been involved with the area around Hastings and that night she thought long and hard about the advice that Morris might have given to her.

She looked again at the notice:

---

[42] Country house in Cheshire, England, built in 1829.

EMPLOYMENT: SCOTTISH REGISTRY, WELLINGTON

EMPLOYMENT OFFERED TO MATURE DOMESTIC, AGED OVER 35 TO ASSIST MRS LOWRY, WIFE OF JAMES LOWRY, ESTABLISHED FARMER, OREKA SHEEP STATION, HASTINGS, NR. NAPIER, NORTH ISLAND, NEW ZEALAND

Two weeks later, Eva received her reply from a Mrs Lowry, offering her the position, which would commence on 9th September. Eva replied immediately accepting the offer. Her wages would amount to 27 shillings and 6 pence a week, which was reasonable pay, especially for the times, and would enable her to continue to save.

She received another letter almost immediately from Mrs Lowry, informing her of another new appointment, a cook named Miss Jamieson who would travel north from Wellington and meet Eva at Hastings Station where a taxi would be waiting to take them the few miles to the sheep station.

Packing her brown trunk and her suitcase with neatly folded and laundered clothes, Eva felt a tinge of excitement. She was already resolved not to mention her work at Brereton but she sensed that the Lowry household would be run along English lines. Sitting down in her hostel room, she wrote to George with details of her future employment.

28th August, 1934

Dear George,
At last I have found a suitable position for myself, working as an experienced and senior housemaid on a sheep station. Please tell mother and father that I am well and happy, as living in a new country for a second time is much less stressful. For a start, I have friends and know the country and also my considerable savings are here. You have a rich sister, George! Even after all my travelling and not working for several months I still have over £300 in my various bank

accounts.

You reminded me before I left to listen out for any mention on the radio of George Bernard Shaw. Well, it would be difficult not to know he had arrived as he has voiced a number of very outspoken opinions, some of which have made me smile. He first noted that people here refer to England as 'home' and suggested to the people of this country that the term should apply exclusively to their own land! I agree with him but it takes time to think like this when you are a migrant.

He gave his vision of the future of the world as a whole, becoming increasingly bound together by the common needs of civilization in things frontiers could not stop. I know you would agree with this opinion but would human nature allow it I wonder. Finally he made a very amusing statement, which I have here in front of me as headlines in the local paper. 'New Zealand would be an ideal place but for the extraordinary mistake of bringing animals into the country. It is over-run with sheep.'

The sheep farmers would not appreciate that remark. He went on in his latest interview to praise the literary press in this country which he feels is immensely superior to the best English newspapers and also warned New Zealand to make its own films or it would become Americanized, or even Anglicized!

Auckland has experienced a very dry summer again, but we hear that you are also having a drought in England. I can hardly imagine it. Now we are approaching the spring rains and I look forward to working out in the country even though it might be isolated. There is much hare hunting here on the North Island. Indeed the entire agricultural situation would interest you greatly George and I am holding you to that visit you promised!

Tell Mother and Father that they can contact me c/o Mrs L. Lowry, Oreka station, Fernhill, Nr Hastings, North Island, New Zealand. Send any future letters to that address George and as promised I will always destroy them as we agreed.

How is dear Joe? Is his medical condition the same or has

his mental state deteriorated? I think of him often.

My best wishes to Edith.
Your loving sister,
Eva.

Oreka Station

Eva travelled across the North Island to Hastings in early September to take up her new position. Arriving at Hastings Railway Station, she found a taxi that had been engaged to take her to the Lowry home, and waited as instructed by Mrs Lowry until the Wellington train arrived. She was joined by a Miss Jamieson, a woman younger than herself, who proceeded to chatter and ask personal questions of Eva during the entire drive.

Eva tried her best to answer the questions without really giving any information away. Besides, where answers involved information about England or Canada, the girl really had no idea of what Eva was talking about. The question about why she wasn't married at her age took a little more thought, but then Eva just answered the way that would cause the least amount of discussion: "Because I've given my life to service and travel and have been far too busy to settle with a man."

As the incessant chatter and questions went on, Eva barely had chance to glance through the taxi window, catching brief glimpses of green countryside, gum trees and rolling hills, which would soon turn yellow then brown as summer approached. Then they were bumping up a rough drive, beneath English trees, including a great oak tree, and were set down in front of a very modern house, fronted by a magnificent verandah. The taxi driver explained that the great earthquake of 1931 had obliterated the original mansion of the Lowrys, to be replaced by this very lovely home.

Eva fell silent at the thought, lost in memories of that dreadful time and realising that what had been taken from her was much more than a house in that earthquake.

But she was pleased nevertheless that she had come here, so near to where Morris had lived out his last happy days.

Mrs Lowry came out to meet them, smiling and very pleasant and Eva felt relaxed, knowing at once that it had been the right decision. Both women were shown to their separate bedrooms, built in the servants' quarters adjoining the main house, pleasant rooms next to each other. Later Eva emerged from her room, glancing into Miss Jamieson's bedroom to see chaos as clothes and belongings had simply been poured out onto the bed and not unpacked properly. She smiled to herself, wondering if this was indicative of the cook's character. She was not surprised as the days went on to be proven correct.

Entering the kitchen to a log fire and afternoon tea, prepared by the scullery maid for the newcomers, she was delighted to see that Mrs Lowry had already posted their duty lists onto the pantry door, for the cook was busy moaning that she had to do Eva's washing and prepare the meals including the staff as from tomorrow.

"I mean, I just got here and she wants me working first thing in the morning! What about a bit of time to settle in?"

Eva looked at the girl and spoke. "You're being paid from today and you're here, so you may as well be working. It's what's happened at every place I've ever worked."

"It's alright for you, you don't even have to do your own washing according to this list," she replied, pointing at the list of duties. "You won't be slaving away in a hot kitchen with other people's washing to do between meal times."

She could hear the sternness in Eva's voice. "I'll be busy enough thank you. And I'll launder my personal clothing myself if you don't mind." Eva couldn't help but think what Audrey would do to the clothes she'd worked so hard to buy or spent so many hours making.

"It's only the staff uniforms you'll need to attend to. And if that's too much for you, I would be more than happy to help you with your job and see to my own."

With that Audrey stood up, clearly angry, "I can certainly manage my job without your help, thank you! Now, I'm going back to my room to finish unpacking." But as she walked from the kitchen she could be clearly heard muttering in a mocking voice, "I'll launder my own personal clothing if you don't mind. Just who does she think she is?"

As Eva checked the list again, she realised that she would only be concerned with the main household duties, including guests. A mention was made of a ball that would be held in the second week of October. Extra staff would be hired on this occasion but the grand house must be immaculate before that time. Eva glanced with appreciation around the warm kitchen where she would take all her meals, pleased by the coziness and warmth.

Since arriving in New Zealand she had again experienced increasing pains in her chest, which she knew was the rheumatism of the heart returning. On warmer days the pains would ease, but at times she had felt lethargic and irritable. Confident that this new position would improve her health, she set about organising her work.

James Lowry wasn't expected back for two weeks. He was away on the South Island seeing to family business interests. The cook was busy finding out all about the Lowry family, and was quick to inform Eva that there were no children. This gave her all the more time to run her home with care and attention. Mrs Lowry was a gentle lady, who made a point of regularly checking on her staff. September may have been a quiet time of year, but in a few weeks when her husband was back, there was the grand ball to be arranged. Meanwhile she busied herself with charity work, taking bunches of flowers from her gardens to the hospitals in Napier and Hastings and delivering gifts and food to the elderly.

Springtime at Oreka station was a wonderful experience. Unlike an English spring, which unfolded subtly, there was an abrupt end to the New Zealand winter.

The greening of the surrounding hillsides, plum and peach blossoms in dazzling white and every shade of pink, willows bursting into leaf and hiding their golden twigs delighted her. Young lambs frisked in the fields reminding her of home. Clumps of wattle and japonicas lined the drive and the huge English oak tree, against which Eva would lean, reminded her of the Lowry's English heritage and made her all the more fond of the Lowry estate. All this was explored during long walks on the estate whenever the weather was fine. She felt that her life could continue on, and decided she had definitely made the right decision to return to New Zealand.

Eva set about perfecting her work. Reverting to many of the traditional household duties she had not practised since the days of the old hall, she felt at ease. In addition to the many tasks she was used to, she learned flower arranging from Mrs Lowry. Working alongside her employer, and finally on her own, she filled the long dining room with magnificent floral arrangements in readiness for the ball. In the process she formed as much of a friendship as a woman in service can do with her employer.

Mrs Lowry didn't bother her, leaving her to her own devices to get the work done that was necessary to run the household. It was quickly apparent that she'd hired a very experienced maid who could be trusted. She often asked Eva to help her in the gardens where they snipped flowers and talked. Eva liked what she knew of Mrs Lowry, a kind young woman who cared deeply for her home and the people around her. She explained that soon the estate would be very busy with the shearing. Guests were expected for Christmas, coming from England.

"Eva, I think you'll enjoy your work here. My English guests are quite delightful. They are friends of my husband, from the time he lived in England a long while ago." She chattered on as they moved among the flowers. Eva waited for more information about the English guests or about Mr Lowry's time in England, but nothing else was forthcoming. So she took the initiative.

"So Mr Lowry lived in England?" she enquired politely.

"Oh yes, but he's not English. He was born near here actually. He has two brothers and their grandfather first settled these parts. The boys all continued the family tradition of going to England for university, Jesus College, Cambridge actually, as their father had before them. It was a family tradition."

She smiled, "I'm afraid I never went anywhere after school. Study, I mean. I did train for nursing, but marriage is a full time occupation. Have you never married, Eva?"

"No Ma'am. There have never been any prospects of marriage for me. Now I'm too old for marriage and children."

"My dear Eva! Too old for marriage and children! You don't look like you're any older than your mid twenties."

Eva smiled, but moved away with the basket. There were many reasons why she wasn't married, many reasons why she kept moving, why she had left her family again. And there were many reasons why she had returned to New Zealand and accepted this job. But they were impossible to explain to anyone.

On her first free day, Eva had decided to go into Hastings. She'd asked how long it might take to walk, but when Mrs Lowry heard about it, she found Eva and talked her into going with her in the car.

"Oh no, dear! You'll not be walking. It's not safe! Not safe at all, a young woman on her own. I'm going into town to visit the hospital. I'll take you in the car and leave you to look around. We can meet up a couple of hours later and travel back here together."

"Certainly Ma'am. That's very kind of you. But I am prepared to walk if need be."

"No, it's settled. We'll go together in the car."

Once in Hastings, Eva made her way to the Hastings cemetery, carefully checking all the headstones for Morris's name. She even asked about the unmarked graves, but there was no trace of him. So she spent her time there wandering around, putting a few spring wildflowers on the unmarked graves before leaving to walk into the town to meet Mrs Lowry.

The Library might be a good place to start, she thought. She was determined to discover whether Morris had ever been found. The last she'd heard from his sister was that he was lost. But Eva was sure he would have been found eventually. If only, she thought, there was a place where I could sit for a little while and be close to him. Remember all the things we said to each other. At last she found something promising. The pain in her heart eased a little, though her sadness was tangible, the Librarian sensing something tragic in the woman who pored over the details of the earthquake and its aftermath. But Eva presented a wall of aloofness around her, deterring anyone from coming close.

Within just a few minutes she had what she was looking for, seven graves that had been made on the edge of Napier, several months after the disaster. Maybe Morris was there? Thanking the Librarian politely, she left quickly to meet up with Mrs Lowry for the drive back to the station. Her mood had lifted. She may not have found Morris, but at least she was closer.

Both women were initially silent in the car on the way back to Oreka. Mrs Lowry seemed lost in her own thoughts while Eva stared from the window across the hilly landscape, thinking of Canadian mountains and happier times. Finally Mrs Lowry broke the silence.

"Eva, we both seem to be lost in our own worlds. I can feel it. I think you're as sad as I am, but I won't pry. Privacy, being able to keep your thoughts private, is very important, don't you think?"

Perhaps it was only a clever way to get a conversation about secrets started, but even so her kind words released all the emotion pent up in Eva. But she was determined not to cry so she clutched her bag tightly and turned away.

"Yes, Ma'am, you are so right. You're extremely kind to me."

She paused a moment, before taking a deep breath. She couldn't tell her about Morris, it would be like giving a piece of him away.

"I do carry a great sadness. But it's not one I can share. But Ma'am, you look very upset. Are you ill?"

Mrs Lowry pulled over to the side of the road and turned to Eva. "Eva, I have to tell someone, and I know by the way that you protect your privacy, that you'll protect mine. Because nobody can know this."

"But of course, Ma'am."

"Today when I visited the hospital, it wasn't to see the patients. It was an appointment for myself."

Eva waited, knowing that the story would come out in her own time. Several minutes passed as Mrs Lowry just looked down at the papers she was holding. She continued to stare at them as she began to speak. "Eva, today the doctor told me that I'm barren. There will be no children at Oreka Station, ever. No heir for James to pass the estate to. Whatever am I to do?" she sobbed, turning to her maid in her desperation.

"Ma'am," Eva was resolute, her voice controlled and showing no emotion. "You will live and find joy, despite there being no babies. Your husband married you to be with you, to share his life with. You just need to find another road to travel together."

Mrs Lowry stared at Eva, amazed by her determined words. "You really believe that Eva? You think we could be happy with no children? The expectation is so enormous. I've been married more than four years already and the family hints are becoming almost too much."

"Mrs Lowry, you have your own life. You are doing so much good in the world for other people already. I see how people love you. Isn't that the finest thing, to be loved by others? To care about others? Sometimes we are just not meant to have children. Your husband loves you and you will be fine."

With that Mrs Lowry smiled weakly and they continued their journey. As they approached the house Mrs Lowry took Eva's hand. "You are a very special person Eva. We're very lucky to have you here in this house. Thank you for what you said earlier. I won't forget it."

Eva turned and watched her employer as she made her way into the house before turning towards the servants' quarters. She had felt such grief that day, yet she'd been able to help someone. Her own loss was immeasurable, but it was behind her. Now Mrs Lowry must face the inevitable, a childless marriage within a wealthy family where inheritance was perpetuity. The land was everything. Its control over people was enormous because it gave them their power. Human sacrifices were made many times over its possession. She knew all this from Brereton Hall. There was a terrible price to be paid for wealth and inheritance and nothing was different in the newer lands where tradition was younger. She'd reassured Mrs Lowry, but in reality she wasn't so sure.

Eva's relationships in the kitchen were not as easy as they were with Mrs Lowry and once again she gained a name for herself as a prig. It was a repeat of what had happened in Wellington so many years before with another cook. Audrey Jamieson despised Eva's quiet refined ways and her refusal to participate in any local gossip and she let all who would listen know that Eva was, in her words, a prig.

Determined one day to find out more from Eva about her personal life, she launched into the subject of eligible men, pointing out in the local paper the photographs of the local brides. Eva responded by studying the paper carefully, then looking up she smiled a sad smile, "I'm simply too old to ever get married."

A deep voice spoke from behind her, causing her to turn in alarm. She found herself facing a strong handsome man, brown eyed with a determined mouth and an almost arrogant air about him. He was dressed in working clothes but even those were worn like a uniform and with style.

The cook shrieked with laughter, suddenly quite coquettish. "Get out Charlie, back to the horses. This is women's conversation!" Then turning to Eva she made a brief introduction. "Charlie, or if you prefer, Charles Edwards, is the main farm hand here, a real genius with the horses, but I don't know about women!" And she laughed again.

Edwards stepped forward to shake hands with Eva and for a brief moment she was reminded of the three men in her life for he seemed a combination of all of them. He looked down at her quietly.

"Trying to get rid of me so quick, Audrey? Normally you can't get enough of me popping in to your kitchen for a cuppa. You couldn't be just a bit jealous, could you? Trying to keep me all to yourself? Eva here is about thirty, very lovely, could be the lady of the house. Someone you'll never be." And then, throwing back his head, he gave a laugh that echoed around the kitchen. "Now there's a good girl, put the kettle on the stove and make us a cup of tea. I've been up since three this morning helping with the lambing."

From that moment, Audrey set herself against Eva. How dare he say she's better than me? She thought.

"I'm sorry if I've embarrassed you, but Audrey can be a nasty little handful sometimes."

"You haven't embarrassed me, not at all," Eva smiled. She could cope with women like Audrey Jamieson. In fact Eva and Charles were almost oblivious to Audrey Jamieson at that moment. Turning to Eva, Charles settled back for a conversation, intrigued by the new housemaid. He'd already seen her in the gardens, but she had disappeared back to the safety of her room before he could speak to her.

"I see you're very fond of flowers. I've seen you a time or two out in the flower gardens. Spring is a good time around here, all the new life and plenty of good grazing for the stock."

"Is that what you do, Mr ..."

"My name is Charles. Yes, I help with the stock, but most of the time I work with the horses. Mr Lowry took me on because he has some very valuable and highly bred stallions. You have to know how to handle animals like them or they escape you very quickly, which is what I think you are about to do Miss Madden."

Eva paused, as she had been about to do just that, escape. She quickly sized him up: charming, but intense and gentle, she could tell that from the way he talked about the horses.

"Thank you Mr Edwards. I'm sure we'll talk again, but I have to attend to my duties now."

For her part Eva was furious that she could be so affected by this man who was a stranger to her. She excused herself and left the kitchen, returning to her room.

Audrey returned with a tray of tea, banging it down on the table. "Where's she gone then? She's a right cow, little stuck up thing! Anyway, no good for you Charlie; prim, flat chested, and nothing to say for herself!" She laughed. "I don't think she'll be lifting her petticoats for you!"

"The trouble with you Audrey is your mouth. I'll leave you with the tea. Maybe you can drink the lot because neither Miss Madden or me want to share it with you."

Alone then, Audrey muttered to herself about snobbish English maids who thought they were above their station. She had respect in her last place of employment.

For her part, Eva was very cross with the cook who had placed her in this uncomfortable situation with Charles and for the next few days as everyone prepared for the spring ball, she avoided Audrey whenever possible, giving her dark looks that denied any kind of communication. Fortunately, she didn't see Charles Edwards either.

The entire staff was caught up with the social occasion. The preparations made a pleasant change from the routine running of a sheep station, and nobody objected to helping. They saw another side of their employers, one of class and status. Eva organised the temporary housemaids, even congratulating Audrey on her plans and how she was managing the six hired kitchen hands. No expense had been spared, including the cost of the ladies' gowns.

Eva lay down on her bed, exhausted by the evening's events. Finally all the festivities had ended. The spring ball at Oreka Station had been a resounding success and she knew that she had played a part in it. Her fastidious attention to detail and hard work had been part of that success and privately she felt a great sense of achievement. She thought of the rooms decorated with balloons and trails of coloured paper, the verandah lit by Chinese lanterns and the supper room arranged with individual tables decorated with bowls of blue delphiniums and a mixture of pale pink blooms.

It had been a happy night for Eva but she was troubled by an unexpected event. She had taken a short break before she started her evening duties in the dining room. She walked quite often now, so took the opportunity of climbing the small rise in front of the house to look down on the lighted rooms. Someone stepped from the shadows, startling her.

"Looks really grand. And you helped it along. Flowers everywhere. I've been watching you these last few days Miss Eva Madden".

She turned and faced him. "You mean you have been spying on me Mr Edwards?"

"Not at all," and his laughter was reassuring. "You know, the only thing that separates you and them is the uniform. You'd look a million quid in one of those gowns."

Eva smiled in the dark. Charles Edwards was a kind man. She decided he meant no harm. She shivered in the cool evening breeze, the cold air causing her to cough.

"Mmm, I've noticed that cough. Here, wrap yourself in this. Might smell a bit of the horses but it'll keep you warm." He'd removed his jacket and wrapped it around her shoulders. They returned to the house and thanking him she handed back the jacket as he turned to go.

Why am I worrying, thought Eva. It was simply a thoughtful act of kindness. Finally she fell asleep, not even waking when Audrey Jamieson slammed the outside door on her way to her own bedroom.

The following week passed normally as the station got back to its regular business. Eva talked to Charles often; occasionally walking on the estate after her work was done. She avoided any personal conversation with Mrs Lowry, who was preoccupied with preparations for the visit of her English friends. James Lowry checked the stock, often riding with Charles when he exercised the horses. There were no more conversations, much to Eva's relief.

November was a hectic month, with all hands working long hours at the shearing, which took place on all of the stations of the Northern Island. Eva was becoming more interested in Charles, wanting to know him a little better. The opportunity arose at the end of his long days when they began to take what would become their regular time together walking around the property. The evenings were warm as summer approached, leaving them with a short time together between nine and ten o'clock.

Eva always headed for her room by ten because she had to be up by six o'clock in the morning and she didn't want disapproval from the Lowrys. Charles seemed on good terms with James Lowry, who recognised an experienced worker. No one could handle the horses as well as he could. He spoke softly to them in a language Eva did not recognise, calming them down so that he could groom them and inspect their hooves.

When he handled the black stallion that everyone else was afraid of, he would snuggle into the side of the great beast, muttering "no foot, no horse" before lifting its hooves for inspection. Eva loved to watch him with animals, sensing his deep understanding of all creatures, which reminded her of her father and George.

She found herself telling him about England and her family, for he had many questions. But she kept her secrets

The Price

about Ellen and Joe and even about Morris. In return, he told her only about his mother and sister, who both lived in Hastings. But Eva was not one to pry, believing that he must have his reasons and that he would eventually confide in her, as she might with him some day.

Sheep shearing finally finished, and with it came the disappearance of Charles Edwards along with the other men. Eva asked where he might be and Audrey replied spitefully that he would be drinking all his money away in one of the local hotels. Seeing that she had managed to penetrate Eva's defences, she pursued the subject.

"He gets the devil in him, does Charlie. It's the demon drink. Anything goes down well when he's on a binge. Most men are like that you know, but then you wouldn't know would you, little Miss High and Mighty. You set him up on a pedestal and you're in for one mighty fall, Miss Swanky Madden. Don't tell me your father never had a drink or two to get away from your mother! My dad lived in hotels, only came home for his meals and sex."

Shocked at the attack on her parents, Eva advanced on Audrey who was twice her size, grabbed hold of her breast and twisted it until the cook screamed.

"Don't you ever speak of my family like that again and yes, you can tell Mrs Lowry if you want to, but don't expect her support!" and she left the room shaking in anger. Audrey wailed so loudly that the poor kitchen maid had to comfort her with hot sweet tea. But the subject of Eva's family never arose again.

Things change at Oreka

Eva accepted Mrs Lowry's offer of a ride to Napier on the pretence of visiting the shops, while her mistress attended to her charity work. She made her way to Park Island Cemetery and there she finally found what she had been looking for, a small patch of earth with a simple cross, and the name Morris Miller painted on it.

Eva slowly sank to her knees, the tears for so long denied finally pouring down her cheeks. With only the sound of her sobs to keep herself company, her memories flooded in, every moment she'd spent with him flashing through her mind. She ran her hands through the soil, letting it run through her fingers over and over. Then she traced the letters of his name on the cross at the head of the grave. Already it was weathered. How soon before even this memorial was gone?

Why did this happen to us Morris? If there were some kind of God, why would he give me your love and then take it away so quickly? I'm so lonely, so alone, without you, but I am trying. I'm travelling on, but who knows where? I can't seem to settle anywhere without you. She sat in silence for a while, the memories of her all too short time with him running like pictures in her mind, the emotions attached to each occasion washing over her. My life is taking some very strange twists and turns, Morris. Going back home only to feel like it wasn't home. Coming back here.

She sat there for hours, telling him everything. The family secrets she'd thought she had a lifetime to tell, about their baby and about their stones in the tree in Stanley Park. Their two hearts bound together forever. Finally, she took a small amount of the earth and put it in her handkerchief. The revival of all those memories of love and happiness swept

The Price

through Eva with such intensity that as she tried to stand up, she swayed with dizziness. Looking at the small cross again, she said her goodbye, finally. The goodbye she had been denied when she thought he was only going to be gone for a few weeks. She walked to the cemetery wall and leaned against it, breathing slowly. She took one last look at the graves and then walked through the gate and went to wait for Mrs Lowry.

She spent a lot of time thinking about her future. She knew that she could never return to Crewe, except as a visitor, so she faced a life in New Zealand. But it couldn't be with the Lowrys. She had to leave their employment as soon as possible. And she was tired of going from job to job. She deserved to settle down somewhere. But no matter how much time she spent thinking about it, she still couldn't decide what she was going to do to change her life.

Her friendship with Charles deepened quickly as her need to have some sort of future became clear. His drinking, although she had never witnessed it, disturbed her. It didn't affect her and she felt she could control it if need be. If he really cared for her, he would stop, she reasoned. She enjoyed his company and was becoming more attracted to him. Their friendship was as yet uncomplicated.

During one of their walks, Eva confronted Charles over his drinking. He confessed quite openly. "Since meeting you Eva, I have hardly had a drop. It's a way of life here for single men. Work hard, drink hard. If it's important to you, I promise I won't do it again."

His voice softened to the gentle tone he used with the animals. "Eva, you're very special to me. We walk out as friends, but I really want to hold you, you know, be with you, and possess you. And don't tell me that you don't feel the same because I know you'd be lying."

"I can't." Eva then turned to look at him defiantly. "But if there's to be anything at all between us I won't have you drinking. I hate it. I hate the smell of it. I hate what it does to men. It turns them into groping idiots. It makes them destroy their families. I just won't have it."

She'd maintained an even tone as she spoke, but she was surprised by the ferocity of her words. She turned away and felt tears in her eyes for she recognised the words of her mother, the anger of her mother and the insidious control that she had never eliminated, perhaps because she'd been so damaged by the curse of drinking herself.

But just as suddenly she turned into his arms, and he laid her gently on the grass. They kissed and undressed each other. He was as gentle as she had imagined, kissing the tiny palms of her hands, removing her laced up shoes and stockings. He lifted her skirts and petticoats and removed her drawers before undoing the buttons of her blouse and exposing her breasts. He kissed her all over her body, stopping briefly to run a gentle finger over the faint scar on her breast before entering her. She shut her eyes smelling him, feeling him and knowing that despite the drinking, some part of her had fallen in love with him.

They lay together on the grass afterward, she looking up at the stars, he dozing lightly. He wasn't the great love of her life, but she needed him and it would be as good as it could be with anyone but Morris. She rolled on her side and looked at him. The great oak tree moved in the rising wind far above them, causing him to turn his head to the side and open his eyes to stare directly into hers. Looking carefully at him, she noted the tiredness and sadness about him. Now he was the vulnerable one and she felt the strength within her as they made love yet again, briefly and fiercely, living only for that moment. The tension that had been rising between them for months still needed quenching.

Finally exhausted, they lay still, their bodies touching, unable to talk. Eventually Charles leant over her body, tenderly replacing her stockings and shoes and smoothing down her petticoats and linen dress. "Eva, you are wonderful. Better than any woman I have ever had and yet you never told me. That was the first time, wasn't it?"

Eva smiled, a slow sad smile, thinking back to her

unfulfilled love for Morris. "Why do you ask if you know?"

Together they walked slowly back to the house, a little apart from one another, each to return to a solitary bed. But Eva now knew that she had crossed a barrier that had kept her from danger or risk. While she had not let any men but Morris into her life, she had been safe, but now she had discovered a passion within herself, an insatiable longing for this man and she knew she would want him again and again.

The following morning Eva went about her routine duties, outwardly simply the efficient housemaid, but within in turmoil. How could this possibly end? She longed to shout out that she had at last found a path to happiness but all her inhibitions and survival instincts protected her from doing so. She would not even rise to the constant jibes from Audrey when she ate her meals.

"Well, well, Miss High and Mighty. What are you up to? I heard you come in last night, sneaking into your room. Come on, let's be friends shall we? Is Charlie getting fond of you? Might there be an engagement in the making? You can trust me," she laughed, winking at the scullery maid. Eva's reply was to walk quietly from the kitchen, leaving her meal half uneaten.

"Stuck up bitch! Who does she think she is? Anyway, why would Charlie want her, flat chested prim little woman, not his type at all?" She laughed bitterly as she turned back to her own meal.

Eva was relieved to find a letter from her brother waiting for her in the hall. She looked longingly at the Crewe postmark. It had arrived on the new air service, the date showing that it had taken only seventeen days in transit. That evening she read her letter, seeking familiar contact with her past, sensing the security offered by her brother.

November 17th, 1934

My dear Eva,
It seems a long time since I saw you off at Southampton. We all miss you and look forward to your interesting letters. I am sorry that I missed your 38th birthday, Edie did remind me but I have been working nights on the railway but nothing of a personal nature seems to be achieved during those times when night becomes day and vice versa.
Edie doesn't like being left on her own but the money is double time and I am resolved to pay off the mortgage on this house as soon as possible. The Ford car, which Tom and me bought between us, is working out well. If Tom keeps up the maintenance and we pay the bills together then we can afford it. The Arial bike has been sold at last and the money paid off the mortgage.
But tell me Eva, what is work like out there? I always interpret your silence as happiness. In Canada you went for quite a while without corresponding but I always reassured mother that you were fine.
This last summer developed into a drought which was so fierce that sheep were dying in their hundreds. Streams disappeared, rivers became mere trickles and trout could be picked from the water by hand! From all parts of the country, families were living on a pint of water a day! Even milk was threatened for there was no water to cool the milk on the farms. We saw our first rain in late September. It certainly gave everyone an idea of the harsh summer conditions experienced in Australia and New Zealand.
I saw an interesting advert for teamsters required in New Zealand. I would love to have tried my hand at that but Edie will have none of it. Her horizons only extend as far as Crewe town and up to Neville Street to visit her mother every day! It is a pity, as I would love to come out to you.
The rest of the family are well and nothing has changed at Chester I'm afraid. It is as we anticipated.
Write to me soon.

Best wishes,
Your brother,
George.

Carefully folding the letter inside the envelope, Eva made her way to the kitchen where she prepared to burn it on the fire. Then she realised that there was no news in this letter that could be misused by gossips or the snooping Audrey Jamieson. She looked at the letter again and smiling, folded it. She was just beginning to slip it into her pocket when suddenly strong arms enfolded her. Turning round, she stared into Charles' eyes.

"Eva Madden, my little Eva, you remind me of a little bird, so fragile but yet so determined to thrive. Come outside and I'll show you what I mean," and he led her outside into the kitchen gardens. "Now look up."

Eva did so and saw a row of tiny birds, lined up on the branch of a willow tree, all waiting to be fed. They wobbled and chirped but hung on with their tiny feet to the thin twig. Swooping down, the fat mother bird plunged worms down their gluttonous throats, never managing to silence them for a moment.

"We never go far wrong if we look around us. We will thrive Eva, you and me if we don't break the rules. I can't say God's rules, because my only religion is nature. I was born a Roman Catholic of course, but I don't practise it. Or any other religion as a matter of fact." Then he smiled. "Now come here, Miss Eva Madden, because I want you right now."

In a hollow beyond the kitchen garden, witnessed only by the birds singing their spring songs, they made love quickly and frantically, eventually lying back exhausted in the grass. Gathering Eva up in his arms, Charles held her close so that she could hear the pounding of his heart, and he hers. They didn't speak but they both knew that they were venturing into unknown territory and it would not be easy. Eva stirred, anxious to finally ask him if he was married. No man as exciting as this could have escaped such a commitment.

She must know and steeled herself for the truth. It was slow in coming but yes, he had changed his name from Price to Edwards four years previously when he left his wife and three children. He had married young and into appalling poverty, once imprisoned for four months for stealing a bag of potatoes in order to feed his young family. Finally his wife moved in with her mother and circumstances became intolerable. He felt in the end that he had no wife or family as others took over his role as father and husband.

All of this was said dispassionately but Eva looked into troubled eyes, knowing that he was telling the truth despite the chance of losing her. She understood the situation. Divorce was impossible, life was impossible. She had seen too many men in the same situation, wandering the countryside, seeking work, pride and honour gone through searing poverty. Compassion welled inside her.

As she looked at his sad face and heard his broken voice, she barely spared a thought for his wife, who despite her hard attitude towards Charles, was undoubtedly finding raising children single-handedly as difficult a job as her own mother had. Instead she saw her father, who had been beaten down by a wife who disapproved of him and the poverty that made it so hard to support his children as he should, the poverty that in the end had all but emasculated him. And in that moment she would have done almost anything to save him.

Taking his large well-worn hand in her tiny one, she looked at him directly. "Thank you for being honest with me. I can't ask for anything more from you." There was a slight pause then and he almost panicked, wondering what would come next.

Quietly and slowly, Eva said, "I want you Charles. I want to share my life with you, no matter what the past. I have savings, you know. We could buy a place together, here near Hastings. And live as man and wife. There will not and cannot ever be children, but we'd have each other."

Charles leant forward, astonished by this reaction. He had already steeled himself for the end of their relationship. Never had he expected this. "Eva, do you mean it? You of all people! If you mean it, really mean it, you'll want for nothing. I promise you. I'll look after you. I love you Eva. I felt it from the day you set foot on Oreka last September. All the other men had their eye on you too, but you had no idea, going about your business in your own little world." His whole face had lit up. "So what have I done to deserve this? Why me?"

Eva saw tears in his eyes. She was shocked that she'd been the subject of the men's speculation, but even more shocked by his tears. "You told me the truth and we'll gain our strength from that," she said defiantly. "We'll make plans. We have the means. No one here need know about our relationship and we'll leave this place for our own."

He smiled sheepishly. "I think they already know about our relationship, Eva."

"What have you said?" she asked, her temper threatening to flare.

"Me? I haven't said a thing! But ... but everyone knows we go for long walks together, even after dark. They have to think something's going on. And don't think that Audrey's not talking about us."

Her relief was palpable. "But all they have is gossip. Nobody knows for a fact that we're lovers. And that's the way I'd like to keep it if you don't mind. As for us going away together, not a word. There's a dim view taken of domestic staff that runs off with other hired help and I don't want a reputation that might stop me getting work if I ever need to in the future. Remember, not a word about us. Or I may have to change my mind about trusting you."

"You have my word, Eva. Absolutely."

That night in the isolation of her room, Eva wept fiercely, beating her pillow in frustration and rage as she finally accepted the suffering of her family, letting go of the powerful religious influences that she had suffered under for so long. But she had to let go of that too and accept that Charlie was the best she was ever going to have and he wasn't bad at all.

"I will be happy," she stormed. "I don't care about what anyone else thinks any more. When I'm with him, I'm loved and safe. Even though I could end up being hurt. Charles isn't Morris, he isn't my father, he isn't George, but I can see some of all the men I've loved in him. He's strong, but he still needs help. He still needs me. He's honest even though he's done bad things. Who am I to condemn him? I'm only Eva Madden. What right do I have to judge him? What right do I have to turn away from the man I love because of his human frailty? I ran away from England because I couldn't cope with the burdens of my family, how can I criticise him for doing the same thing?"

All these questions frayed at the fringes of her decision. But in the end she knew she wasn't happy as a single woman and that she deserved not to spend her entire life in service to others, unable to make decisions about her own life even about her day to day routine. She deserved to be free and make her own path in life. Even if that freedom came with the price her mother always said had to be paid. After hours of crying, finally she came to terms with her lot and felt peace in her decision to make the best life she could with this man. Finally she could sleep and find rest. At least with Charles she could have some kind of future. There could be no going back now.

Exhausted by crying, she fell asleep. In her hand were small flowers that she had picked from the spring grass where she had lain with Charles. As she had lain in bed she had held them tightly as some sort of reassurance against things going wrong. They had comforted her in an inexplicable way. The next morning, very early, she rose and wrote to George as honestly as she was able.

20th December 1934

*Oreka Station,
Fernhill Near Hastings,
North Island, New Zealand.*

*Dear George,
I received your letter and noted the contents. This is only very brief but I wish you to tell Mother and Father that I have met a man whom I wish to marry. His name is Charles Edwards. You would like him George; he has something of you in him. He is a strong man, a teamster and farm hand who works here. He is 44 years old and is a man of the land like you. We intend to buy a cottage near here and will start to look soon but as yet no-one at the station knows our business.
I love him George and I will be with him no matter what. I hope you give me your blessing in this matter,*

*Your loving sister,
Eva.*

Over the following weeks, Charles and Eva made careful plans. She made a point of telling Audrey that she was suffering with her heart and needed to see a doctor in Hastings. Very soon, the entire station heard about her failing heart and how if she didn't stop working that she'd likely die! How lucky the station was to have Audrey to take on some of Eva's work as her health failed. As usual, Audrey had made herself the heroine of the story, but more importantly she had not failed Eva and had elaborated on the story beautifully. In the process she had turned it into irresistible gossip!

Eva handed in her notice just before Christmas, but Charles waited until the New Year so that their leaving would not be connected. Mrs Lowry begged Eva not to go, but on the pretence of returning to her family in England, Eva managed to convince her. She needed her, she said. Where would she find another person with Eva's experience? she argued. But Eva wouldn't be swayed. James Lowry simply looked at her after she gave her notice, but not a word was spoken between them. Not then and not until she left.

Eva and Charles made plans to stay in Hastings for a few days, in order to look at some land that he knew about. He was very enthusiastic about it.

"It's only about twenty-three miles west of Hastings. It'll take a few hundred sheep. And there's a little cottage already there. It's broken down and needs some fixing up, but we could live in it while I fix it up. Then maybe we could rent out the land for agistment until we have money to stock it."

"I have some money Charles. The farm could start paying for itself sooner than you think."

"I reckon we could get it for just thirty quid down, Eva. Take out a mortgage, pay it off in ten years or so. And I can earn a bit extra doing work on the other farms nearby."

Eva was pleased. £30 was easily affordable from her savings. And if Charles was right and they could make a living from the property through agistment and eventually stocking it, then she could leave the rest of her savings intact in case she ever needed them. She wouldn't even need to let him know that by now she could almost pay for the property outright.

Christmas passed by almost unnoticed for both of them as they planned their new lives together in secret. They spent hours walking around the farm after dark, discussing their plans and carefully laying down a false trail in order not to be seen as a couple. Charles explained to James Lowry that his father was going to be arriving from Australia soon, with money to buy a farm. But he was not deceived. He had seen the two of them out on the estate in the evenings and he was deeply troubled. Charles was an excellent stockman, but he was no saint. Eva was vulnerable and he feared for her safety but she was a mature woman and he could not interfere.

Audrey Jamieson also knew that they were going away together. She had seen a great change in Charles. Protective and caring of Eva, he would not tolerate any unkind words about her, warning Audrey in threatening tones to say nothing about their prolonged walks. Jealous and angry, Audrey could only watch, but she dared not spread gossip about the two of them.

Leaving the Lowrys

It was finally the 3rd of February, the day when both of them would leave. Since their resignations coming at the same time was simply a coincidence, it was perfectly natural for them to share a lift together as far as Hastings Railway Station. Understandably, Audrey was not part of the party to come outside to farewell them. She'd considerably gone off Charles since she realised that he'd been going for walks, and goodness only knew what else, with Eva. She'd never liked Eva's refusal to participate in her gossip and the breast twisting episode had completely finished it for her. Eva's departure from Oreka Station was a case of good riddance as far as Audrey was concerned. But Mrs Lowry and a number of the other staff were certainly outside to wish them both well for the future.

James Lowry took them into town in his car where Eva made a point of leaving her luggage at Hastings Railway Station. Charles also left his kitbag at the Left Luggage Office as they had planned, then hardly bearing to look at Eva, he set off in search of suitable lodgings for her. They had decided that they would be noticed in town if they stayed together. But the lodgings in Heretaunga Street they'd decided upon were depressing.

Their whispered conversation on the street outside was heated. "I don't care what people will think, Charles. I'm not staying here. It's dingier than my parents' house in Crewe."

"Well it was you that said we couldn't stay together. What else will we do?"

"I'll go back to the Hastings Hotel and you can register me under a different name. That way the Lowrys won't know that I didn't go on after I was dropped off today.

And they won't know we're together if I use a different name. Come on, let's go."

Charles turned to the boarding house owner who still waited on the doorstep and called, "Thank you for your time. My friend has decided not to stay after all."

So they walked back to the Hastings Hotel in the February heat. When they got there, Charles mischievously asked Eva what new identity she would like to assume and then settled on Miss Malcolm. It still started with an 'M' like her real name and would be easy for Eva to remember, but Malcolm was common enough that it wouldn't stand out. It would also match the initials on some of her luggage.

"If you have to use a different name," he told her, "it's better to use something fairly common and not too far from the truth."

Since the Lowrys were expecting him to stay at the Hastings Hotel for a few days, he booked himself in under the name of Edwards. He hoped the use of an alias for Eva would further muddy the trail if someone were to start gossiping about them.

Sweaty from the walk, Eva washed and changed as soon as she got to her room. After a quick check in the mirror, she hurried down for the evening meal where she found Charles already waiting for her. They sat opposite each other, smiling but not touching even though they longed to. To other guests they showed every sign of propriety, just two acquaintances dining together since they happened to be in the same place at the same time. Later that evening, when the hotel guests had gone their separate ways, Charles visited Eva in her room, excited to be with her. He brought her a gift of a pair of walking shoes, which had cost him thirty-five shillings. It was more than his weekly wages but Eva couldn't walk about the property in her town shoes.

This time their lovemaking was measured and prolonged and silently they caressed each other, smoothing away the anxieties which each felt. For the first time they could make love to each other at leisure, instead of the rushed and furtive episodes that they'd had to resort to at Oreka. Eva felt tired, even exhausted, by all the changes and prolonged excitement and she fell asleep quickly. But after dozing for only a few minutes, Charles gently left the bed and silently dressed. He then tiptoed out of the room to walk about the town he knew so well. He visited his sister but said nothing of Eva, keeping the promise they'd made to keep their relationship a secret. His sister was anxiously waiting to tell him about a warrant that had been put out for his arrest. The police had called at her house only a few days before.

"Charlie, you'd best get right away from here. They don't know you're working out at the Lowrys, but it won't take them long to find out. Just disappear for a while like you've done before when the police have been looking for you."

Charles smiled, seeming quite indifferent to the news. "Don't know why they don't just give up. They keep on about all this maintenance I owe for the Missus. Well I just haven't got it."

He took the drink that she offered. "I'll be in touch. Don't worry about me. I've never been as happy as I am now. And I'll make sure they never find me."

"Take care of yourself Charlie. Here, I've filled a hip flask with a drop of whisky for you. Just in case you need it."

Restless and worried by the news of the warrant, he made his way back to the bar where he drank several whiskies before retiring to his room. He looked a forlorn figure sitting in the bar by himself, talking to no one. The warrant was a worry. But surely they wouldn't find him when he was now Charles Edwards and especially if he was the 'husband' of Eva and living on an isolated farm. He couldn't say anything to Eva about the warrant, because she wouldn't let the matter drop like his sister did. The problem of payment wasn't a new one and he was skillful at disappearing. He'd done it often enough. As he drank more, he began to feel more annoyed about the news. Hundreds of men were in the same position, it was a common enough thing. Why the warrant for him? Finally he retired to bed, quite drunk, and able to sleep soundly.

After a lifetime in service, Eva awoke at dawn as usual, and tiptoed along the corridor to Charles's room. She silently turned the doorknob and walked carefully across the carpet to wake him with a kiss, but immediately smelt drink on his breath. Horrified, she moved away from the bedside to stare at him, confused that he had broken his promise not to drink any more. Then she fled to her room, locking her door while she gathered her senses together. She'd given up everything for this man and now he'd let her down the very first day she'd had to rely on him. Was this going to be the pattern, or would he change for her? Her own father, who'd loved her mother deeply, hadn't been able to change for love, he'd still visited the pub for a couple of beers even though he knew how much her mother hated it.

By the time they met over breakfast, she had calmed down, but Charles noticed at once that she wouldn't look at him and guessed the reason.

"So that's why I wasn't woken up by my lovely woman," he lightly protested.

"You promised me Charles. You gave me your word."

"Eva, I know I did and I'm sorry. But last night I called to see my sister and she and her husband insisted I have a New Year drink with them. Please let this go, just this once. Come on, I'm begging you. What did you expect me to do? I hadn't seen them for months," he pleaded.

Eva forgave him, but she was still cross with him for doing the one thing she hated. Her mother's powerful influence stayed with her even though she fought against it. His eyes carried a forlorn hope, but her voice was flat. "Drinking is the one thing I absolutely won't tolerate, Charles."

"Eva, I've given up the grog for you. I'll never be

drunk again in my life. I promise you." Her face softened and he knew he'd won, even if he was still in her bad books.

His description of the land they hoped to buy soon cheered her though and she made plans to cash her cheques for her wages from Mrs Lowry, also calling at the Hastings Post Office to make an application for £30 to be withdrawn from her Post Office Savings Bank account at Wellington. She made arrangements for this money to be sent to her by Money Order telegram, addressed to her, care of the Girls' Friendly Society at Napier, and the book to be forwarded to the Post Office at Waipawa. To anyone who cared, it would look like she was going to work in Napier.

As she wrote the note to the Post Office in Wellington, she sensed Charles watching as she wrote that she had £300 in the account. There were also the £100 savings bonds that she'd continued to invest in over the years, but she decided there would be time enough to tell Charles about those. Besides, some didn't mature for a few years. They may be needed if the farm took a while to become profitable. Best she keep it to herself for now she decided.

Later that morning Charles called at the Labour Registry Office in Russell Street Hastings and left the two suitcases belonging to Eva. If anyone were looking for them, they'd assume that the woman at the hotel was someone different. Why would Eva be staying there if her belongings had been left at the Labour Registry for a couple of days while she checked on the prospects for a new job?

Eva watched Charles, tall, long limbed and fit, step lightly down the steps of the Registry and she realised perhaps for the first time that he would be attractive to most women and felt a small burst of pride that such a man was hers. Nevertheless, she knew she had to stick to her resolve about his drinking. She couldn't have a man drink away everything she had worked for since she was thirteen years old and then leave her to wither and age as her mother had.

Together they boarded the bus for Napier where Eva called at the Girls' Friendly Society Hostel. She had booked

The Price

a room there when she was still at the Lowry household, but today she cancelled it as she and Charles had planned and made the excuse that she had met friends and intended staying with them. She also told the housemaid that she was expecting a telegram, asking her to hold it for the next day.

Their plans were going ahead perfectly. The Lowrys would never suspect their relationship and although they avoided any physical contact with each other in public, both Eva and Charles were excited at the thought of their new life together, exchanging knowing looks on the bus journey back to Hastings.

Eva gave Charles her wages for safe keeping, assuring him that the £30 would be used for the deposit on their land buy. As she handed over the money, she reflected for just a moment that this was the first time in her life she'd done anything like it and that it was somehow the final surrender to the relationship and their plans. She was no longer an independent woman who had to take care of these things alone.

That afternoon they visited a taxi driver that Charles knew, and arranged a taxi for the following day to take them out to Taheke Station, Argyle East.

"I'll not be able to take you tomorrow. Got to do some work for the Missus. You know how it is Charlie." Charles had heard about Mrs Dooney and she was indeed a formidable woman. "But I can arrange for someone else. Name's Guild. He can pick you up at the hotel. If you let me know what time you want to set off, I'll give him the message."

"Actually, how about we meet him here at ten o'clock?" Charles replied. "That'll give us time to get ourselves up and washed and have some breakfast." Eva nodded as he looked at her.

This arrangement fitted their plans perfectly. They could look at the land without any gossip spreading in Hastings, buy it if they both agreed, and settle there without anyone being any the wiser of their whereabouts. Eva knew that she would eventually have to tell her family more about the arrangements, but for now she was determined to go ahead with their relationship and hopefully a future together. That night they sat closer together at the dining table in the Hastings Hotel. Charles leant over the table to stare deeply into Eva's eyes.

"You don't have any regrets do you, my darling? You're going to be brave enough to see this through?"

Eva sat quite still, watching him carefully. This was it, she decided. This is my future. And the only way to commit to it is as if Morris never existed. She took a deep breath and looked Charles in the eye. "Charles, I've never felt so happy or so hopeful. It's as if I've journeyed all my life to reach this point to find you." She paused for a moment before leaning closer and whispering. "Can you tell how much I want you right now? I know I have to, but I'm not sure I can wait to touch you until we can finish dinner and get back to our rooms. We would be quite the scandal if I did what I wanted to you right now!"

Charles smiled, reaching over and gently taking her hand. "You can wait if I can." She could hear the teasing laugh in his voice. Then, more seriously, "it won't be long. Nothing's going to separate us now. Nothing, my little Eva." He leaned back in his chair. "It's been a long, hot day. The one thing that would quench the thirst is a beer."

"Charles!"

"Eva it's just the one, I promise. It'll be cold and take the dust from a man's mouth, that's all."

She thought for a moment. If it were only one beer, it would be refreshment, not real drinking.

"Of course. One beer is fair enough at the end of a long day."

He smiled as he rose and walked to the bar and ordered a long beer. As he talked to the barman, the man made mention of the English lady who was his companion.

"You're doing well for yourself aren't you?" joked the barman enviously. "What a good looker! What have you

The Price

got going for you or need I ask?" And with that he laughed aloud. He continued, "These English women, some of them are right little ladies, brought up different from the local women. I know of a family near here. All English, by the name of Hollis. Their women are just a bit hoity-toity, but nice all the same. I always watch my language when they come in here for a meal."

Eva glanced up, shrewdly observing both men, with no idea that she, and English women in general, were the topic of their conversation. She thought again about how strong and handsome Charles looked. She began to smile to herself for the second time that day, thinking about how other women admired him, but he was all hers. Her smile spread as she realised how her mother would react to such a vain thought. But the smile turned to a frown when she saw the beer in his hand. The glass was almost full. She was sure the last time she had looked up there had been less in the glass.

As he sat down, Charles spilled some of his beer on the table, the smell reaching Eva instantly. For one dark moment she was pulled backwards and downwards into that pit which had held her for so long. Her temper boiled over and she stood up, her face reddening. Suddenly, she thumped the table, unable to control herself. She felt the same deep anger rising within her that had brought her to physical violence twice before but she could do nothing to restrain herself. Her voice was quiet, but full of menace. "You're drunk, Charles. You're drunk and you've been secretly drinking behind my back." Tears filled her eyes. "I'm leaving and going to my room. I'm finished with you."

Storming out from the empty dining room, she left Charles feeling devastated. What on earth had brought such anger and even hatred to the surface? He followed her to her room but the door was locked. He could hear sobbing and tried to talk to her through the door, but there was no answer. He lifted his hand to bang on the door, but slowly let it fall to his side as he realised that other guests would hear and Eva still wouldn't let him in.

    For her part Eva was desperate. She lay on her bed as sobs wracked her body. She knew she couldn't spend the rest of her life in service. She had lived by the rules of others her whole life and she deserved her independence. First her mother, and then her employers. Was she never going to have her own home? Charles was her chance and yet she wouldn't be ruined by a man who couldn't resist the drink. She felt so trapped. Like being at the bottom of a well, being able to see the light that she wanted so desperately, but not quite being able to find her way out. Her rage was more frustration, surely. Yes, it was justified since at this point she had so much to lose, but it was almost overwhelmingly frustration. She wondered if this was how Ellen had felt when she used to lose her temper so spectacularly. This scared her and brought fresh sobs as she realised that they were more alike than Eva had ever imagined. For not the first time Eva questioned whether she might too have a touch of the madness present in her family. To react so violently about a drink surely wasn't rational, was it? It scared her most that she'd had no control over her reaction. Yet surely it was borne of the stress she'd been under and the risks being taken in the next few days.

    For hours she tried to make sense of all she was feeling, finally falling asleep from exhaustion. She had heard Charles knocking and softly calling for her and later skulking outside her door, but she ignored him. Her grief and confusion could only be compared to the morning she awoke to discover she'd miscarried Morris's baby.

    Charles was distraught. Surely she couldn't mean it? He didn't know what to do. He stood in the corridor outside her room for what seemed like an age before leaving the hotel and walking for hours in the dark summer night. He didn't notice the scent of flowers that perfumed the dark or even where he was going. Suddenly he stopped in his tracks, forcing himself to lean against a wall. And there he sobbed, feeling Eva's suffering, knowing that he must calm

The Price

her in some way, rid her of this terrible consuming anger or it would end their future together and he couldn't bear to even contemplate that happening. He knew he'd caused it, but having a drink was a natural thing to him, a lifelong habit that would be hard to break. She had to give him time. Surely he could convince her.

Much later, he finally reached the hotel and made his way to her bedroom. All was silent inside. He paused at her door, deciding that he had to leave her alone that night, even though he wanted to make love to her, to wipe away the ugliness that had surfaced when she seemed at her happiest.

Early the next morning when he woke he crept down the corridor to her room. The door was open! Stepping inside, he looked for signs of packing but there were none. He walked forward to look behind the screen to the little hand basin and there stood his little Eva, pale but calm. Nothing was said between them as if each did not dare to broach the subject. Silently they each packed, leaving the hotel to meet the taxi at ten o'clock. Nothing was resolved, but at least they were together.

Charles sat in the back with Eva, glancing quickly in her direction, noting her blue coat and small white hat pulled down over her curls. He knew that within an hour she would be too hot but he didn't dare say anything, he knew he was very much on probation with Eva at that moment. In silence, the taxi set off on the long journey across bumpy, unmade roads, but Charles reasoned that at least she was sitting next to him. She wasn't running away. They still had a chance.

He searched for something to break the ice, suddenly remembering the conversation with the barman. "Eva, have you ever heard of an English family names Hollis?"

Hearing that well known name brought a smile to Eva. "Why do you ask? I knew of a Hollis family who lived in Crewe, a few doors from me. I used to play with the children. Their uncle came out to New Zealand and they used to ask me to look him up, but I've never been able to trace him."

"Well, the barman mentioned a family named Hollis and I know the name. They live quite near to where we are going. Maybe if you're up to it and wearing your new shoes," he paused as Eva suddenly laughed, a flood of relief sounding in her voice. "Maybe we could walk over there and see if you know them."

The ice was broken. Eva snuggled nearer to him and he could hardly hear the whispered words, "I'm sorry." But it was enough for him.

"No need to say any more," he reassured her, knowing that the dark moment had passed. She'd given him back the future again.

The remainder of the long journey was spent discussing the countryside with veiled comments about the land they hoped to buy. Eva grew increasingly excited in the hope that the Hollis family may be the very one which had emigrated from Crewe all those years ago. It would be so wonderful to have neighbours from the old country even though their farm might be several miles away.

Charles talked about finding work, stopping on the way at the Plough camp at Taheke. Eva stayed in the car, feeling slightly carsick from the rough journey, while Charles asked about ploughman's work. Unfortunately, the farmer was out at Hastings at the sales, but his wife promised to pass the message on to him. While Charles talked to the farmer's wife, Eva sat back in the car, looking at the house in the distance, partly hidden by tall blue gums, wondering if their own property could be developed into a similar home. This one was quite impressive and was all that she could want. All around her were the strange small green hills and winding roads. Young willows shrouded the creeks that seemed to run everywhere and where the water was deeper, tall willows swept the edges of the streams. It was very remote but very beautiful and she knew that she could settle here and be happy. She felt more at ease now, smiling as Charles strode back purposely along the track, lifting his hand in a greeting as he drew near.

She was lost in thought, making plans for their future as Charles and the taxi driver talked about the supply of water to the land. She picked up snippets of conversation about how the creek that bordered the properties originated from springs and was not affected to a great extent from floodwaters. She drifted off again, only to wake moments later to more conversation about water, finding herself reassured that the heavy rains of the last week had not caused it to flood and it served as a permanent watering hole for sheep throughout the year. The creek ran within two or three chains of the main road, passing through the Monk property and into the Nestor Estate. She realised that Charles knew this land well and had worked on many of the farms. She was pleased when he whispered to her that he knew he could confidently show Eva the small property in question even though there weren't any fences to mark the boundaries.

Finally arriving, Charles asked the taxi driver to wait for a couple of hours, and he and Eva left the car. The sun was already well up in the sky, but Eva insisted on carrying her coat, and left her hat on to stop her unruly hair from blowing in her face in the breeze. The taxi driver lay back in the driver's seat, preparing to sleep, realising that they would be quite some time. He wasn't worried. He had the newspaper and a sandwich for later. Eva and Charles joked that it would be quite a treat for Mr Guild to be paid for sleeping and eating as they looked back again to see him pulling his hat brim down over his eyes.

Treading carefully near the fast running stream, Charles crossed in a narrow spot, carrying Eva across in his arms. "This'll be part of our stream. Just think Eva, I'm carrying you over the threshold of your new home." They both laughed then, realising how silly he sounded. Together they struggled up the bank until they lost sight of the taxi as the land dipped suddenly into a hollow.

"Look Charles, I can see some caves. Can we look into them? The last time I saw caves like that was at a place called Beeston Castle, all the way back in England."

"Of course we can go up there."

"We'll have to build our own castle here, right here on the hilltop!" Then turning to look at him she smiled and sang out, "Oh, Charles, I am so happy! I've never felt so happy!" and Eva twirled around until she sat with a bump on the ground feeling very dizzy. She looked up at him and spoke in a quiet voice, "My brother would love this place. Of course he'll probably never see it, but it's everything he would want. Land of his own, working outside with animals and the earth. This is the place. I know it."

Charles knelt beside her, the two of them looking steadily into each other's eyes. Slowly he removed his jacket for Eva to lie on, feeling for any stony outcrops for the ground was littered with rocks. Passionately, they made love, lying on the earth that was to be theirs, each reaching out for the other to rid themselves of any guilt, any doubt. Eva leant over Charles, kissing his eyes until he laughingly protested. "Eva, stop! We've come to look at the land. Hand me my jacket and let's decide today whether we'll buy this place or not. But I think your mind is already made up!"

Something small, but heavy, fell from his jacket pocket, rolling onto the grass. He reached over to grab it but Eva lifted it slowly. Her face darkened.

"Charles, what is this?" She opened the cap and smelled the small hip flask.

For a moment Charles was lost for words, he could barely remember having it. Then he recalled his sister giving him the whisky to keep him warm on the night he had called in to see her. He stared at Eva feeling awkward and embarrassed, wanting to say that it didn't matter, and praying that she wouldn't flare up into a violent temper.

Eva scrambled to her feet. "Are you the man I was thinking I could live with? You liar! You're a drunkard, a womaniser! You are everything I hate in men. You don't love me. If you did love me you'd stop the drinking. It's the only thing I've asked of you and you can't even do that! You just want to use me. And my money. I hate you! I hate you Charles Edwards!"

"Please Eva, my sister, " but he knew that it was too late. Eva had lost all control.

Picking up a small stone, she hurled it at him with all her strength, then she approached him, hitting him as hard as she could with her handbag and then with her fists. Charles tried desperately to hold her arms but she fought him, beating him about the head as he stumbled.

"You think that I love you? Well, you're mistaken. I loved Morris. I still love Morris. But I settled for you! What do you think about that? You're not fit to clean his shoes!"

"I don't believe you Eva. You're mad! Stop all this right now! We've come here to buy this place. Who is Morris for God's sake?"

"I'll kill you," she screamed for the last time as everything within her was repulsed. "You've ruined everything! You've ruined me!" Then she heard her mother's voice. "You are the sinner! You are the evil one!" She couldn't believe she had thought she could make a life with this man and that because she willed something, that it would be so. She had defiled Morris's memory and this was her punishment. Her rage, fuelled as much by realising how irrational and like her mother she sounded at the collapse of her dream, burst through any attempt to control it once more and she flailed at him again.

Suddenly she was beyond coherent thought. All her life lived in emotional restraint, all the years of nothing for herself broke her. The only thing she saw was this creature who had denied her everything. Who had charmed her and then like everybody else, discarded her needs as unworthy of their attention. It was as if everything evil in the entire world was focused for that moment on his face and she had to destroy it.

Staring at this raging woman who was suddenly a stranger to him, what Eva had said about this Morris fellow finally sunk in and Charles realised she wasn't the virgin he had assumed she'd been when they first made love. He stepped back away from her, furious, and fell back, hitting his shoulder on a rock. She advanced toward him. He was desperate and panicking now, he could see that Eva really did intend to harm him. He scrambled about him looking for help, barely even thinking. Finally he saw it. He reached out and grabbed a Manuka branch and scrambled back to his feet. Lifting the branch, he brought it down on her head, hoping to stop her. Her denture flew from her mouth, but she didn't seem to notice. Still she seemed to come at him, staggering, her hand shakily moving upward toward her head and blood now appearing through her woollen hat. Again and again he hit her until she lay on the ground calm and still.

Panting with exhaustion, Charles crawled over to her, lifting her broken head into his arms. "Eva, my little Eva, what have I done? Please, please Eva, come back to me," and rocking her in his arms he shut his eyes in grief. "What have I done? Why did you have to mention other men? Tell me it isn't true. Oh, why did I have to hit you on the head? What have I done?" he kept repeating to himself.

Her small body lay like a dead bird from a nest, twisted and awful in death. Her clothes were still partially off from their lovemaking. How could they have gone from making love on the grass to this? He felt the blood seeping down and matting her hair. He touched her chest and felt a faint heart beat, but he knew enough about animals to know that she was dying. He was dying too. Leaning over her, he kissed her sweet mouth, tried to close the dead staring eyes, kissed her small nose, and rocked her to and fro until in grief, he howled like a dog.

Finally, he slowly carried the little body carefully down towards the stream. He felt that by washing her he could clean her, make her happy again. She would be horrified to have her hair all matted like this. And the blood would flow down the stream and with it all the hate and unhappiness she had carried within her.

Stepping into the stream, he found a deep pool beneath one of the willows. There he laid her body, floating gently, washing all the unhappiness away. Her cotton printed dress floated outwards, revealing her petticoat, her pearl beads shining round her small neck as she lay face upwards in the water. He thought how beautiful she was, the most beautiful thing in his entire life, and he had killed it.

Charles crouched back on the bank shivering, then he began to think clearly again and scrambled up the bank to find her belongings. Quickly he hid the hat, coat and handbag in nearby bushes. He covered her face with branches, not being able to bear the thought of her staring upwards, and then he ran back towards where the taxi was parked.

As he ran, Charles could think of nothing but Eva, no longer by his side but lying in the water, gone forever. He was numb with horror, not even able to think about the nightmare he was going through. He slowed down, hardly feeling the soaking cold from the stream into which he had stepped. Walking towards the car, he saw the taxi driver stir and look at his watch. They had only been gone one hour and twenty minutes, and Charles had told him they'd be at least two.

He spoke quickly, gasping and answering his own questions before the driver had a chance. "Take me to Hastings. Yes, yes, I know. I'm on my own. Where is Miss Madden? She insisted on walking over to the Hollis place, said they would bring her back to the railway station tomorrow morning." And he settled back in the front passenger seat.

"Been in the water Charlie?"

"What? Oh, yes. I slipped in the creek coming back."

As they drove through the isolated countryside, Charles searched for normal conversation, fighting back the urge to vomit.

"Miss Madden gave me £30," he muttered, almost absentmindedly, thinking of that huge amount of money lying in a postal order, to be used for the deposit for their property. "Stop at the Te Aute Hotel and I'll stand you a drink. We could do with one in this heat."

Once there, Charles drank silently but within his head the screaming voices had begun. He was suddenly aware of the taxi driver's questioning about Miss Madden. He felt sick but remained outwardly calm.

"Oh, she'll be fine. I'll be meeting her at the railway station tomorrow." He paid for the drinks from one of the £5 notes from the wages that Eva had given to him for safekeeping. Mr Guild bid him goodbye and went about his way. He'd heard the whispered conversation with Eva about his breath in the car and Charles was scratched. They'd clearly had an argument before she'd gone off to her friend's place. He was grateful for the day's work and he'd heard Charlie was a good bloke, but this was one situation he didn't want any part in.

Charles barely noticed him leave. Alone or with company, he didn't care. Only grog might numb what he was feeling. Charles began to drink heavily, relying on gin to ease and maybe even obliterate the horror of what had happened. Beer was never going to be enough to deal with the grief of this. At closing, he went to his sister's house and asked to stay there. Horrified, she listened to his rambling story, urging him to cover his tracks and go and get Eva's cases. She told him he had to stay indoors and kept reassuring him as she bathed the scratches on his neck and hand and cleaned the blood from his clothes. She feared the worst for him. To think that a few days ago she'd been worried about a warrant for maintenance payments. Love for him would keep him safe in her house until he recovered his wits.

The following day he left early, collecting Eva's suitcases and storing them at the house. From the time he returned to the house he began to drink constantly, relying on gin to ease and at times even block out the horror story he was living.

"I want to join her," he repeated over and over.

Distressed, his sister obtained some laudanum[43] from a friend, slipping some into his drink. Charles was relieved of his suffering for a few hours while his sister carefully planned out an alibi for him. Charles's days passed by in a fog of remorse, guilt and suffering, finally forcing him from the house to seek work.

---

[43] Until the early 20th century, laudanum, an addictive opiate, was sold without a prescription.

A Body is Discovered

February 14th was a bright Thursday morning, and Herbert Monk decided that after he'd finished his chores for the day it would be the perfect time to go and collect some eel traps he'd set a couple of weeks earlier. He'd modelled them on the Maori traps that were always successful and he hoped for a good catch. He'd pulled some traps out of the creek a few nights before, but had left one of the woven baskets on the bank. He knew that it would only take one good rain for the creek to rise and he'd lose his basket.

He was sixteen and relied on a bicycle to get him around, so he could only carry a couple of traps at a time and needed to wait until the heat of the day had gone. He finished his dinner and at half past seven he left home for the Nestor Road Junction. He left the bike there and walked up the creek. Occasionally he picked up a pebble and tossed it in the water, whistling as he walked. The only other sound came from the willows as a breeze rustled their leaves. He watched as their branches floated on the surface of the stream. Despite the long summer, this particular stream showed no signs of drying up. When he reached the old willow tree that grew across the creek, he carefully balanced and walked across one of its gnarled old branches to the other side.

As he stepped off the branch onto the safety of the bank he looked up and then stopped in his tracks. The stream was blocked just beyond the willow. An object was causing it to swirl and eddy. He walked forward curiously. Something was floating awkwardly in the water, partly submerged. Instinctively he approached by climbing the bank to look down, rather than wade in the stream. The dry twigs cracked beneath his feet and willow branches curtained his view. He stopped suddenly. He knew instantly what he was looking

The Price

at, even while his conscious mind was still asking himself what it was he saw. Time seemed to freeze as he took in all the details.

Only a short distance away was a body, about three feet from the bank and tangled in willow fronds. The head was facing upstream from him and the current had washed it sidewards. At first glance he couldn't really tell if it was a woman or a boy, but looking closer he could see that even though the face was black and gouged, a dress hid most of the trunk. Used to finding dead sheep, Herbert moved forward. He couldn't reach it, but at least he could now be sure that it was a woman. His heart hammered as if it was going to burst from his chest.

"Poor bugger," he said aloud, more to comfort himself. "This was no accident. Best let Dad know. Suddenly all feeling rushed back and he bolted. Back across the willow branch and running to his bike before riding home faster than he ever imagined he could, he took short cuts over hills and paddocks until finally reaching home. He burst through the kitchen door yelling for his father. "Dad! Dad! Dad!"

Mr and Mrs Monk came through the door from the sitting room, the paper still in his hands and some sewing in hers. "What's all the ruckus, son?"

"Bert, are you alright?"

"Mum, Dad! There's a body down in the creek! Just near where I left my trap. It's just floating there! Dad, you have to do something!"

Mrs Monk reached for a kitchen chair to steady herself and shakily put her sewing on the table while the boy's father went around the table to his son and put his arm on his shaking shoulder.

"Now Bert, you need to sit down and tell me what you saw. Are you sure the person was dead and not just cooling off?"

"I tell you Dad, it was a dead body! Just floating there, staring up. Nobody swimming would have their clothes on like that. Nobody could be so still, or smell like that! And the face…"

"It's all right son, I believe you. Was it a man or a woman?"

"A woman. She was small. Once I realised what it was I just bolted back here. Are you going to call the police?"

"Of course! Now you just sit here and I'll make the call." Looking at his wife, who was visibly pale and shaky, he said, "Perhaps you could make some tea love. I think we'll all need it."

His description of the body had alarmed his father. Murder was unheard of in these parts. This was definitely a matter for the police. Leaving Herbert to drink his tea and retell the story to his mother, he made his way to the neighbouring farm. They had recently had a phone installed and it was the only way he could get the information to the police quickly. By the time the police were notified, it was too dark to go out to the body. It was a sleepless night in the Monk household, but Herbert led them to the scene the next morning.

When the police reached the creek at first light, they found the body of a young woman, about twenty years of age they thought. One of her stockings was on the bank and a partial top denture was found six paces from the creek, lying discarded in the grass. A woman's garter also lay nearby. The general consensus among the officers was that she'd been raped because her dress and underskirt were up around her waist and her bloomers, stocking and shoe had been removed from her right leg, but still remained on her left one. At odds with the rape theory though, was that there didn't appear to be any signs of a struggle as no clothes had been torn.

The unpleasant job of retrieving the body began. The local doctor, Dr Rowland Cashmore examined it on the bank of the creek, making only a cursory examination. He noted the wound on the scalp and thought that it was most likely the cause of death. Any more information was hard to determine because the length of time in the water, combined with the hot weather, had caused the body to decompose. He'd been told that the police thought she was a Maori woman because of the colour of the skin, but as soon as he saw the body he knew they were wrong. Her face was almost black as a result of putrefaction. And the skin and hair were peeling off. The eyes and mouth were also almost eaten away by maggots. Although he was cautious by nature and wasn't fond of conjecture, he thought that given the conditions, she might have been in the water up to a week. He recorded it all in his little notebook, carefully going about his business in silence before nodding to the waiting policemen to take the body away.

They wrapped the corpse in several blankets and carried it carefully to the police car. From there they drove it to the Hastings mortuary and by mid morning most of the district knew about the murder. The police continued to search the surrounding area and noted that two small willow branches were floating on the pool and had been partly on the body. It was clear that they had been deliberately broken off the willow tree growing in the pool and apparently thrown on the body, possibly to hide it to some extent.

A post mortem was carried out almost immediately Dr Cashmore reached the morgue. It was then discovered that there were several other wounds on the head of the body, which he believed were blows from a blunt instrument. As his grim task proceeded in silence, he made notes that told an awful story of the end of a woman. As a local doctor he'd never seen anything like it and knew that he had to be as detailed as possible in order to give this woman some chance of justice at some point in the future. He meticulously noted that her skull was fractured in two places, one fracture running from the bridge of the nose backwards over the top of the head, while the second fracture ran crosswise from the right ear. Either fracture would have likely resulted in her death, the two combined absolutely ensured it. Photographs were taken of the body and he tried to obtain fingerprints, but the skin was missing from some of the fingers and peeling off the others, so only a few were obtainable.

He stopped several times, feeling a tremor starting in his hand. He was a little overcome by his task and his horror at what had been done to this young woman. He turned away from the corpse, pretending to fuss with his notes and implements as he forced himself to calm down. This woman was relying on him to do his best work in order to get justice. He also realised that if he didn't do his best to gather all the evidence that could lead to a conviction, what was to stop the animal that had done this from striking again? Each time he stopped to calm himself, he took a deep breath before going back to his work, his jaw set and his mind focussed again on the job and not on the poor woman laid out on the bench in front of him.

He wrote in his notes that the body was clad in a print dress, two petticoats, and two singlets. He revised the police's initial assessment of a twenty-year old Maori and recorded that it was the body of a well-nourished white woman of about thirty years of age. Despite his personal feelings, he matter-of-factly noted that putrefaction had destroyed most of the facial outline, and the upper jaw was toothless, making facial identification impossible.

Finally, almost as an afterthought, he added that the examination revealed no sign of pregnancy and that apart from the head injuries, there was no sign of injury about the body. In his opinion, death was probably due to extensive laceration of the brain brought about by a fracture of the vault and base of the skull. He went pale at the thought of the considerable force that would be necessary to inflict such wounds. Job done, he covered the body and went home, trying to remove the image of her from his mind.

On the Friday night, within twenty-four hours of Herbert Monk first sighting the body, the police's investigations led them to the Lowry property. James Lowry agreed to go with the police to view the body. He felt sick with fear for Eva. Surely it couldn't have ended like this? He stared down at the small figure lying on the mortuary table, just a body, decomposing and hideous. He was horrified by what he saw. There was no doubt in his mind. There was little to recognise but the shape of her nose and wisps of hair identified her. Still he could not bring himself to be the one to say Eva had ended like this. So he lied. He told the officer that although he was "of the strong opinion that it was Evelyn Mary Madden," he couldn't be sure.

His mind was reeling. How could this remnant of a human being be the Eva Madden he'd known? The woman, who just a few days before, had been cutting flowers in the garden with his wife. It couldn't be. His wife would be devastated. He couldn't tell her. So in the end he wasn't really sure whether he didn't identify the body as being Eva because he couldn't or because emotionally it was just too much for him to do.

Turning to the police officer again, he offered to bring in the cook in the morning. He thought she could make a positive identification. Neither he nor Mrs Lowry would be able to identify the clothes of this woman. The following morning he drove Audrey to the morgue, waiting outside in the car, unable to look at the body or clothing again. The cook's reaction was instantaneous and she positively identified the body and clothing as that of Miss Madden.

"No doubt about it sir. I know them clothes. Washed 'em enough times. It's definitely her."

"Yes, yes, Miss Jamieson. Thank you. We'll contact you again." Even the police quickly tired of Audrey Jamieson's crudeness.

Returning to the car, she merely nodded to James Lowry and said quietly, "It was her frock, Mr Lowry. I saw her making it. She's gone."

The ride back to Oreka Station was made in silence. Audrey thinking about the hateful things she'd said about Eva, and James thinking about the light that had left the world. How was he going to tell his wife? In the end, he couldn't tell her. She ran to the front door when she heard his car arrive and broke down as he walked through the door

A Body is Discovered

and looked at her, nodding only slightly.

Audrey had returned to the kitchen and was already thinking about her important role in all the events. People all around would know her now. She couldn't help thinking about whether Charlie had been involved. Even if he had, she reasoned, he must be innocent. If he was with Eva when it had happened, then it must have been an accident she decided. In the middle of her reverie, Mr and Mrs Lowry summoned her to the sitting room.

"Audrey, we've asked you to come in here because we want to impress upon you the importance of not discussing these awful events with anyone," began James Lowry.

Her face fell. This was not what she was expecting. She thought this conversation would be in praise of her and a discussion about her future role in the investigation and trial.

"Mr Lowry, Sir"

"Audrey, my wife and I will not have our family linked to these evil events, or what might have led up to them, any more than we absolutely must. You will not discuss what might have happened here at the station or what you saw today at the mortuary with anyone except in reply to police questions. Am I clear?"

"Yes, Mr Lowry." Audrey's face showed all her disappointment.

"You need to know that there is no place in the employ of this household for anyone who cannot be discreet. And without a satisfactory reference from Oreka Station, future employment in these times might be a hazardous proposition."

"Of course, Mr Lowry. I understand."

"Thank you Audrey. You may return to your duties. Please let Mrs Lowry know if you need some time away from your duties to grieve and come to terms with the difficult task you performed this morning."

"Thank you Mr Lowry. Mrs Lowry. I'll be all right

to get back to work now."

And as she left the room James turned to his silent and grief stricken wife and said, "That should fix the little gossip."

Audrey returned to the kitchen fuming. Had she just been threatened with the sack if she talked about any of this? Again her thoughts turned to Charlie. If he hadn't been involved, where was he?

Charles spent days hidden in the house of his sister, wondering if Eva's body would be found. He sweated and couldn't sleep. He shook and was only quieted by the cheap whisky that his sister provided him with in copious quantities. His sister assured him that by now it would have washed down the stream. Maybe it had even reached the sea. The rains were due any day now and the sooner the better.

Two weeks passed until the pain was unbearable. In his alcohol-fuelled state, Charles decided to end his life next to Eva. He should have done it in the first place he reasoned. He'd lost the only person he'd ever truly loved was how he saw it now, and he couldn't go on living without her. So he found a thick rope in the shed and waited until his sister left the house for groceries. Then he set off across country, his pockets filled with all the alcohol the house possessed. He walked in a half circle across the landscape, so that he could approach the creek from Nestor's farm. From time to time he took a drink to ease the pain and he talked to himself almost incessantly about how he hadn't meant it, how much he'd loved Eva, about how much he wanted to be with her now. Sometimes he rested, his head in his hands, but by evening he had covered miles of rough country and was nearing the creek.

Desperately tired, he climbed a small tree, wedged himself in the lower branches and slept until dawn. As the sun came up he made his way downhill, dreading what he thought he would see. He reached the willow, but he saw nothing. She was gone. His darling Eva no longer lay in the stream. Far away he heard the crack of dried branches.

Someone else was here. But he wasn't afraid. It was just a young lad with some eel traps who stared at him curiously as he passed. Charles stumbled on, searching upstream for any sign of his Eva, his mind not registering that floating upstream would be impossible. Bewildered and drunk, he rested, waking as he felt the first cool breeze of evening. He wandered in a daze along the stream, deciding to return to the willow tree.

But on Saturday the sixteenth of February, the police were still working around the site where Eva's body had been found. What a man would be doing walking in such a lonely spot was a matter of curiosity to one of the officers. As soon as the man saw the police, he walked away, clearly drunk. But his rambling gait made it easy for Constable Dawson to intercept him about five hundred yards from the creek and the two men exchanged greetings.

"What brings you here today, Sir?"

He muttered unintelligibly and then: "Ah, I'm very crook, mate. I been on the booze for days and it does ya no good, you know." He then took a bottle from his coat pocket and took a swig before carefully putting it back.

Police dealt with drunks frequently, but for one to take a drink in front of an officer was almost unheard of. Constable Dawson frowned. "What's your name, please sir?"

"Edwards. Me name's Edwards."

"Do you have a Christian name, Mr Edwards?"

"Charles. Charles Edwards. Charlie."

The smell of his breath was putrid and at some point he'd clearly relieved himself without unbuttoning his fly.

"Well, these are lonely parts to be in Mr Edwards. What might you be doing hereabouts? And with that big rope?"

"I've walked five miles, shorter across country than following the roads. I'm going to see a settler about getting me old job back." The question of the rope was ignored. "I was asleep in that tea-tree over yonder," he said, pointing towards the creek.

Constable Dawson followed Edwards as he walked drunkenly back to the creek, where he sat down and drank a long pull from a gin bottle, produced from another pocket. Finishing it, he tossed the bottle into the water. The policeman was astonished as Edwards then produced a bottle of methylated spirits, mixed it with creek water and drank.

The policeman was still a distance from Charles. He was a big man and could deal with at least two officers at once if he wanted to. Yet he was not only very drunk, but also deeply depressed. He kept muttering about the stream.

"What's the rope for Charles? Not thinking of stringing yourself up are you? Don't want to be doing that."

Another officer walked over and asked, "What you got here, mate?"

"Says he's Charles Edwards, on his way to see about getting his job back on a farm near here," replied the first officer.

"Charles Edwards, you say?" He leaned forward to look at him more carefully. "I reckon he might be William Price. There's a warrant out for him. Default of maintenance payments. His likeness is in at the station house."

"You're joking. What's William Price doing out in these parts?"

"There's probably only one reason he'd be right here mate. We'd best take him in."

He gestured to the two detectives at the murder scene to come over and together they quietly approached Charles and suggested he come back to Hastings with them. He gave no resistance.

Price gave a rambling statement about leaving Miss Madden at the railway station and then going on a drinking binge. When confronted with evidence that they'd been at the hotel together, he changed his story, confirming that he'd checked her in there, but that she'd left him because of his drinking. The taxi driver was a liar he said, as was the farmer's wife at the ploughman's camp. There had been no woman with him.

When he was asked what kind of a girl Eva had been, Price answered, "Very respectable. Very respectable girl."

"Was there any intimacy between you and Miss Madden?"

"No. Thought never entered my mind."

But despite his statement, William Price was formally arrested and charged with the murder of Evelyn Mary Madden. He was silent throughout the arrest procedure.

Based on information William Price had given them, the police conducted a wider search of the area around where the body had been found. On Saturday, February the twenty-third they started cutting away Manuka bushes and about five chains from where Herbert Monk had discovered the body in the creek, a number of items were found. Screwed in a bundle was a lady's blue coat and hidden inside was a shoe, a lady's white hat and a handbag. Inside the handbag was a newspaper cutting, a smaller purse with no money and a mud stained handkerchief.

The following day Audrey Jamieson was able to identify all of the items as belonging to Eva. It seems that Audrey's meddling and interest in other people's business had served a purpose after all.

The News Reaches Home

The *Crewe Chronicle* received the news by telegraph within hours of the formal identification of the body. Billboards about the town announced the sensational news of the Crewe girl who had been murdered in New Zealand.

FEBRUARY 16th
GIRL DEAD IN A STREAM
CHARGE OF MURDER ON SHEEP RANCH
Auckland (New Zealand), Sunday.

A teamster at a remote sheep station of the Hawkes Bay region of New Zealand was today charged with the murder of Eva Madden, an English domestic servant, whose decomposed body was found in a stream near Waipawa. The accused man, Charles William Edwards, also known as William Price, was employed at a ranch where Eva Madden formerly worked.

Before being charged he was taken many miles to the waterhole where the body had been found. Miss Madden was 20 (sic) years old. Her head had been badly battered. Her home address in England has not yet been traced.

British United Press.

Joseph spotted the billboard first. Scrawled on the blackboard over the boy selling newspapers at the top of the railway station entrance were the words, *Crewe woman murdered in New Zealand.* His world stopped for a moment. Then as everyone does when confronted with the possibility of some horror being done upon a loved one, he thought that it couldn't possibly be his Evie. Maybe one of those

Hollises, he thought. Or a complete stranger.

He quickly groped in his pocket for a few pennies to buy the paper and was half relieved when his hand came out empty. While he couldn't read the news, his Evie was still alive.

What will I tell Martha? was his next thought. Then he decided that he couldn't tell her anything. Not until he was absolutely sure. George was the answer. He'd go and speak to George about it.

As soon as Joseph managed to get the story out, George rushed from the house to buy a paper. His heart was thumping as he paid the newsboy and when he saw Eva's name, his stomach lurched and he thought he was going to fall to the pavement. He all but ran back to the house and from the stricken look on his face as he walked through the door, his wife and father knew what he'd found. Edith staggered backward to sit down and George steadied his father, who looked like George imagined he had as he read the news. Still, they reasoned, it could be a mistake. They weren't completely sure. It could be a mistake they kept repeating.

"Dad, this is doing us no good. You're going to have to go home and look after Mam. Someone has to stay there with her. What if one of the neighbours tells her first?"

"By God you're right. But George, what will I say to her? How can I tell her this?"

"I don't know Dad, but you have to find a way. Some of the neighbours must know by now and it's only a matter of time before someone knocks on the door to ask her how she is. Shouldn't she hear it from someone she loves and trusts? And you can tell her we're not sure yet, that maybe there's still room to hope. Now go. Please Dad."

As soon as he closed the front door behind his father Edith all but collapsed. Her little body was wracked with sobs and she could barely catch her breath. All she could get out was "Oh George, oh, poor, poor Eva!"

As he comforted his wife, George realised just how

strong he'd have to be. Martha was incredibly frail and Joseph would need every bit of his energy to care for her. And Edith had lost one of her best friends. She may not have seen much of Eva over the years, but his wife thought of Eva as much more than a sister-in-law. No, just like with Ellen and Joe, it would be up to him to see to all that needed to be done right now. He'd wait until they were absolutely sure to tell Gussie and Tom, but he'd better make it soon. Once it was all settled he'd find a moment to grieve. He was used to family tragedy and he'd deal with this one the only way he knew how, at a distance. Only by not allowing himself to get caught up in the emotion would he be able to do what needed to be done. His train of thought was broken by Edith.

"Charles Edwards. George, it says the man's name is Charles Edwards. Isn't that the name of the man Eva said she was going to marry?"

"It couldn't be. She couldn't decide to marry a man who would do something like this. Eva's sensible, a good judge of character."

"But George."

"I won't have it, Edith. I won't have people thinking Eva would run off with a murderer. What would people think? They'll think she was loose or even worse. She couldn't have been meaning to marry him. I won't hear any more. If he murdered my sister then he deserves to be punished! Edie, if Eva's dead because of this monster, he'll hang."

With that, George cut the story from the newspaper and picked up the only photograph that the family had of Eva and went to make enquiries at the Crewe Police Station. His enquiry was duly noted and they would look into the matter immediately. Would he mind giving a statement, they asked. George replied that he would do anything that helped them shed some light on the truth of this story. George was taken to a quiet room near the back of the station, where an officer typed his statement on an official form.

19th February, 1935

GEORGE WILLIAM MADDEN, states, I am an engine-cleaner and reside at 100 Ernest Street, Crewe.

On Saturday evening 16th February 1935, I was shown a newspaper cutting containing an account of the murder of a Young Woman named EVA MADDEN in New Zealand.
On Monday 18th February 1935 I saw the attached Newspaper cutting taken from the "News-Chronicle" dated 18th February 1935, referring to the same murder, and it states that the home address in England of the Young Woman is not known.

My sister EVELYN MADDEN, single, aged 38 years, about 5' 3" in height, slim build, dark hair, pale complexion, left England on 21st February 1934 for New Zealand, she had been in New Zealand for 5 or 6 years, probably between the years 1925-1930. The family have corresponded with her in New Zealand and her last address was:

Miss. E. Madden
C/o Mrs Lowry "Oreka,"
Fernhill, Hawkes Bay New Zealand

from which address we have also had replies.
We should like to know, if possible, if enquiries could be made by the police in that district (Fernhill) as to whether the Young Woman described in the Newspaper cutting attached is my sister, or if not, any information concerning her.

My father's full name is:
Joseph Madden
Retired plate layer
23 Chamber Street, Crewe

And my mother's full name is:
Martha Madden, who also resides at 23 Chamber Street,

Crewe.

Both my parents are seriously upset and at present not in a fit state for even me to ask questions about my sister.

The photograph handed in, is a good likeness of my sister but I am unable to say when it was taken.

Witnessed

Signed
GEORGE WILLIAM MADDEN

18th February 1935 at 2pm
R.S. Howard Acting Sergt 223

    Three days later, early in the morning, two policemen arrived at the home of Joseph and Martha. They knocked on the door and with eyebrows raised, both noted the flutter of the net curtains in several houses nearby. The neighbours had all been watching the house since the article in the *Chronicle* and within minutes the entire street would know of their visit.

    Joseph quickly showed them inside to the rarely used sitting room. The policemen gently explained that they needed to interview both parents. Joseph fetched Martha and sat her down in the most comfortable chair. Joseph and George had told her the news, along with Gussie and Tom two days earlier. Martha was grief stricken, and even more so now the police had come to the house looking so grim, but Joseph calmed her and they sat patiently waiting for authority to announce the death of their daughter.

    Yes, the identification of the body had taken place and sadly it had been identified as Eva Madden, formerly of Crewe.

    "But you could be wrong," persisted Martha. "Our daughter is named Evelyn, not Eva!"

    The policemen looked to Joseph for guidance, for they too were very upset by the terrible news. Joseph nodded and rose. "I'll see to things here," was all he said. He quietly showed them to the door. "You need to speak to my son George. He'll have to deal with all your enquiries. If the police keep coming here every time there's a bit more information or you need something, it'll kill her. You need to speak to George," he repeated. "One hundred Ernest Street. He'll help you with whatever you need. I need to look after my wife."

Closing the door, he leant for a moment on the wall before entering the room to comfort his wife. How much more did the family have to suffer? First there had been Ellen, then Joe and now his first born, his beloved daughter whose letters about her travels had given so much joy to them. She was gone, murdered in a foreign land and they couldn't even reach her to say goodbye. Even if they had money for travel, it would be months before they could get to New Zealand and his daughter would be cold in the ground by then. His mental anguish was all but overwhelming, but he knew that ahead of him now lay the religious suffering of his wife, who would lay the blame at the feet of the sinner, namely herself.

George suggested to him that he should burn all of Eva's letters that he could find. It wouldn't do any good to have the family's private business become entertainment for newspaper readers throughout the Empire. And if the police could get them, that's surely what would happen. They'd be read at a trial and everyone would know about Ellen and Joe. And worst of all, it would just give people the opportunity to tell stories about Eva. If the Maddens had had practise at keeping secrets before, they now resorted to new lengths at protecting their own.

While Martha rested the day after the police visit, Joseph gathered any letters from Eva they'd kept and fed them one by one into the kitchen fire, feeling as though he was slowly burning away pieces of his daughter. Later that evening, when Martha was safe enough to leave for a short while, he visited Betley Woods, grieving silently by

The Price

the pool and remembering Eva as a little girl busy making the winter warmers under his laughing instructions. He also remembered the conversation he had with her just before she left for New Zealand and vowed to be a better husband and father for the rest of his days. Martha needed him, really needed him possibly like she'd never done before. And he wouldn't let her down. Not for a minute.

The next news the family received from New Zealand was of Eva's funeral. George read the letter first and then he and Edith told the rest of the family.

"She was buried in the Hastings Cemetery on the 18th of February 1935, under the name of Eva Madden," George read.

"Evelyn. Her name is Evelyn. Can't they get that right?" asked Martha.

"Mam, everybody there would have known her as Eva. That's probably what they thought her name was," answered Gussie gently. Then, "Go on George."

"The funeral left St Matthews Church, King Street, Hastings at 11am on that Monday, and the body was interred in plot No. 865 Block D of the Church Of England Ground in the Hastings Public Cemetery. The service was conducted by the Rev Mortimer-Jones, Vicar of St Matthews Church."

"Church of England! She's a Methodist!"

"Mam, I'll see to it. I'll write and tell them her proper name and I'll see if the police there can find a Methodist Minister who can visit the grave. I'll see to it."

He knew she was trying to focus on the small things because she couldn't face the enormity of the real situation, that her eldest daughter had been brutally murdered in a land on the other side of the world alone and without the comfort of her family.

Joseph was less visibly distraught. "Thank you George. We know you're doing what you can son." He reached across and touched Martha's hand, stilling the wringing.

George continued. "Amongst those who attended

the funeral was Mr Ebbett, Coroner, and wreaths were also placed on the grave by Mr Ebbett and Mr James Lowry, with whom the Deceased was last employed. A number of other acquaintances that the Deceased had made during her time in New Zealand were also present, though no record was kept of their names."

"It also says here that The Reverend Mortimer-Jones has written to you Dad. Have you got any letters from New Zealand?"

"No son. You'd have whatever's been sent to me."

What the message didn't say was much more than what it did. All the letters that had been sent and received since Eva had first left England had sung with life and adventure; now the correspondence was reduced to cold facts. They were so far away that it couldn't have been any other way. Had they been able to be there, the family would have known so much more that might have given them some comfort.

For instance, among the mourners who gathered beside the grave in the burning heat of that February day were the Bruce family, farewelling the friend that they had made so long ago and seen so little of in recent times. Finally they realised that they knew so little about her, not even where to send their condolences to her family. Mary Bruce and her son Tom vowed that day that in death they would do for Eva what her blood family couldn't and attended each day of the court proceedings, trying to ensure that she received some justice.

Eva's photograph was returned to George once the full identification had been made and the Madden family settled in and awaited the outcome of the trial. Joseph and Martha became ill with grief and anxiety, hardly leaving their home. The full responsibility was now given to their son George, who would manage Eva's estate. Even Edith bought and delivered what food and other supplies they needed. At times neighbours wondered if they were in fact still in their house. Martha spent most of her days reading and re-reading passages of the Bible, while Joseph seemed to spend hours sitting at the kitchen table, staring into space. The grief was overwhelming.

Outside the home the Madden family were much talked about in many Crewe homes and pubs, but as the weeks passed, other news made the headlines and people's attention waned. Finally the family were left to grieve without questions being asked by neighbours and friends all the time. But still, each new piece of information was like peeling a scab off a wound.

There were many things that George learned in the months before and during the trial that he kept to himself. Joseph and Martha were fragile and what he could spare them he did. There were things they just didn't need to know he thought. In the process he bore much more of the burden than the others. Just as he'd done when he'd suggested that any mail that Eva had sent be destroyed, he went about erasing her from their lives. Already the Madden family habit of keeping secrets was beginning to assert itself again.

The Head

Forty-two witnesses were interviewed in readiness for the Lower Court hearing, which would precede the trial. But there were some people who were sure that even more evidence was needed. The solution came from a pathologist from Auckland Public Hospital. And the solution was gruesome. The pathologist was due to give expert evidence as to the cause of death and contacted Dr Cashmore, who had done the autopsy on Eva. As letters and telegrams were exchanged, Dr Cashmore, in consultation with Dr Whyte, who had assisted him in the autopsy, agreed that Eva's body should be exhumed and the head prepared as an exhibit for the trial.

Both local doctors had initially protested that their report of the post-mortem had been extremely thorough and full. They argued that the injuries could be demonstrated on a skull from a demonstration skeleton. But they soon became convinced that it would be a disaster if any loophole were to be left. They came to agree with the pathologist that the head would furnish valuable information as to how the fractures were caused. The doctors were finally in full agreement and an approach to the police was made.

As the Inspector of Police pointed out to the Commissioner of Police, "A gruesome crime has been committed and it must be met with a gruesome exhibit. Only the head of the deceased woman will do." He went on. "The head would be of great assistance to the Pathologist when giving evidence, and I submit, Sir, that such evidence be obtained to strengthen the evidence given by the doctors. We can't leave any chance that this blaggard could get away with it."

After a week of telegrams and telephone calls,

Doctors Cashmore and the pathologist finally met. They discussed their positions and the actual logistics of how they were going to procure the head. The police may still need to be convinced and there had to be an element of secrecy. The public couldn't be told or they'd turn up to watch and there would be sure to be at least one busy body who would complain that they were desecrating the poor girl's grave. Never mind that they were doing it for the girl. How could she rest in peace if there was any chance the murderer was to escape his punishment?

Nobody considered how her family might have felt about this; for all they knew, she had no family. And nobody considered what the local Maori view would be, that she couldn't rest in peace without her head. What the natives might believe was hardly more than silly superstition. No, for the sake of the murdered woman, they needed the head.

Following the meeting, Doctor Cashmore made a telephone call to the Inspector of Police saying that the two doctors were in agreement. The exhumation and removal of the head was essential. The pathologist then returned to Auckland. Only two days after his lengthy meeting with Doctor Cashmore, he wrote to the Inspector of Police in Napier, confirming his position, referring to Eva as the 'victim of Waipawa murder' and affirming that he was 'anxious to examine the skull' himself. The Inspector of Police joined the calls for exhumation.

They informed the Crown Solicitor of their decision and he requested that the exhumation of the body occur as soon as possible, and the exhibit in question obtained. He made an immediate application to the Minister of Health under the Cemeteries Act of 1908 for the remains of the body to be lifted from the plot in the public cemetery to enable the severing of the head to take place.

Without a thought that this had been a real person, violated terribly and deserving of a peaceful rest, and without questioning the motives of the pathologists and police officers about to take their part in such a spectacular trial, permission was given via a stroke of the pen on the 29th of March. The only qualifier was that it was decided that the detective on the case would take the head of the deceased by motorcar to Auckland as it would be offensive to the travelling public if conveyed by train.

The body of Evelyn Mary Madden was exhumed at 4am on the 31st March 1935. The Police, the Pathologist and Crown Solicitor had been granted permission and at that time of the morning, there were no spectators from the community.

It was cold for that time of the year and steam rose from the mouths of the men gathered around the grave in the dark. Standing around in silence, as the macabre activity was conducted, were Detective Sergeant Bickerdike, and other police officers, Doctors Cashmore and Whyte, the Sexton of the local Church of England parish, undertakers and the Town Clerk of Hastings. The Pathologist had not travelled from Auckland. They shuffled their feet and avoided looking at each other instead focusing grimly on the undertakers as they boarded the sides of the grave to prevent the earth falling in. The coffin was lifted out by ropes and laid at the edge of the grave. One of the detectives examined the plate on the wooden box to confirm the name of Eva Madden.

"Let the record show that I agree that this is the coffin of Eva Madden. Doctors?"

Doctor Cashmore and Doctor Whyte stepped forward and looked at the plate in the weak light cast by the lanterns. Doctor Whyte looked at Doctor Cashmore and nodded.

"We agree. This is the coffin of Eva Madden," said Doctor Cashmore clearly.

Sergeant Bickerdike then handed a screwdriver to Detective Farquharson. "You may open the coffin now."

The Sexton and one of the undertakers stepped back as the coffin was opened. Their discomfort was palpable. But they understood that this poor violated woman needed peace and justice and the doctors and police would surely know best. If doing this was the only way to get justice for her, then they were prepared to go along with it.

"Doctors Cashmore and Whyte, is the person in this coffin the same woman on whom you performed a post mortem examination following the recovery of a body from a waterhole at Argyle on 14th February last?" Sergeant Bickerdale read from his instructions.

"Yes it is," both men uttered clearly.

Doctor Cashmore then opened the paper with the notes he'd taken during his meeting and discussions with the Pathologist once again just to check on what procedure they'd agreed to. Suddenly he felt less confident, now it came to the moment, had they covered all contingencies? He cleared his throat and held the paper up to one of the lanterns with a slightly shaky hand. Then, opening his bag, he removed the tools he would need and proceeded to remove the head and first couple of vertebra, including the entire throat down to the clavicle.

The Sexton closed his eyes and whispered prayers to himself as he tried to block out what was going on and one of the police officers moved position so as to be out of the line of sight of it. Even the Sergeant, who held the lantern close for Doctor Cashmore to see what he was doing found himself looking away at several points.

Finally Doctor Cashmore lifted the head and placed it in a metal container provided by the police, actually an Arnott's biscuit tin. As decided, no disinfectant was used during the procedure. He washed and wiped his hands with the water and disinfectant he'd brought and then with a sigh he removed his apron. Then in company with Doctor Whyte, he witnessed the sealing of the container. The gummed tape was dragged through the water that Doctor Cashmore had only moments before used to wash his hands and laid across the joins, making it airtight. Both doctors then signed a declaration as to its contents. The head and declaration were then placed in another, larger tin and both tins made airtight.

Sergeant Bickerdale then signalled for the

undertakers to reseal the coffin and re-bury it. The Sexton, still shocked by the businesslike manner of the whole proceedings, stayed with the men as they went about their work in the early dawn. As the last sod was replaced, he said a prayer over the grave and before leaving made a promise that as long as he lived, the Sexton of his church would watch over the grave and that he would be there for her when the body was reunited with its head.

The head had been taken to the police station from where Detective Farquharson was to have driven it to Auckland. Despite the original decision being taken to not use a public train because it would be seen as an affront to decency, he decided that the hiring of a public taxi would be an unnecessary course of action and so proceeded to Auckland by the excursion train leaving Hastings on the following Sunday at 3.40pm, conveying to the Pathologist the head of Evelyn Mary Madden.

As he placed the container on the luggage rack he smiled to himself. Nobody on the train was any the wiser and it was a smart idea to save the money. People might object if they knew, but who would ever find out? He was just a man travelling with a parcel. Besides, he would be in Auckland in a few hours and as soon as the exhibit was delivered (he'd stopped thinking of it as a head), he could settle into a pub he liked to stay in whenever he was in Auckland and still have some time for drinking and entertainment in the big city before catching the train back the next day.

The Pathologist took possession of the parcel and went straight to his laboratory at the university, despite it being a Sunday night, and prepared the head for flensing[44] and maceration.[45] He kept the head in Auckland until the trial in May.

Hardening the Doctors' resolve to see the perpetrator come to justice was that just a few days before Eva's head was removed from her grave, Charles had escaped from

---

[44] To strip the blood or the skin from the flesh for forensic purposes.
[45] The softening and breaking down of skin resulting from prolonged exposure to moisture.

the Napier gaol where he was being held before the trial. He had appeared before the Court at Napier following his arrest for the murder and was remanded for one week. A further remand order was granted when he came before the Magistrate after that week and it was thought that the police would be ready to proceed with the charge against him on March 21. On that date however, a further remand order was granted. He was to have been brought up in Court on the Thursday, but escaped on the Tuesday.

His head finally clear after weeks without grog, he realised the situation he was in and climbed the roof of the prison while the warden was answering a telephone call and jumped down to freedom on the other side, setting off in the direction of the Napier General Hospital. It was a pretty half-hearted attempt at an escape. He realised quickly that with only prison clothing, no food or money and no plan for a place to go, he had no chance. The thought of robbery crossed his mind for only an instant. Despite what he'd done to Eva, and even despite deserting his wife and children, he wasn't a monster and the thought of harming someone through robbery wasn't one that appealed to him. Unfortunately, that wasn't how the police and press portrayed the whole episode

After three hours of searching, carried out by thirty policemen, he was recaptured. Exhausted and wandering about aimlessly in a paddock, he was handcuffed and returned to the gaol. The Napier police expressed their appreciation for all the assistance private citizens with motorcars had given them. More vehicles than could have been used were offered for the search. It seems locals were horrified that something like this murder could have happened in their neighbourhood and were eager to make good their reputation.

As with the murder itself, Eva's family heard the news of Price's escape via newspaper headlines in Crewe. For some of them, they had just had their first full night's sleep since they'd heard the news of Eva's murder. And then the wound was opened again. It was a bad day for all of them when they heard that Charles William Price, alias Charles Edwards, made a short attempt for freedom from Napier prison. George's anger burned in his throat when he read the newspaper. This man had murdered his sister and now he'd come so close to getting away! Then he calmed himself and resolved to not tell his parents, but Gussie and Tom were another matter. They would see the news for themselves in the *Crewe Chronicle*.

    Gussie, usually so strong, was beginning to show nervousness and it was clear that Percy didn't know how to help his wife. But George had to ignore her. His burden with a grieving wife and parents who just couldn't cope with any of it was as much as he could bear. Especially when coupled with his own grief for the sister he'd loved so much. When his anger burned, as it did with the escape of Price, he'd just have to put it with his grief, in a place deep inside where it could wait until he had time to deal with it.

    The date of the hearing was set for the 11th April, to be held at the Magistrate's Court in Napier. Forty-two witnesses had been summonsed to give evidence and a list of exhibits was prepared in readiness for the trial. The Napier hearing was a mostly dry affair and ended on April 17th. Price was committed to the Supreme Court for trial.

The Trial

The trial commenced on Monday the 20th May 1935 at The Supreme Court in Napier, and continued until the following Saturday the 25th May and Monday 27th May. On the first day alone, twelve witnesses gave evidence, a constant stream of people telling their small piece of the story.

There were reporters present throughout and the newspaper articles and radio news items were sensational. The 'Trial of the Century' one reporter had called it. Usually reporting on the court proceedings in Napier was considered one of the more lowly assignments at the paper, but more than one reporter saw this trial as a chance to make a major career move. There was competition among reporters as to who would be the one to get the line by-line statements each day. Nobody cared about the victim, only the story.

Pencils moved furiously as they recorded details the witnesses gave, such as the victim's clothing being bunched around her waist and one stocking being missing. As the reporters gathered during the lunch recess on the first day, they speculated on Price's guilt.

"The fact that when the coppers searched his kit bag and found the keys to her suitcases should be enough to hang him all by itself. I mean what's he got her keys for?

"Never mind that, what's his sister doing with her cases?"

"Leaving her trunk at the train station was a mistake. Once the coppers had that, they had proof that she hadn't left town like he said she had."

"S'pose he couldn't pick that up. He could get back and get her cases, but he could hardly be fronting at the station and asking for the trunk of a dead woman, now could he?"

The speculation was a daily event between the reporters, in between phoning in their stories to the newspapers around the country in time to make the next editions.

The jury was, as is usual in murder cases, strictly kept together during the whole period covered by the trial. They were a group of ordinary men, a mix of rural landowners and townspeople, the sort of people that may have known an Eva and a Price in their lives. They made two visits to the scene of the crime, the first visit on the first day of the trial and the second on Saturday the 25th May, after the taking of the evidence had been completed.

Quietly sitting in the corner of the galleries each day was Mary Bruce, unnoticed by everyone and keeping the silent promise she'd made at Eva's graveside. Her son Tom came with her the first day, but it was too much for him. Grimly he took his mother to the courthouse each day and each day she told him that she would be all right and that he should leave her there. Tom had loved Eva, but he didn't understand what drove his mother to care so deeply for her that she would endure this trial. After all, the Eva that he loved was dead.

"She was a woman and what happened to her could happen to any woman at the hands of a man, Tom. Men have so much more brute strength than women. But they never realise that we're the stronger sex. We endure everything. When someone is sick, who cares for them? When someone is hurt, who cares for them? When disaster strikes, who cleans up? It's always women. And so we have no choice but to look after each other. Eva's mother or sister can't be here for her, so I will keep the watch. You don't have to come." And so no more was said between them about the trial, and Tom got his news of the trial from the paper, like everyone else who was neither compelled nor chose to attend.

For her part, Mary wanted to contact Eva's family somehow. As she sat in court each day, she kept wondering to herself how to get a message to them as she had no address. Would the police give her an address she wondered? Probably not. All she knew of Eva's family is that they were from Crewe in England, but Eva had rarely ever mentioned them. Come to think about it, apart from having had parents and a brother who worked on the trains, she wasn't sure she knew anything else at all. For all her warmth with the Bruce family, Eva was a very private person, Mary realised. Probably all that upstairs-downstairs training she had from that big hall she worked in for all those years.

Then she would quietly wonder to herself what she might say to these strangers. All that she could say was that Eva had had a family on the other side of the world from her own family and that she had been loved and would be remembered. She could never tell them of the trial. It was almost more than she could bear. So in the end she never did write a letter, just kept her vigil for her friend.

The Pathologist was called immediately after lunch on Wednesday 22nd May. When the grisly exhibit of Eva's head was taken from its container, the same one it had been sent to Auckland in, the people in the upper and lower galleries shifted their positions, so that they might see it and hear what the medical expert had to say about it.

Several women who were sitting close had been knitting furiously throughout the trial. Upon seeing the exhibit, they screamed and one of them fainted. In the commotion as the two women were taken from the courtroom by a doctor and police officers, Mary Bruce sobbed and lifted her hanky to her mouth, tears running down her cheeks. What had they done to her poor friend?

The Pathologist carried the head over to the jury benches, showing the fractures in the different areas of the skull and explaining their nature. He talked quite conversationally, pointing out particular features, including the spaces where the front denture had been, the advanced tooth decay in one of her molars and the extent of the fractures, particularly the one from the bridge of the nose running six inches right back to the crown of the skull.

Not noticing the men becoming more uncomfortable, he practised his expertise, using technical and anatomical language that most jurors didn't understand, demonstrating on the skull as he told of the force and direction he believed would have been needed to cause the injuries. Continuing, he pointed out how the force of the blow to the top of her head had even split the bone below the nose, so that the upper jaw was broken in two.

"I believe the blow probably came from the left," he concluded dispassionately.

Some of the women upstairs found the ordeal too much for them and two of them were seen to leave the court. Even the more hardened of them shuffled their feet and looked a trifle discomforted.

In cross examination, the defence asked if the Pathologist agreed with the opinion of Doctor Cashmore, who in his evidence could not rule out the possibility of the numerous fractures being caused by a fall from a height.

"In fact," he went on, "these blows are quite homicidal in character. There is evidence of several blows and they could not possibly have been accidental. It is my opinion that it is highly likely they were caused by a large piece of wood."

Later in the week, Audrey Jamieson finally had her day in court, glad that no rules set by Mr Lowry could keep from her moment in the limelight. She told the court that, "Mr Edwards and Miss Madden often went for walks together," and "I talked to Mr Edwards on the morning they left. He told me that he was going to Auckland and we were joking around, and he said that he was tired of Eva and sick of her."

Arthur Hollis, who Eva had looked so long for when she first arrived in New Zealand, gave evidence to support his wife's statement that they were both home for all meals on the 6th of February and that nobody else stayed with them. Nor did any woman come to their house at any time.

Neither of them knew Charles Edwards and had never seen or known of Eva Madden, although he understood that his brother's family in Crewe had known Eva's, as his brother had written to him shortly after news of the murder had become known in England.

Herbert Monk had given his evidence, with his parents proudly looking on as he told in measured and clear terms what he had seen. But the Crown didn't ask him about the second evening he visited the spot when he had seen Price with the rope. And no mention of it was made in the evidence of the police. Herbert couldn't help wondering if they just didn't want to show that Price might have had a shred of humanity or contrition. He had hoped that the Defence would ask, but they evidently didn't know about the rope. In any case, despite his parents' congratulations on the excellent way he had conducted himself, he left feeling as though he hadn't been taken seriously by the court or the prosecution and that there was something not right about not telling the whole story.

Throughout the days of evidence, including the showing of the head, Price had mostly sat looking at his hands, fidgeting. He didn't look any of the witnesses in the eye and barely looked into the galleries. When called as a witness, he seemed affable, though confused. He yelled out "No!" in response to some particularly persistent questions from the Crown. But apart from that, he was reasonably contained, talking in his deep, quiet voice that had first led Eva to trust him. A number of people even said they could understand why people liked him. But for the most part, during his own trial he behaved as though he was merely a disinterested participant.

Under the onslaught of forty-two witnesses in four and a half days in the court, the Defence was resigned that getting an innocent verdict would be almost impossible. However, both the Crown and Defence in their summing up of the case were in agreement that there was no proof that the murder had been premeditated on the part of the accused.

When he instructed the jury, Justice Blair was careful and measured. He told them that although there had been some conjectural evidence given by the police regarding the probability of rape, they must be clear that they were trying a case of murder, not one of rape. Similarly, he went on, the jury wasn't to take into consideration any ideas they might have about the victim if they believed that consensual sexual relations had occurred between the victim and the accused. Their only job was to decide whether or not Charles William Price, also known as William Price and Charles Edwards, had wilfully murdered Evelyn Mary Madden.

When the jury left the courtroom, their faces solemn and heads down, there was a deadly hush. Barely anyone left the court and there was little conversation. The tension in the courtroom was tangible; Mary Bruce felt as though she had to keep checking to make sure she was still breathing. She kept wondering what was taking so long. It should have been obvious and they should have been able to decide as soon as they left the courtroom. Then she'd realise that they were deciding whether a man would live or die, a man like them, with children. She kept looking at the clock and found herself surprised again and again that it had hardly seemed to move.

Despite not knowing whether a decision would be made today, tomorrow or next week, people sat still, with barely a word between them. So quiet was the courtroom, that Mary Bruce, in her quiet corner at the back of the courtroom, could hear the clicking of knitting needles from the women who had again taken up their seat at the front of the gallery. It seemed that they had not been so deeply affected that they would miss any more of the spectacle than they needed to.

As the minutes ticked by, the tension in the courtroom increased. Mary Bruce wasn't the only one who wondered what could be taking them so long. On the other hand, Price's sister wanted them to never come back. For a while the jury stayed locked in their room, there was still hope. In the end, the jury only deliberated for one hour and twenty minutes before they returned and announced their verdict of 'Guilty'.

Mary Bruce, unlike most of the others in the courtroom, who hadn't known Eva, cried silently. She would receive her justice. And in a few minutes she would return to her life as mother and farmer's wife, but forever touched by the events at the creek and by what had happened in that courtroom.

Price's sister gasped and sobbed as the verdict was read. She knew it was coming, but actually hearing the words was a different thing.

"Charles William Price. You have been found guilty of murder. Do you have anything to say as to why a sentence of death should not be passed on you in the matter of the murder of Evelyn Mary Madden?"

"No," Price replied in a calm clear voice.

Mr Justice Blair donned the black cap and slowly pronounced the words that condemned him to die by hanging. Price received the dread sentence with outward calmness, his only sign of nervousness being the drumming of his fingers on the dock rail.

The Death of William Price

William Price spent the two months after his sentencing quietly in his cell in Crawford Prison, Wellington, where he'd been taken after his trial. He didn't sleep much and when he did, it was only for short periods before only the slightest noise nearby would wake him. He was brought things to read, but ignored most of them. Generally, he spent his hours smoking and pacing in the confines of his cell. He rolled cigarettes compulsively and when he had no more of his own to see to, the guards would give him tobacco and papers to roll theirs. They resorted to this in order to stop the drumming his fingers resorted to when his hands weren't busy.

There were a number of people who were interested in what he was thinking, but the chatty Charlie of old had disappeared. William Price was a broken man and he talked little, preferring to keep his thoughts to himself. If he told anyone how he felt about his fate or even the events that had led him to his current situation, they weren't telling. There was some interest from reporters in talking to him after the sensationalism of the murder and trial, but none were permitted to enter the prison.

There was some speculation when people heard how much money Eva had in her various accounts and savings bonds that he'd murdered her for her money. Others, like Audrey Jamieson, suggested that he was only with her for her money. The cook she'd had a disagreement with so many years before in Wellington wrote to the police stating that it was her view that Eva could never have had such an amount of money without having done work that paid more than a servant or housekeeper. She quite openly questioned Eva's morals and went on to state that with a temper like hers, it was no wonder he'd turned on her. This was despite the fact that she'd personally been a witness to Eva's habit of banking all of her wages.

Overwhelmingly though, mail to authorities and speculation about both Eva and Price was that they were genuinely nice people and that everyone who knew them was at a loss to understand how it had all come to the murder of one and the pending execution of the other.

A few of the prison guards spoke out and gossip in the pub in Wellington was that their most famous prisoner was a 'quiet bloke, pretty friendly, but not one for talking much.' More than one person that had known him or met him after sentence was passed commented that it was hard to imagine that he could kill a little woman like the one described in the paper. He was a big man, but seemed gentle.

"Just goes to show, you can never tell about anyone." This was the refrain heard often about William Price.

A number of letters, which pleaded for the death sentence to be commuted, were sent to the Solicitor General of the Crown Law Office in Wellington, the Minister of Justice, the Governor General, the Acting Prime Minister, the Executive Council of the Dominion of New Zealand and to the New Zealand police at both Napier and Christchurch. If the case had been sensational as a murder and trial, the execution was about to become one of the most divisive issues in New Zealand history, even though William Price seemed largely unaware of it all.

The flood of letters were very significant, because New Zealand was about to abolish the Death Penalty and there were many voices raised on Price's behalf to prevent him from being the last man hanged in New Zealand before the legislation abolishing the Death Penalty was enacted. There were open meetings about the case in some towns and both those who wanted to see Price receive the ultimate punishment for his horrific crime and those who believed that the State has no more right to take a life than any person, pursued every angle. Life imprisonment was the only humane and just solution was the argument of the abolitionists.

Price's niece even wrote to the Governor General of New Zealand:

To His Excellency
The Governor General

Dear Sir,
Please forgive me for the liberty I am taking in writing to you. But dear Sir, I am desperate, and I am asking for your help. Please, please, give us that help, we need it so badly, my dear Mother, is so hopelessly unhappy.
It is this way dear Excellency, my poor uncle, Mother's brother was yesterday proved guilty on a charge of murder. We all loved him so, we cannot believe the worst in him, he was so kind to everyone and such a good brother to Mother, don't let him die, be merciful. I've prayed so fervently for help, but our prayers were unanswered, won't you please try and give us hope, not for freedom dear Excellency, but imprisonment anything rather than a death like that.
I am afraid for Mother, she is so broken-hearted I am sure she will pine away, save her for me please.
I shall ask God to grant you the help to save him from death and us from bitter unhappiness.
Dear Excellency try to realise just how we are suffering and please don't be angry with me for writing to you, no-one advised me, only a little spark of hope helped me.
Please, please don't forsake us, and it is with this last plea that I sign myself and Mother as,
Your Humble Servants.

Mr Averill, the solicitor that represented Price at his trial, presented three foolscap pages in appeal to the Solicitor General. Among the points he made was that the

Death Penalty should be commuted in consideration of the fact that Price had had no designs or intentions on murder when he went out with Eva on the day she was killed. He also reminded the Solicitor General that Eva had travelled with Price from Oreka as a matter of convenience, but then had insisted on staying at the hotel with him and that they walked about town and dined together in Hastings and Napier.

Further, he went on, had the crime been premeditated, why would Price have not tried to conceal her presence in the car on the journey to Argyle East. He went into some detail about the state of Eva's clothing, making it clear that she must have removed her bloomers herself or they would have been torn. There had been an inference throughout the trial and in the press that Price had raped Eva before murdering her and Mr Averill felt that this might have prejudiced the judge toward the Death Penalty, rather than imprisonment for life, although he never would have committed this opinion to print in an appeal to the Solicitor General, especially given the instructions the judge had given the jury.

Price, for his part, continued to tell his lawyer that he couldn't remember anything about killing Eva. Mr Averill believed him and formed the opinion that he had acted in some sort of automatic state brought on by extreme emotion and so couldn't be held mentally accountable. His submission to the Solicitor General also added that Price's actions after the event were clearly those of a man who failed to grasp the true meaning of what he had done.

Mr Averill told Price on one of his visits that there had been a meeting of concerned citizens in Christchurch on the 9th of June and that they had voted unanimously to appeal to the Prime Minister for a reprieve and the prompt abolition of capital punishment in New Zealand. Also from Christchurch, he told Price, was a letter from the New Zealand, 'No More War Movement'. They argued that twenty countries had already been wise enough to set aside the Death Penalty, a 'remnant of barbarism' as they called it. As they said, the sacredness of human life should be considered paramount and that the commandment 'thou shalt not kill' should apply equally to the State. But Price was unmoved, remaining quiet and introspective, no matter what news Mr Averill brought.

Even Audrey Jamieson, emboldened by her day in court and the reactions she had received from people she'd told her story to, wrote to the police station following the sentencing. She described the day when she had provoked Eva, resulting in Eva grabbing her breast and attempting to twist it. She wondered whether Eva losing her temper could have provoked Price. She finished by saying that she hoped her story wouldn't be a joke all over Napier and with a PS saying, 'of course if anything like that happened, they could hardly hang him'.

Towards the end of his two-month imprisonment following his trial, Price was obviously showing signs of stress. He was smoking heavily, often lighting one cigarette from the butt of the previous one. He slept less and less and when his hand wasn't busy with a cigarette, the tapping of his fingers on any surface in his cell could clearly be heard. To quiet the increasingly disturbing effect the drumming had on the nerves of others, the guards continued to have him rolling cigarettes for other prisoners as well as themselves. To all who had contact with him, he was clearly unravelling, despite how little he still had to say.

Throughout the period following the trial, Price was visited by authorities asking whether he was ready to tell them what had really happened the day of the murder. He maintained that he couldn't remember. But that changed when he was visited by his lawyer with bad news. Mr Averill explained that he had made every appeal for clemency, how he'd stated that Price was not himself and that the killing was some sort of horrible accident. That he'd even inferred that people might have judged him harshly because they thought he raped the victim. Or that people judged him and thought he was a brute because he was such a big man and Eva so tiny. But all had been to no avail. The death sentence stood. There would be no life spent in prison, with possibility of release some day in the distant future. Price would die on the gallows and nothing his lawyer could do would stop it. After Mr Averill left, Price decided to tell the story to the prison's governor.

The Office of the Undersecretary of Justice reported to the Minister of Justice on the 11th of June that Price had made a full confession. In it he had stated that Eva had felt carsick and he had suggested that a walk in the fresh air would 'fix her up'. He then stated that they had sexual relations upon the ground. Afterwards they had quarrelled about his drinking and Eva had told him that his rotten breath made her feel sick and then slapped him with her purse. He had gone on that he really didn't know what had come over him, because they 'were pals', but he had 'grabbed a piece of Manuka and banged her over the head'.

That was the extent of it. He'd told it all in a matter of fact voice and seemed as confused and mystified by the whole turn of events then as he had likely been when the murder happened. And yet, while Price had already given this confession, he still had his lawyer convinced that he remembered nothing of the actual killing. He continued to lobby for the death sentence to be commuted, even stating that Price had made the confession as a way to get some peace. He believed his client utterly when he said he didn't remember murdering Eva Madden.

That he could be so likeable and yet so dishonest as to desert his obligations to his wife and to be so believable when lying was only ever really pondered after his death. During the time between his trial and execution date, there were no easy answers. People either wanted him hanged or his sentence commuted to a life behind bars with no hope of release. But everyone who met him commented on what a nice man he seemed.

After describing the killing in Price's words, the

Undersecretary went on to say that he was convinced that Price wasn't a deliberate criminal. In fact he wrote that he felt 'bound to add that of all the murderers I have seen in prison for some years this man has the most pleasing personality. I feel confident that he is not a lascivious sadist nor normally of a brutal disposition, but a man whose inhibitions were temporarily impaired through drink.'

However, he was also of the view that this should not and could not be taken into account as "it would be unwise from a social point of view to allow 'uncontrollable impulse' to enter into the matter. To do so would be to weaken one of the most important props in the protection of society from a deterrent point of view. There is a social obligation on persons possessed of normal wits to exercise self-control." Drunkenness or uncontrollable behaviour could never be allowed to be an excuse for criminal behaviour or harm to others in the eyes of New Zealand law and so the death sentence must stand.

On the morning of Thursday 27th of July, exactly two months after the day he was sentenced, a priest visited William Price at a quarter past six in the morning. Price hadn't slept at all the previous night and as the two men sat in the cell with only a pale light bulb pushing away the predawn darkness, he made his final confession in hushed and shaky tones. The priest then administered the Last Sacrament.

As the priest left the cell, he turned around and looked back at Price who just said, "Goodbye Father."

The Priest nodded, deciding not to mention that he would see him again at the gallows. Every moment Price could push away the thought of what was about to happen to him, the easier it might be. He didn't need to be reminded of his appointment in just over an hour's time.

At seven o'clock he ate breakfast. He hunched over his plate, moving the fork from the plate to his mouth in a steady rhythm, almost that of an automaton. There was no chatting with the guard who took his plate away, just another

The Price

cigarette lit from the last and the constant tapping of his fingers.

At four minutes to eight he looked up as his cell door was opened. He dropped his cigarette and stubbed it out. His hands shaking, he held out his hands to be cuffed, without saying a word. His breath was ragged as he tried to maintain some composure. As he was led from his cell he started to feel weak in the legs. Knowing what was going on, one of the warders quietly said, "C'mon mate," and he and his partner both supported Price as he began the walk to the gallows. The medical officer and prison superintendent led the procession, studiously ignoring whatever difficulties Price might be having.

With the support of the two warders, he walked erect down the corridor, through the yard and up the scaffold under the cover of the high prison wall. He mounted the steps to the gallows platform with the two warders and the priest. His arms were strapped to his body and the noose positioned around his neck. He took a moment to look at the yard and at the witnesses present. Strangely, he thought there would be more, but there were only a few, none of his relatives, and once again nobody to speak for the woman whose life he had taken. Realising he was now completely abandoned and alone, he turned to the priest, who nodded as the rosary beads moved through his fingers over the Bible he held in front of him.

As a loud, clear voice suddenly broke the silence, Price turned quickly. The Sheriff was standing near the top of the steps, and began to read aloud his sentence. "Charles William Price, having been sentenced 'that you be taken to the place of execution and there hanged by the neck until you are dead.' Have you anything to say before the sentence is carried into execution?"

"No," Price said in almost a shout, his nerve having completely failed him by then. He then turned to the priest and shakily whispered, "Goodbye Father."

"Goodbye. God bless you," replied the priest.

The Death of William Price

A white hood was quickly placed over the prisoner's head and at precisely eight o'clock the lever was pulled to operate the gallows of the Crawford Prison and William Price was hanged.

Death was instantaneous.

A perfunctory inquest was held before the Coroner an hour later and his body was buried at Karori[46] later that day.

---

[46] Cemetery near Wellington, North Island, New Zealand.

For those left behind

Each revelation of the investigation, trial and sentencing of William Price caused further trauma to Eva's family. These people who had spent so much of their lives trying to avoid being the subject of neighbourhood gossip were now unable to avoid it. Every time there was a new revelation in the *Crewe Chronicle* it felt to Martha as though she'd been wounded, and the open wound had been paraded around to every neighbour for them to pour salt into it.

Each gory detail of the trial was reported in the paper. The family had to learn from the newspaper that their daughter and sister had been dug up from her final resting place and her head removed. They had to learn from the newspaper that her severed head had been paraded around a courtroom when a description and drawings would have sufficed. Who was there to whisper to her grave that she was loved, or to speak for her in the court or even to care that she had been alive and brave and adventurous and bright? All these things broke down the family a little bit more each day.

Being the times that they were though, the family didn't make any objections known to the police. In the 1930s, law abiding working class people like the Maddens believed that if a policeman or a doctor said something was necessary, then it was. They bore their horror, believing that there was no choice and in Martha's case that the trial was a personal one sent to her to test her faith and devotion to God. But being Maddens, very little of it was ever said. They each knew that their thoughts travelled the same paths over and over only by the haunted looks on each other's faces. There was no more news in the *Crewe Chronicle* after the guilty verdict and sentence was delivered. At least the daily attention brought by the newspaper stories had stopped and the family could try to heal.

Joseph and George tried to spare Martha the worst of it, but she demanded that she be told things that no mother could bear to hear and she became frailer and frailer, dying less than two years after the death of her eldest daughter.

George was left to deal with all communications with the Crewe police as Joseph withdrew and became less able to manage all the details. So much did George endeavour to shield the family that he didn't even tell Edith that Price had been executed. Of course, he had been notified by the New Zealand police via their Crewe colleagues, but he never mentioned it to anyone in the family. The burden was immense on the young man's shoulders. He was not yet thirty, but too much of his life now revolved around an insane sister and brother, a murdered sister and broken parents.

Percy tried hard to look after Augusta, but she was emotional and in private would rage about the silence among family members. Outside her home, she remained the only one unafraid to speak her mind, but what had happened to Eva was too much even for her and her eldest sister became a secret even she couldn't speak about.

Tom had barely known his eldest sister, but his grief was terrible, magnified by the public way in which he had to wear it. It seemed everywhere he went people knew about it, knew it was his sister and would whisper about him as he passed. In time, he would move away from Crewe, perhaps eventually the burden of being a Madden was too much.

Edith did whatever she could to support George. She understood what he needed to do and worked hard to provide an escape from the strain placed upon him by his family. She grieved deeply too. She'd lost her brother to the war and now her friend in an equally senseless way. Whenever George could get a break from his job with the railways, she tried to organise something to do, such as a trip to the country, a picnic or a ride on a motorcycle through the narrow country lanes of Cheshire.

When the pain had faded a little and laughter took its place in their lives again, Edith convinced George that they needed faith in the future and they started the family they'd for so long decided against, bringing twin girls into the world close to what would have been Eva's forty-fourth birthday. They would have their treasured childhood for almost a decade before the horror of what had happened to Eva entered their lives.

Eva's personal belongings and savings were forwarded to her family in Crewe following the end of the trial. Edith unpacked the trunk she had so carefully packed all those months before, tears streaming down her face as she looked at all the beautiful clothes packed in such a haphazard way that Eva would never have approved of. Eva's last act was to help George, Gussie and Tom pay off their mortgages and have the financial security that Martha had so wanted for them all.

The Pathologist applied to the Inspector of Police at Napier asking for Eva's head for his museum. He also asked that if the weapon was identified whether he could have that too. The Inspector of Police replied that he would send the skull with a detective who was soon transferring to Auckland. Local Maoris accused the Pathologist of denying Eva her right to rest in peace while her body was incomplete. But the irrepressible Doctor Gilmour paid no attention to such things, if he heard them at all.

The fate of Eva's head was unknown to her family who assumed that it had been returned to her grave. Its whereabouts is still unknown, despite an exhaustive search instigated by the New Zealand Prime Minister in the 1990s at the urging of Eva's niece. There is some suspicion that it was destroyed with many of the Pathologist's specimens after his death. Eva's family and their descendants nevertheless always had to deal with the grisly display in the courtroom being the best known thing about the family among many people in Crewe.

The murder of Eva Madden and the trial and

For those left behind

execution of William Price was not forgotten in the local area and for more than fifty years it was taught as part of the Social Studies and History courses in the local schools. Textbooks with references to the events still survive, but they can't ever do more than present facts. The fact that Eva Madden could read at age three, that she was the much loved eldest of six children of Joseph and Martha, that she had been supporting her family since age thirteen, that she had once served in one of the great halls of England, and that she had travelled the world alone at a time when most women had to ask their husband's permission to go to the store. These things were not known and never acknowledged.

Eva's personal effects were quickly disposed of after being returned, only two photographs surviving. And then the Maddens did what they did best. They made Eva a secret. She was not talked about, her grave remained unmarked and if it weren't for the memory of other people who'd known her, she might never have existed.

Except for hints like winter warmers that were made and the little song her nieces sang as they skipped around the edge of Betley Mere, just as Eva had so many years before.

'When day is done and gone the sun, remember me.'[47]

THE END

---

[47] An adaptation of a popular scout song.

Postscript

Finding Eva

I am coming to the end of a long journey that has carried me across the world in search of Eva. She has haunted me for too long. Even now I feel the cold breath of her death and cannot really bear to think about those terrible events so far away from her homeland.

My search for Eva began many years ago when, as a child of nine, I was walking to school one day when a woman from a nearby street asked me if I was related to the Eva Madden who was murdered in New Zealand. "You know ... the one where they held up her decapitated head in the courtroom for everyone to see?"

I remember asking my mother about Eva. She took me into the privacy of our front room and closed the door in great secrecy. She spoke in short sentences and I sensed the emotion and difficulty involved in telling me the story even so many years after the events.

"Yes, you did have an aunt. She was lovely, quite a lady. She and I were close friends. But you must never tell your father that you even know of her existence. He has forbidden the subject in the house. She travelled, working as a domestic in New Zealand. She was murdered out there. I believe she fell in love with a man, a teamster who looked after horses. They went to look at a cottage, but he murdered her. I think he was hanged, but I'm not sure. Your father doesn't talk of it, ever. Promise me that you won't either. It's for the best."

Very occasionally if asked, my mother would tell me details of the times she spent with Eva, but always in confidence, for she now trusted me never to discuss the existence of his sister with my father. I remember looking at my father carefully for days following the initial conversation with my mother, wondering how he felt having to carry such sadness and secrecy in his heart.

I never knew my grandmother, Martha Madden, for she died before I was born, and not long after Eva's murder. I have a dim memory of my white haired grandfather, Joseph Madden, standing on the step of his house, smiling kindly at me. But as far as I know I never went inside that house that had such an impact on the children raised within its walls.

Forty-two years after the words spoken so thoughtlessly by a neighbour changed my world, they came back to haunt me again. I was teaching at a school for newly arrived migrants in Adelaide, South Australia, and there I met and made friends with a woman from Auckland, New Zealand. One day I asked her about the North Island and mentioned my aunt, hinting that it was my belief that she may have been murdered there.

My friend returned to New Zealand during the school holidays and spent some time researching old newspapers and sure enough she found news of a Madden woman's death, informing me at once by letter.

Realising that it was a journey that I must take alone, I slowly and tentatively began to make enquiries. I wrote to the national Archives in Wellington, New Zealand to ask about information that may be printed in newspapers. I discovered articles relating to the murder, and was informed that a box of detailed notes on the trial was available. It had not been committed to microfiche, but if I went to Wellington I would be able to carry out my own research on the papers at my leisure.

Excited, but very apprehensive, I enquired through the Hastings Council on the whereabouts of my aunt's grave, which I discovered did exist at the local cemetery. I had finally begun to travel along the road of discovery. Little did I know at this point that it was not being planned by me. The journey that I was about to undertake would be complex, frustrating, frightening at times, but revealing.

I began to question my father's authority, for it had

been his wish that I never knew of my aunt's existence. My father, George Madden, died in 1977 but still his presence guided me. I needed his blessing to continue the search, in order to unravel the mystery of his sister's death. I sensed that if there was disapproval, then I would not be able to complete my writing. If it went ahead it would be with his blessing, but I would know one way or another. Resolute, I planned a trip to New Zealand, intending to place a headstone on Eva's grave. A Maori undertaker did this for me whilst I was travelling to Wellington.

The archival material was contained in two brown boxes, the seals of which had been broken. I began the long and painful task of lifting out the old typewritten letters relating to Eva's death and subsequent trial of the man who murdered her. Again and again I replaced the lids on the boxes, shocked by the grief that swamped me.

The descriptions of Eva's body were vivid and horrifying. At night I fell asleep to dream of her floating upwards on the pool as maggots ate out her beautiful brown eyes.

*'The eyes were putrefied and their anatomy
is unrecognisable'*
(The water had carried away parts of the skin.)
'The putrefaction about the face and neck is probably due to the fact that the head was not completely immersed with the rest of the body. The liquidation of the brain is quite likely to occur early, in cases where the skull is fractured, particularly at the base and where the nose is involved. This would also be accelerated, if the head is not immersed in water.'

Was this really my aunt? Why had she suffered such a monstrous end, and more importantly, how? In horror and disbelief I shut my eyes again and again as I sat in front of the boxes, bewildered and angry. When I came to the list of her suitcases and trunk, my first reaction was one of guilt. There

Finding Eva

I was, picturing the clothes and possessions, yet Eva was dead. The woman began to come alive through her neatly organised belongings, the sum of her life journey, and yet I could find very little on the list that was personal. Prolific as the contents were, there were few clues to Eva's life. The two sixpences and a small newspaper cutting intrigued me, but I was astonished by the wealth of clothing she owned.

At times I felt intrusive, reading about the contents of her suitcases and trunk, finding small details that tied her to me as her niece. I began to recognise another Madden woman, as I worked on throughout the day, sifting through the matter of fact detail that uncovered her life in New Zealand. Without warning I came across hand written letters from my father, the same dear handwriting that I treasure in letters he sent to both his grandchildren and me. I wept for the terrible loss of Eva, thinking of her brother at the age of twenty-seven, dealing with the death of his eldest sister.

Then there was the photograph, followed by many personal details of her life in New Zealand. I noted that she returned after five years yet the passport details mentioned Canada. No one had ever mentioned Canada.

Who was Eva Madden? She was not just a murder victim, though is anyone who loses their life this way ever only a murder victim? It was at that point I realised the enormity of her life. A woman before her time, a brave and beautiful woman who travelled far on her own. I examined the only photograph of her that I possessed, staring closely at it. She was a traveller as I have been. I grew closer to her that day, determined to honour her memory and life.

Towards the end of my research I slowly and painfully realised that her remains were not complete. Her head had been severed from her body, but never replaced in the coffin. For all the time I had been reading about her I had assumed, like my family had too I supposed, that it had been replaced with her remains. How had this happened? How could her spirit be at rest? Was this the reason why I was so unnerved by her existence? I had planned a small ceremony over her grave, but now I felt it would be meaningless.

The deep and growing anger concerning the violation of Eva's body beyond death grew within me. Silently and steadily the prism was changing, illuminating her world. As the shafts of late autumn sunshine spilled onto the papers in front of me in the Turnbull Library in Wellington, I began to feel that Eva had set me on this journey, gently allowing me to have my initial dreams of putting them to rights. She had protected me from the awful truths, leading me forward slowly until I was capable of coping with the deeper implications surrounding her death.

Now I was faced with a Christian service that I had arranged to take place at Hastings the following day. I felt hypocritical and knew that it would now be meaningless. I wanted to feel that Eva was at peace, but how could she be, when such violation had taken place?

How appropriate were Emily Dickinson's words now engraved on Eva's headstone:

'Ample make this bed. Make this bed with awe;
In it wait till judgement break, Excellent and fair.'

The full implication of those words had been lost on me, even though I had chosen them. Now I understood. I'd chosen them because of the reference to judgement breaking, but now I knew that they were there because this would only ever be a temporary resting place until justice is really done for her.

Left alone by her grave, I dug a small hole, laying within it a piece of my hair, a scrap of material from my father's motorcycle jacket and an old handkerchief belonging to my mother. I took her photograph from the grave where I had carefully placed it during the service, and left feeling frustrated and bitter.

The journey continued. I discovered the pool where she had lain after her death. The willows old and rotten lay on the banks, but the spot was virtually unchanged. The area was lonely and deserted until a girl's voice calling from the road startled me. I walked over to her to tell her the story, which she knew nothing about. In return she took me to her grandmother's house, a cottage that must have been built even before Eva's time.

It was here that I discovered the details of Herbert Monk, who was still alive and living in Rotorua. I was determined to see him, as he was the sixteen-year-old boy who had discovered Eva's body in the pool, so I took his telephone number.

The grandmother recalled the trial, which had been sensational. The entire district talked about it for months afterwards. She also knew about the Lowry family and gave me directions to Oreka Station. In the late afternoon, I made my way up the long drive to the Lowry household. I walked up the drive, as I'm sure Eva must have done many times.

Here I met the son of James Lowry, by his second wife. Following a detailed explanation, he and his wife made me very welcome and over tea he told me what he knew. Once again, like Eva's family on the other side of the world, James Lowry had thrown a veil of secrecy over the murder. No one was allowed to speak of it, but the son remembered being told how his father had been greatly horrified by it.

Determined to tread on the same earth as my aunt, I excused myself from tea, climbed the bank to where the lake used to be, and walked around to the servants' quarters. I found what had been her bedroom, looking out over the property, as she would have done, at a landscape which had yet to receive the autumn rains.

The following day I met Herbert Monk, who told me the disturbing news of a dream he'd had of the body, only days previous to hearing from me. We chatted together like old friends. Then I asked him to draw the pool and the surrounding area. Proudly he told me that he had ended up owning most of the land where we had been, but that now he was in his eighties, he had retired to Rotorua. His memory was precise. He described my aunt's body with great sadness then pushed the piece of paper towards me. In exchange I gave him my sketch of the pool. The drawings were identical! He also told me about the rope that Charles Price was carrying when he revisited the scene of the murder, still puzzled why he hadn't been allowed to tell of that detail in his statement so long ago. Herbert was convinced that Price intended to hang himself, but the existence of the rope was never mentioned during the trial.

Finally, I visited several Maoris at Rotorua, telling them the story of my aunt. They were very disturbed about the removal of the head from the grave, emphasising to me that her spirit could not be at rest in New Zealand as her remains were incomplete. They urged me to find her head.

My journey back to Adelaide was troubling. Carrying the copies from the box, films of the various places I had visited, and experiencing a deep feeling of unrest, I contacted Mr Bolger, the then Prime Minister of New Zealand about my aunt's head. He promptly wrote back to me, offering to help in any way he could. He contacted the Auckland Hospital, the consultant Pathologist telephoned me and we began the search, which ultimately proved unsuccessful.

I took up my previous life in South Australia, distancing myself from the life of my aunt. The boxes and letters were put away for a future time when I could reconsider why I felt it so necessary to write the story of Eva. Then the writing finally began, taking me to archives and libraries across New Zealand, Canada and England. My research of Eva's life revealed an articulate, well-travelled young woman of considerable means, who escaped her working class background through her work and ambitions for a more interesting life.

Steadily the Madden secrets bubbled to the surface, explaining my father's attitude to his family in a far more complex way than I could ever envisage. The depth of his sadness can never be fully realised. He strove to protect his family from their hereditary identity by hiding the truth. All of the adults in my childhood were bound to these secrets in some way or another so that I might live a trouble free childhood, not haunted by the implications of madness and murder.

The sun shone on me always. It was only my father's story telling that revealed the human condition of loss, pain, suffering and the meaning of love. Not for me the traditional tales told neatly from a book, but rather the troubled stories whose words were buried deep in my subconscious. At times these incredible stories ran from bedtime to bedtime, lasting as long as a week, and I was enthralled with them. Every tale contained a life lesson; every character gave me wisdom.

I often wondered about his words and their meaning. Entrenched in them were the well-taught lessons that I carry with me to this day: independence, fear, the ability to love unconditionally, bravery fought for at a high price, integrity, honesty and an insatiable curiosity.

Looking back to those times, I feel that my father gave me the meaning of Eva's life and death through his incredible story telling. It only remained for me, a Madden woman, to unravel the messages, decode the words, and make the journey.

Now I have returned the incomplete remains of Eva Madden to the land of her birth, as her last resting place. They lie in Crewe Cemetery, Cheshire, England, in the grave of her parents, my grandparents. Finally the spirit that has haunted two generations will be put to rest. She will no longer lie in foreign soil, but has come home in dignity and peace.

Her violation beyond her human existence has now been sanctified in some way through the uncovering and telling of the story of her life. She has enabled me to give her a voice so that in death the life she lived will have meaning.

Reflections

2nd Edition, 2016

The publishing of a second edition of *The Price* has given me the opportunity to reflect on the story of Eva Madden. I wanted to present a second edition in a way that would facilitate deeper realisations in the reader. The form of this second edition has changed including its overall presentation. The original photographs have been removed, for the most powerful images lie within the written word. For those readers who wish to pursue historical facts and language definitions I have included factual references where I thought they were needed.

In today's society we are far more aware of the impact of mental illness in families and individuals. Acceptance of mental illness has been slow in coming and even now it is easier to discuss physical illnesses. Unfortunately, a stigma still applies to mental illness at all levels of society. There is far more medical knowledge available to the community but much more work needs to be done in this area. In the case of Eva Madden, in the early 1900's the mystery and shame associated with mental illness resulted in silence and even more effectively in secrets.

Eva searched all her family to come to terms with the torture that they were undergoing in order to follow Martha's wishes. Those close to Martha grew up in a very restrained household. Love, grieving, discussion and sharing thoughts did not sit comfortably within the Madden home. Poverty took Eva out of school at the age of thirteen. She lived an entirely different life in wealthy circumstances even though she was a mere servant. So she became the observer of her family's poverty and a keeper of secrets. She saw poverty from a distance whilst living in a great hall in Cheshire.

Her mother Martha was not born into a working

class family and proceeded to press upon her children the need for education, social correctness and above all religion. A staunch Methodist, she enforced her strong views and way of life onto her children, none of whom pursued religion through choice. She alienated herself from her neighbours and barely tolerated the street life around her.

As Eva grew into a woman, she developed her own strong views and ambitions and could barely cope with her mother's imposing ways. Eva loved her family and ultimately kept the secrets as part of her unconditional love. She certainly didn't agree to secrets but she had no choice. She coped by burying them along with her mother's fanatical belief in Methodism and hatred of alcohol, which she saw as a sin. By ignoring her mother's wishes and demanding way of life, Eva was able to survive and travel. She was a great saver according to the remainder of her financial records, and by her growing finance she was able to experience life in the colonies of New Zealand and Canada. It was a remarkable feat for a working class woman and only achieved through discipline and determination.

So what was the reason for her premature death on the grassy bank on the North Island of New Zealand in 1935 There are many opinions, but it is my belief that deep subconscious feelings flared to the surface in her mind in reaction to a small metal flask of alcohol, which fell from Price's pocket. They were both happily seeking out a cottage, which they hoped to purchase, and then the flask fell to the ground. It precipitated a violent reaction in Eva, opening up all of the unbearable secrets and trauma, which she had hidden for most of her life.

She had searched all of her family in Crewe in order to accept the family's grief but she had no means with which to help them. On the grassy bank on that fateful day her mind became a hell. Her mother's words leapt out of the darkness and flung Eva backwards into the pit of fear she was running away from. She physically attacked the man she had hoped to live with for she totally lost control thus sealing her own fate.

Following her death, yet again poverty stalked her family preventing them closure by not being able to travel to her funeral in New Zealand. Poverty prevented them from placing flowers on her grave, talking to the local people and, in time, forgiving William Price. Poverty never allowed them the choice to challenge the legal system for having removed her head from its resting place, severing it from her body and using it as bizarre evidence in the trial. The family probably never knew that the head had not been returned to the grave.

Such violation of her body after death, such injustice and ghastly acts hardly bear thinking about.

As a writer and Eva Madden's niece I have presented Eva as an amazing woman before her time, a human being, full of thought, laughter and kindness.

Let us celebrate her incredible life beyond her death, the life of a brave, resilient woman.

And let us remember her.

Janice Madden

20 June 2016

Reflections

Also written by Janice Madden

Circles within Circles

Knights of the Road

Just a Girl from Crewe

The Price 1st edition

Reared in Chester Zoo

Enter

The Red Carpet

Grandad's Letters

Books may be ordered from www.janicemadden.com